Francis Aidan Gasquet

The old English Bible

And other Essays

Francis Aidan Gasquet

The old English Bible
And other Essays

ISBN/EAN: 9783337171391

Printed in Europe, USA, Canada, Australia, Japan

Cover: Foto ©ninafisch / pixelio.de

More available books at **www.hansebooks.com**

THE
Old English Bible

AND OTHER ESSAYS

BY

FRANCIS AIDAN GASQUET, D.D., O.S.B.

AUTHOR OF
"HENRY VIII. AND THE ENGLISH MONASTERIES"

LONDON
JOHN C. NIMMO
14 KING WILLIAM STREET, STRAND
MDCCCXCVII

CONTENTS.

ESSAY I.

NOTES ON MEDIÆVAL MONASTIC LIBRARIES.

Study equally with labour a monastic work—First beginnings of libraries—Special places set apart for books—The creation of English libraries—Arrangement of book-cases and making of catalogues—Chained books—The librarian—Size of mediæval collections   1-40

PAGES

ESSAY II.

THE MONASTIC SCRIPTORIUM.

Book-making a peculiarly monastic occupation—Scriptoria proper—The great English historiographers, Matthew Paris, William of Malmesbury, &c.—The work of the Scriptorium—Cloister writing schools—Cost of MS. making—English writing schools in early times   ... 41-62

ESSAY III.

A FORGOTTEN ENGLISH PREACHER.

Mediæval sermons serve as useful side lights to history—Bishop Brunton of Rochester in the fourteenth century—His account of manners and morals at the end of the reign of Edward III. and the beginning of that of Richard II.—New lights upon the period and work of the Good Parliament—The orator's plain speaking... 63-101

ESSAY IV.

THE PRE-REFORMATION ENGLISH BIBLE (1).

The Wyclif origin of the old English version traditional—No vernacular version supposed to be authorised—Lollard persecution for the Scriptures—The evidence connecting Wyclif and his immediate followers with the version examined—The attitude of ecclesiastical authorities to the version—Evidence for an authorised vernacular version 102-155

ESSAY V.

THE PRE-REFORMATION ENGLISH BIBLE (2).

English historical review, criticism on the last Essay examined—Mr. Matthew and Mr. Kenyon, admissions that the church permitted the use of the version now known as Wyclifite—Their reasons for thinking that Wyclif was the author of the version examined ... 156-178

ESSAY VI.

RELIGIOUS INSTRUCTION IN ENGLAND DURING THE FOURTEENTH AND FIFTEENTH CENTURIES.

English people better instructed in their faith than commonly supposed—Various injunctions on this point to the clergy—Familiar character of the religious teaching—Various books to assist priests in the discharge of this duty—Character of mediæval sermons—Sermon aids in England—Some English preachers and their work 179-225

ESSAY VII.

A ROYAL CHRISTMAS IN THE FIFTEENTH CENTURY.

Henry VI. at Bury St. Edmunds in 1433—The reception of the royal guest—Account of the religious services in the abbey church—The King's amusements ... 226-259

CONTENTS.

ESSAY VIII.

THE CANTERBURY CLAUSTRAL SCHOOL IN THE FIFTEENTH CENTURY.

The cloister the monastic schoolroom—The inconveniences and hardships of mediæval education—The treatment of books—A monastic school boy—His lesson book—Teaching as to polite manners—His writing and Latin lessons—Proverbs—Scribbles—Reginald Pole ... 260-285

ESSAY IX.

THE NOTE BOOKS OF WILLIAM WORCESTER, A FIFTEENTH CENTURY ANTIQUARY.

Interest and value of a properly kept note book—William of Worcester—His birth and early life—His travels and notes of places and people, and his description of places, buildings, and knowledge of architecture—His notes as to classical manuscripts—His friendship with Prior Sellyng of Canterbury—The revival of Greek in England 286-318

ESSAY X.

HAMPSHIRE RECUSANTS, A STORY OF THEIR TROUBLES IN THE TIME OF QUEEN ELIZABETH.

Recusant laws—Their purpose and origin—Their incidence illustrated in regard to Hampshire people, rich and poor, to the commencement of the reign of James I. 319-384

I.

NOTES ON
MEDIÆVAL MONASTIC LIBRARIES.[1]

IT is by no means uncommon for certain writers to assume that the ideal monastic occupation was agriculture. They appear to consider that it was only in process of time that study, writing, and other forms of intellectual work were allowed by the monastic order to usurp the position of manual labour. It is perhaps hardly necessary to say that such a notion is, at the least, inaccurate and misleading. St. Benedict from the first, as may be seen in his legislation for the daily work of his monks, contemplated a mixed occupation of hands and head for such as entered "the school of divine service" under his Rule. Times for "reading" entered largely into the disposition of his day, and he treats it as quite exceptional "if the situation of the place or their poverty require" his monks to give up their intellectual pursuits "to labour in

[1] Reprinted, with additions, from the *Downside Review*, vol. x., p. 87 seqq.

reaping their corn." How it came to pass that in process of time the labour of the hands gave way almost entirely to that of the head is a story altogether foreign to my present purpose. And all that I would insist on here is that according to St. Benedict's conception study or reading was to form a part, and a large part, of each monk's "accustomed task."[1]

Now reading implies the existence of books, and so, as a necessary consequence of this provision in the Rule, every properly constituted monastery must from the first have looked to the formation of such libraries as were then possible as a matter of primary importance. That they did so in fact can hardly be doubted by any one taking the trouble to look at any series of monastic annals. It was many centuries ago—somewhere in the 12th century, if I mistake not—that an abbot, writing about the establishment of a new abbey, said that "a monastery without a library is like a castle without an armoury"; for "our library is our armoury." And although he goes on to explain his meaning as specially referring to books necessary to prosecute those Biblical studies in which the monks would find defence against the assaults of their enemy, there can be no doubt from the beginning of his letter

---

[1] *Rule of St. Benedict*, Cap. 48. Of Daily Labour. "Idleness is the enemy of the soul; hence brethren ought, at certain seasons, to occupy themselves with manual labour, and again, at certain hours, with holy reading, &c."

that he had before his mind at the time, the principle which St. Benedict lays down in his legislation for the daily work of his monks, that "Idleness is the enemy of the soul." And in this point of view the library was the "armoury" against this foe.

Considering the importance attached to the collection of books in every monastic establishment, it may not be without interest if a few pages are devoted to an attempt to sketch in outline what such a library must have been in any of "the great solemn monasteries" of England. And first, as in so many mediæval matters, we must begin by divesting our minds of notions derived from this nineteenth century of ours, when the art of printing has so completely changed the conditions of book-making that there can be little comparison between a library of modern books and the small but proportionately precious collection of manuscript. The multitudinous rows of volumes, for instance, gaily dressed out in their cloth bindings of every hue and colour—those studies in cheap blue and silver, or brown and gold—to which the eye is now accustomed in every modern library, must be banished from the imagination as a preliminary step to realizing the mediæval prototype; and the same may be said of every, or almost every, characteristic detail of a modern library. If any books at all were visible in the manuscript collections of a mediæval monastery, they were probably sombre tomes enough. Away then with all notions from this age of ours if we would understand what an ancient library was like, how it was worked, under whose care it was, and what the conditions were, under which the monk in those "dark ages" used the manuscript treasures of his house.

And first it is well to understand that from the earliest Christian times there was held to be a sacred character about books. In fact there was ever a close connection between them and the Church, and the House of God itself was long considered the most fitting place for the aumbry of manuscripts, which men in those days of simple faith regarded as among the most precious of God's gifts. If I might hazard a guess why this should have been so, it would be that these were partly, if not mostly, made up of copies of the Holy Scriptures, or of works of the Fathers of the Church commenting on them; and to the reverential spirit of the early ages of the faith, no more fitting place could be imagined to preserve these sacred treasures than the Church. The very Latin word now used for a library (*Bibliotheca*) was used to signify the Holy Bible itself.

Whatever the reason, the fact is certain that the church was the common, if not the usual, place where in early mediæval days the manuscript treasures of a great church or monastery were to be found. Thus, for example, when Pope Damasus, towards the close of the 4th century, founded his public library in Rome, he raised the hall, or basilica church, dedicated to St. Laurence, from out of which led the little rooms devoted to various departments of his library, and in which were stored the precious volumes.[1]

So, in later times, St. Louis of France, upon his return from the crusades, had many volumes of the sacred Scriptures and of the Fathers of the Church copied by the most skilful scribes, and these he placed in the Sainte Chapelle which he had built to receive the relics of the Passion brought back from the Holy Land.[2] The same disposition of the manuscript treasures of the great abbey of St. Alban's appears even as late as the twelfth century. The *Gesta Abbatum* says of Symon the 19th abbot of St. Alban's, who ruled the house wisely and well from

---

[1] Lanciani, *Ancient Rome*, p. 187. The writer also says: "The finest libraries of the first three centuries of Christendom were of course in Rome. They contained not only books and documents of local interest, such as the *Gesta Martyrum* and *matriculæ pauperum* and so forth, but also copies of the official correspondence between the See of Rome and the dioceses of the christian world. Such was the importance attributed to books in those early days of our faith, that in christian basilicas, or places of worship, they were kept in the place of honour next to the episcopal chair. Many of the basilicas which we discover from time to time, especially in the Campagna, have the apse *trichora*—that is, subdivided into three smaller hemicycles. The reason and meaning of this peculiar form of an apse was long sought in vain; but a recent discovery made at Hispalis (Seville) proved that of the three hemicycles in those apses, the central one contained the tribunal or episcopal chair, the one on the right the sacred implements, the one on the left the sacred books." See also the remarks of G. B. de Rossi, in *Codices Palatini Latini Bibl. Vaticanæ*, pp. xvi., xvii.

[2] Tillemont, *Vie de St. Louis*, iv., p. 48.

A.D. 1167 to 1183, that he did much to attract learned and lettered men to the cloister. He collected many books, chiefly Scriptural, and "their number," writes the chronicler, "it would be too long to name; but those who desire to see them can find them in the painted aumbry in the church, placed (as he specially directed) against the tomb of Roger the hermit."¹ Abbot Symon's book collecting was not in vain, for to him may be traced the origin of the school of St. Alban's chroniclers, to whom we owe so much of our knowledge of English history; and although the first efforts in that direction were, to say the least, crude, what they subsequently accomplished during the course of over three centuries deserves the grateful recognition of posterity. There is no need to enlarge further upon the fact of this close connection between the library and church in the middle ages. The point could be largely illustrated from the English monastic chronicles, but one late example of the existence of a library in a church at the beginning of the fifteenth century may perhaps be given. The story is interesting in itself, and as the books in question do not appear to have been merely biblical or patristic volumes, as they may perhaps be accounted in other instances, it will not be out of place.

On Saturday, August 21st, 1406, at six o'clock in the evening, King Henry IV. arrived at Bardney

¹ *Gesta Abbatum*, ed. Rolls series i., p. 184.

Abbey, Lincolnshire, with a large retinue. "The abbot and convent," says the account we are quoting, "came to the outer gates in procession to meet him. The illustrious king on seeing the procession dismounted, and kneeling humbly kissed the cross. After he had been sprinkled with holy water and censed, the cantor intoning (the hymn) of the Trinity, *Sit honor virtus*, he was conducted with becoming honour by the abbot and his monks through the church to the high altar. There when the singing was over and the abbot had said the prayer, (King Henry) kissed the sacred relics, and passing through the cloister retired to the abbot's chamber for the night."

The next day, "which was Sunday, the king descended to the cloister about six o'clock in the morning, and entered the chapel of Holy Mary in the church near the 'vestibule,' which had been adorned with carpets and hangings of red and other decorations fitting for a king. Here he heard two masses, and in the meantime the blessing of the water before the High Mass was begun; and this over, the procession went to the chapel of Holy Mary, as was the custom each Sunday in the year. Then it went round the cloister, and the most illustrious King Henry and his nobles followed till it entered the choir (again), when the king went back to the chapel, where he remained till the High Mass was finished."

"After the mass he passed through the cloister

to his chamber to dine." Then after transacting some business of state, "the King again descended through the cloister to the church, and there turned over our library. He read in divers books according to his will and good pleasure, and then, by the same way he had come, he returned to his supper."[1]

The love thus shown by Henry IV. for books was transmitted to his sons—even to Henry V. We have two curious instances of this latter monarch's propensity for borrowing books and forgetting to return them. They may be worth recording, although not directly bearing upon the present subject. The first example has reference to a work of secular literature. In 1424 the Countess of Westmoreland petitioned that great book collector, the Duke of Gloucester, that a volume called the "Chronicles of Jerusalem and the viage de Godfray Boylion" might be restored to her. She said that the late King, Henry V., had borrowed it from her, and had not returned it, and that it was then in the possession of Robert Rolleston, the keeper of the royal wardrobe. This petition was granted, and the book returned.

The other instance is still more curious. In the same year, and almost about the same time, the Prior of Christchurch, Canterbury, requested that the monks of the Shene Charterhouse should be

---

[1] Hearne, Appendix to Leland's *Collectanea* iii., pp. 300—1 (ed. 1715); taken from the fly leaf of a MS., formerly belonging to Bardney Abbey.

directed to deliver up to Dom William Molash, monk and almoner of Canterbury, a large volume containing the works of St. Gregory the Great. The King had, it is true, left it to the Carthusians by his will, but the Prior stated that this same volume had been bequeathed to Christchurch monastery by Archbishop Arundel on his death ten years before. The volume had been simply shown to Henry V. by Sir Gilbert Umfreville, one of the executors of the archbishop's will, and the King had simply kept it during his life and left it to the Charterhouse at his death. The petition of the Christchurch monks was granted, and a letter was written to the Prior of Shene to deliver up the book in question.[1]

But to return to our present subject. As time went on, and books began to multiply in the monasteries, places other than the church were arranged, according to convenience, where they were deposited. It was not till the later middle ages, however, that the practice of gathering all the manuscripts of a convent into one special place became at all common, or that one special room, called the library, was set apart for the purpose. It must have struck all who have paid any attention to the ground-plans of our ancient English abbeys that, as a rule, no place can with any certainty be assigned as the site of the library. The fact is that although here and there some such

[1] Rymer *Fœdera* x., pp. 317-8.

special building had often been erected to contain the books of the establishment, more commonly they were placed in presses erected in such parts of the building, as practical utility might dictate. Thus, for example, at Durham we find that the manuscripts were distributed, according to convenience, in various parts of the large establishment. Some were kept in the church, others in the spendiment or treasury, and others again in the refectory, and in more than one place in the cloister.

In the spendiment there were apparently two classes of books—one accessible to the monks generally, the other kept in what we may consider as the inner archivium, more securely preserved. "Within the said treasury," says the author of the *Rites of Durham*, "was a strong iron gate, set fast in the groundwork, in the roof and in either wall, the breadth of the house, so fast as not to be broken; and in the midst of the grate a door of iron with a strong lock upon it, and two great sheets of iron for the said door."

Other books were placed in an aumbry, or press with folding doors, near the entrance to the infirmary. These were taken from the other bookcases when needed, and were intended for the use of the reader in the refectory.[1] Another case of

---

[1] To the interesting library catalogue of the monastery of S. Justina of Padua made in 1453 are prefixed lists of books set apart for public reading. List 1 gives those to be read in the Chapter, with a descrip-

books was set apart for the use of the novices in the part of the cloister opposite the door of the treasury, so that at any time they could have access to them for their studies. The general store of books belonging to Durham, at any rate at the end of the 14th century, was kept in presses set in various parts of the cloister.[1] "Opposite to the carrels, against the church wall," writes the authority before quoted, "stood certain great aumbries of wainscot, full of books, as well the ancient written Doctors of the church as other profane authors, with divers other holy men's works; so that every one studied what doctor he pleased, having the library at all times open to go and study in, besides their carrels." This *Library*, however, was the creation of Prior Wessington, some time before 1446, " in the south angle of the Lanthorne which

tion of the size and the binding of the volumes; List 2 those intended for reading at table in Latin; List 3 those of books in the *vernacular* to be read in the refectory at the first or second table. This catalogue has been printed (but not published), along with the Library catalogue of S. Antonio's at Padua referred to below, in an 8vo volume by W. von Göthe (?) about the year 1864; it is also printed by Mazzatinti as an appendix to the Catalogue of Italian manuscripts in the Bibliothèque Nationale at Paris. Richard of Bury in his *Philobiblion*, speaks of the care taken by the mendicant friars to form collections of books. "Whenever," he writes, "we turned aside to the cities and places where the mendicants had their convents . . . . we found heaped up amidst the utmost poverty the utmost riches of wisdom. They are as ants ever preparing their meat in the summer, and ingenious bees continually fabricating cells of honey. . . . They have added more in this brief (eleventh) hour to the stock of the sacred books than all the other vine dressers."

[1] *Catalogi Veteres*, ed. Surtees Soc., p. 46.

is now above the clock, standing betwixt the Chapter House and the Te Deum window, well replenished with old written Doctors and other Histories, and Ecclesiastical writers."

The picture which may be derived from this account of the disposition of the Durham books will be fairly correct in regard to other monastic houses. Thus at Westminster we know that in the cloister there were presses of books for the particular use of the seniors and the novices, because there is a special order as to a cresset light being set beyond the aumbry of the master of novices, and a special permission for a novice sufficiently instructed to have books out of the presses set apart for the use of the seniors.[1] Many more examples of these cloister libraries might be given from the chronicles of other houses which all go to show that what we know to have been the case at Durham and Westminster was the common and general disposition of the monastic manuscript volumes.

Towards the close of the 14th, or in the first half of the 15th century as at Durham, it is not uncommon to find special buildings, or at any rate rooms, set apart for libraries. Thus, to take St. Alban's as an example, Michael de Mentmore, who was abbot from A.D. 1335 to 1349, besides enriching the common presses of the monastery with many manuscript treasures, collected together some of the books into what is called his "study,"[2] which

[1] Cott. MS. Otho C. xi., f. 84 and f. 86.   [2] *Gesta Abbatum*, ii., p. 363.

apparently was a place set apart for those who showed special aptitude for learning. His successor, Thomas De la Mare, who ruled St. Alban's for nearly fifty years, is said to have increased the collection of books in this study—or "library," as it is now called—with many precious volumes, by the help of Thomas of Walsingham, who then held the office of cantor and scriptorarius.[1] De la Mare was followed in 1396 by John de la Moote, and he, although abbot only for something less than five years, "newly built two sides of the cloister, with the studies, *library* and chapel of St. Nicholas; and over the vaulting of the cloister he designed to build a library; and over that of the chapel of St. Nicholas a small chamber for the monastic muniments. But this," says the Chronicle, "prevented by death, he left to others."[2] It was apparently not for another fifty years, or in the year 1452, that Abbot Whethamstede finally completed the work thus interrupted. He had long desired to see it done, and before the resignation which closed his first abbacy, "had collected much of the materials" requisite. His successor did nothing, and so, "immediately after his installation" for the second time, he set to work and finished the entire building in the second year of his second abbacy. "And upon the mere construction of this building," says the chronicler, "not reckoning the glazing, lighting, or the furnishing with desks, he

[1] *Gesta Abbatum*, iii, p. 389.   [2] Ibid., p. 442.

is said to have expended more than one hundred and fifty pounds."[1]

Almost at this very time the library of Christchurch, Canterbury, described as sufficiently spacious (satis amplam), was finished at considerable cost by Prior Thomas Goldstone.[2] Prior William Sellyng, who held the office for twenty-two years from A.D. 1472, added a special scholars' library. He was a man "deeply versed in both sacred and secular learning, knowing well both Latin and Greek. . . Next to the Prior's chamber he built a tower called the *Gloriet* (afterwards called the Prior's study). The Library over the Prior's chapel he adorned with a beautiful ceiling, and stored within it many books for the use of those most given to letters, whom most anxiously and kindly he assisted and encouraged. The southern walk of the cloister also he caused to be glazed for the use of the more studious brethren, and there made some fine carrels."[3]

So much for the place where the books of an old English mediæval monastery were deposited. The reader's attention is now directed for a moment to the cases in which the volumes were kept. As will perhaps be sufficiently understood already, these were aumbries or closed cupboards, and not the open shelves to which we are now accustomed.

---

[1] *Reg. J. Whethamstede abbatis secundæ* (Rolls Series), i., p. 421.
[2] Wharton, *Anglia Sacra*, i., p. 145.
[3] Ibid., p. 146.

From the earliest times Christian libraries followed in this, as in many other respects, the pagan models. Upon the doors of the cupboards were, not unfrequently, painted the heads of the chief writers or other celebrated persons, as in the Vatican library at the present day, where, when the presses are closed no books are visible.[1] The volumes were placed apparently in a horizontal position on the shelves, and did not stand vertically as in modern times. One description of an English mediæval book cupboard may be given here. "The press in which the books are kept ought to be lined inside with wood, that the damp of the walls may not moisten or spoil the books. This press should be divided vertically as well as horizontally by sundry shelves, on which the books may be ranged so as to be separated one from another, for fear they be packed so close as to injure each other and delay those who want to use them."[2]

Perhaps the most complete account we have of the appearance and disposition of an English 15th century library is that of the White Canons of Titchfield. "There are in the library of Titchfield," says the preface to the old catalogue, "four cases (*columnæ*) to put the books in. Thus on the east face (*i.e.*, opposite the door) there are two—

---

[1] The Vatican Library was fitted up, as we see it to-day, with presses, vases and busts, by Pope Sixtus V., in 1588. It was, however, arranged strictly on the ancient Roman plan.

[2] Customary of Barnwell (Harl. MS. 3061), translated in *Saturday Review*, February 21st, 1891.

viz., (case) one and (case) two. On the south side is case three, and on the north, case four."

Each of these cases had eight shelves, marked with a letter of the alphabet, which represented a division of the library. Thus roughly in case 1 were placed the Bibles and the patristic glosses upon it; in case 2, was what might be termed the theological portion of the library; in case 3, the sermons, legends, regulæ with canon and civil law; whilst case 4 contained the books upon medical and surgical science, upon grammar, logic and philosophy, and the various unclassed volumes. The letters of the alphabet afforded further divisions: thus, B was fixed to seven shelves of case 1, and contained the various glosses on Holy Scripture; and D, affixed to five shelves of case 2, was assigned to the works of St. Gregory and St. Augustine. Lastly, on the first folio of each volume was entered the shelf letter, followed by a number naming its position on the shelf. Thus the volume from which these particulars are taken is called the "*Rememoratorium de Tychefelde*," and has on its first page the press mark "P.X." Turning to the catalogue we find that the volume is entered as the tenth book on shelf P.[1]

[1] Harl. MS. 6603, f. 3 seqq. (extracts from a volume in the possession of the Duke of Portland). This catalogue has now been printed by the Hampshire Record Society. At the end of the 14th century the Library of Lanthony Priory contained some 500 volumes arranged most carefully in subjects. They were placed in five cupboards or aumbries, each with many shelves. The catalogue (B. Mus., Harl. MS. 460, ff.

One word may be said on the practice of fastening books with a chain, although this had to do with public libraries, and had no place in monasteries. In churches the custom of having a fastened breviary or Bible was very common. "Bound with a chain like a common book" was an expression of St. Bernard; and St. Thomas of Villanova, at the beginning of the 16th century, speaks of "the breviaries in cathedral churches left for public use and fastened with a chain." From an inventory, taken in 1483, it appears that the Sacristan of Saint-Oyan had amongst other books a "Catholicum," or dictionary, with an iron chain to it, probably for public use in the sacristy.[1] So, too, in the public library at Oxford, each book had, within fifteen days of its being acquired, to be chained to its proper place, and the keys of the chains kept in the chest of five keys. At St. Mary's Church, in A.D. 1414, the

---

3-11) gives the titles of the books in each aumbry beginning with the bottom shelf, which it calls the "*primus gradus.*" The first aumbry was reserved for Bibles and glosses on the Holy Scripture—the glossed psalters alone filled the fourth and fifth shelf. In the second and third aumbry were the works of the Fathers and theological works. In the fourth, canon law occupied the three bottom shelves; the fourth, fifth and sixth shelves held the classics, grammarians, philosophers and historians. The fifth and last shelf of the third aumbry contained the works on medicine and the fifth aumbry was reserved for future additions. (Cf. H. Omont, *Anciens Catalogues de Bibliothèques Anglaises*, Leipsig, 1892, p. 208; a separate print from Hartwig's *Centralblatt für Bibliothekswesen.*)

[1] *La Bibliothèque de Saint-Claude du Jura* in the *Bibl. de l'Ecole des Chartes*, vol. i., p. 319.

work of de Lira on the Bible was chained in the chancel for the use of the Oxford students. Many donors expressly prescribe such chaining of their books, even in the monastery cloister. Thus Peter III., King of Aragon, in 1382, in presenting a library to the great Cistercian Abbey of Poblet, lays down in his deed of gift that the abbot is not only to have made in the cloister "bels banchs," but is to provide "moltes cadenes," to the end that the books may be chained. Moreover, that the memory of his gift be not lost, he adds that the royal arms are to be emblazoned over the aumbry, with this inscription "in good letters and big: *aquesta es la libreria del Rey En Pere III.*," to distinguish him from other Kings of the name of Peter.[1]

I may now pass on to the *librarian*, or officer having charge of the books. Strange as this may seem to us now, the office was held almost invariably, at least in England, by the cantor or precentor, the chief official director of the church services. Calling to mind the fact of the close connection between the library and the church, to which attention has been directed, it is not difficult to understand the origin of this union of duties now apparently so distinct in one man. Whatever be the explanation, the fact is clear, that ordinarily the *cantor* was the official librarian. "The library," says the custumary of Abingdon,

[1] J. Coroleu, *Documents Historichs Catalans del sigle* xiv., pp. 33-4.

"shall be in the keeping of the cantor. . . . When he is away, the succentor (or sub-cantor), if he shall be fit for the office, shall keep the library keys; but should he be giddy and light minded, he shall give them to the prior or subprior.

"If any shall go a long journey, he shall hand over to the cantor, before starting, the library books he may have . . . The keys of the presses in which the *libri annuales* and singing books are kept, shall be in the keeping of the subcantor."[1]

Further, "the cantor shall examine the aumbries belonging to the boys and youths, and the others in which the books of the community are placed, repair them when damaged, find material for the library books, and mend any tears."[2]

It was the cantor's place also to see that the monks were supplied with books, and that no book was given out from the presses without a proper entry on the parchment roll kept for the purpose. He had also to see that the readers took proper care of the books borrowed by them. Thus, at Evesham it is ordered that: "whenever the community sat in the cloister (the cantor) shall walk round when the bell has sounded, and put back (into the presses) such books as by the carelessness of some may have been forgotten. Let him take charge of all the books of the monastery,

[1] *Chronicon de Abingdon* (Rolls series), ii., pp. 373-4.
[2] Ibid., p. 371.

and have them in his keeping, if his diligence in study and knowledge are such that they may be entrusted to his charge. Let him not take back a book from any one, unless it be entered on the roll; neither let a book be given to anyone in exchange without a proper and sufficient voucher, and let this be entered on the roll."[1]

Even as late as A.D. 1511, Archbishop Warham, in his Visitation of Christchurch, Canterbury, testifies to the continuance of the universal custom by which the cantor had charge of the library. "As to the 6th article," he says—"that is, as to the proper distribution of books to each monk, it is arranged that the precentor, to whom *ex-officio* the distribution of books belongs, shall take care to give to every one suitable books."[2]

The care taken of books in the middle ages, as evidenced by the Evesham customs, may be illustrated by a similar direction to the librarian of the public library at Oxford to see that "every night open books, open windows and the door of the

[1] Evesham Customs in *Penwortham Priory* (Chetham Soc.), p. 105.
[2] Arund. MS. 68, f. 70. The following portions of the admonition addressed to the Librarian prefixed to the catalogue of the monastic library of Admont in 1370 are worth quoting. "The work of the librarian, or, as we call him, *Armarius*, in a monastery is the library; so manage, therefore, that thou, who art made the armarius, mayest have full knowledge of what is given to thy charge. . . The first duty of a librarian is to strive in his time as far as possible to increase the library committed to him." Then after quoting many examples of those who had gathered together large libraries, the Prologue continues: "Every armarius should, as far as his opportunities allow, emulate the foregoing examples. He who is, however, negligent in

library be shut without fail" (*infallibiliter*).[1] It would be impossible here to show fully how completely alive those in the "dark ages" were to the value of such volumes as they possessed. They knew, as well as we do, that every manuscript was *unique*, that it possessed a history of its own and existed in its perfect state only by the labours of many skilful heads and many cunning hands. All this, however, is a story connected with the work of what is known as the *scriptorium* of the mediæval monastery, and well deserves to be considered separately. It may be sufficient for the present purpose to state broadly that, allowing for the difference of money, a manuscript would cost in the middle ages as much as, if not more than, such hand work would fetch in these days. Moreover, it is to be remembered that a single manuscript often contained a number of separate treatises which, if printed, would form as many volumes.

And this leads me to say a word about the size of

this, let him at least beware that the library does not diminish—that is, that the books given to his charge do not in any way get lost or perish. Let him know and have a care against fire and water, which are most hurtful to books. Let him repair by binding, books destroyed by age, let him put them in a sure and safe place that so he may warn readers to treat them properly. What and where they are let him remember, and know the names and their authors. If there are more books than he remember the names of, let him make for himself a list or book, in the beginning of which, if he wish, he can write this Prologue." Wichner (J.), *Zwei Bücherverzeichnisse d. 14 Jahrhunderts in der Admonter Stiftsbibliothek*, p. 4 (a separate print from the *Centralblatt f. Bibliothekswesen*).

[1] *Munimenta Academica* (Rolls series) i., p. 267.

the English monastic libraries. Of course, as in the present day, this varied considerably according to the taste and requirements of the particular house. According to Prior Eastry's catalogue, there were at the beginning of the 14th century some 3000 works in the library of Christchurch, Canterbury. At Glastonbury the catalogue made in 1247, and printed by Hearne,[1] shows, if it be a complete list, that the monks of the great Somerset monastery then had about 400 volumes, and must therefore have been about the same size as that of Canterbury; and, to take but one more example, the list of books belonging to Peterborough, printed at length by Gunton, comprises some 1700 works in 268 volumes. Of some, even of the greatest abbeys—as, for example, of St. Albans —we have no means of estimating the extent, so completely were the literary treasures swept away at the dissolution by the Tudor officials. A few years before the suppression of the house, Leland visited Verulam "to examine the ruins of the old Roman town. When I had done this," he says, "I went to the sanctuary of St. Alban, nigh to the fallen city wall. Here a scholarly monk, called Kingsbery, a diligent investigator of antiquities, most courteously showed me the manuscript treasures of this great monastery." It appears clear, therefore, that up to its last days the library —whatever happened afterwards—was sedulously

[1] *Joannis Glastoniensis Chron.*, pp. 423 seqq.

cared for.[1] Some of the books had evidently left the St. Albans' shelves at an earlier date, for that monastery, on account of its political proclivities, seems to have been marked out for vengeance from the very first days of the Tudor sovereignty.

The Reformation in England, from whatever side it is approached, was indeed, to a degree which is not now inadequately realized, heartbreaking work. It would appear not improbable that the last days of Leland were rendered a sorrowful agony by the mere spectacle of the ruin wrought around him. " Thus John Leland, *antiquarius*," says a singularly well-informed writer, " had a side to his character of which very little is known. He was an ardent lover of poetry, had a great knowledge of classic writers, and was himself a facile executant in the classic vein. But those who chose to regard him only as a picker-up of antiquities looked somewhat askance on the production of his muse, and a correspondent of Bale's, saying that " Maistre Leylande" had " a poetycall wyte," quaintly adds, " whyche I lament, for I judge it to be one of the chefest thynges that caused hym to fall besydes his ryghte dyscernynges." And Bale's sweet curses—

---

[1] Tanner, *Bibliotheca Britannico-Hibernica*, p. 613. The name Leland gives the monk is " *a regia curia*," which at first sight seems likely to be " Kingscourt ; " but it was probably one " *Thomas Kyngesbery*," who took his degree of B.D. at Oxford 4th March, 1511-12 (Boase, *Register of the University of Oxford* I., p. 44). The name of " Thomas Kyngsberd, prior," appears in the list of monks at the dissolution of the abbey (Monasticon II., p. 250).

"God shorten their unprofytable lyves, if they cease not of that myschefe in tyme," and "cursed be he for ever and ever, that shall, in spyght of hys nacyon, seke thereof the destruccyon"—are aimed at those who were enemies of the historical works of Leland. Others may prefer to the suggestion of the Bishop's friend to believe that different causes led to the antiquary's insanity. Is it not more likely that when he had travelled through England, had witnessed the yet untouched splendours of the monastic houses, had pored over the things he most cherished, their chartularies, computus books, and chronicles, his mind gave way when he saw the destruction that very nearly did away altogether with the learned lore of long and toilsome ages of history."[1]

This, however, relates specially to the larger houses, and there is no doubt that many would perhaps consider some of the poorer houses very badly furnished indeed. Thus Deping possessed only 23 volumes, and some, I suspect, were still less well provided.[2] It must, however, be borne in mind,

---

[1] *Saturday Review*, Sept. 5th, 1885.

[2] The catalogue of the Burton-on-Trent House, drawn up about 1175, names some 78 volumes, and contains many items we would gladly possess to-day. (See Omont, *ubi supra*.) There were several Anglo-Saxon translations in the library, Gospels, Psalters, &c. One of these, *Apollonius Anglice*, suggests the possibility of this volume being the same as the only copy of this work known to exist, in C. C. Coll. Cambridge, MS. No. 201, formerly S. 18. There are indications which seem to connect this important manuscript with Winchester, by a colony from which Burton-upon-Trent was founded in 1004.

that only the richer foundations could afford to purchase the costly manuscript treasures at a time when to present 129 books, as Humphrey Duke of Gloucester did to Oxford, was considered a most princely donation. Perhaps, as a general estimate of the size of the monastic libraries in England, the opinion of the antiquary Hearne may be quoted. "No one," he writes, "that reads either Boston of Bury, or Leland, or other authors who say anything of their (*i.e.*, the monks') writings, can justly suppose them to have been illiterate men . . . . We have accounts of the furniture of some of these libraries; and if we may judge of the rest by these, 'tis certain they had a large as well as a noble stock of books; and that many of their libraries might vie for number with many of the best libraries since. And even such libraries as had not so great a store, exceeded divers of our present libraries by reason they were all manuscripts; and upon that score are to be looked upon as a valuable and precious treasure. In short, as the abbeys were very curious, fine and magnificent piles of buildings, richly endowed, and continually found liberal benefactors, so I believe their libraries in every respect answered the other parts of the structures, and were all (notwithstanding the reflexion made upon the Franciscan library at Oxford, just upon the dissolution) adorned with an extraordinary fine collection of books."[1]

Moreover, it must be remembered that gigantic

[1] Hearne, Appendix to Leland's *Collectanea* ii., p. 86.

libraries, such as we find in these days, are quite a modern growth. Even in the last century collections of ten or fifteen thousand volumes were considered large, and the vast libraries of these times have been rendered possible only by the sacrifice of many smaller ones, and by the doubtful policy of gathering in a few large centres what had been spread over the country. A comparison of the public libraries in France and England will show that whilst in almost every district of the former there exist large collections of manuscripts and printed books, in England all have gradually been gathered together to three or four large centres. This may be explained partly by the fact that in England there has been time since the suppression for the tendency to concentration to run a full course, partly by the fact that on the suppression of the French religious houses the old monastic libraries were secured to the nearest town, whilst in the 16th century in England the priceless manuscript treasures were scattered to the winds as worthless rubbish, and the remnants that have been saved from destruction we owe to the zeal of private collectors.

But little need be said about the catalogues of the libraries. Although but few specimens have been preserved to us, there is every reason to suppose that a system of cataloguing, more or less elaborate, existed in every religious house. Some, probably, would be mere lists, like that of Cluny which Mabillon and Martene found there five or six hundred years after it was written. The books were entered on parchment stretched on two boards three and a half feet long by one and a half broad; and much the same practical arrangement existed apparently in the public library at Oxford, where the librarian was directed to enter the names of the volumes and their donors on a " large and conspicuous board, to be suspended in the library."[1] In some of the English monasteries, however, very full and perfect catalogues existed—not mere lists of books, but such as showed the works arranged in classes, and often with such verbal indications as might serve to identify a manuscript. Thus the Titchfield catalogue was so arranged, as the preface says, " that when any book is wanted it may be found in the library without difficulty, on the shelf marked with the letter referred to " : and, to mention but one more example, the Durham catalogues, published by the Surtees Society, not only classify the books, but enable a manuscript to be identified even now, by quoting the first two words of the second folio of each volume.[2]

[1] *Munimenta Academica* (Rolls series) i., p. 267.

[2] The use of this I may be allowed perhaps to illustrate by the following :—In the course of some investigations I was making of the sermon literature of the 14th and 15th centuries, I came upon a volume of sermons, "Magistri Roberti Rypon." From internal evidence I concluded that they had been preached at Durham. I turned to the Durham catalogues, and found, on p. 76, "Sermones Magistri Roberti Rypon, Supprioris Dunelmensis, cum tabula, ii. fo. Vivendo debent." These two words corresponded with the first words on folio 2

It may perhaps appear somewhat unnecessary to mention that the books of a monastic library were freely used by the inmates for study and reading. It has, however, been asserted more than once lately that the unfortunate monk was allowed only one book each year. This probably is a statement founded on that of Sir Thomas Duffus Hardy,[1] that "in some monasteries it was the custom, at the commencement of Lent, for the armarius to deliver to each of the monks a book for his private reading, allowing him one year for its perusal." That the writer could not have meant to imply that this was the only book allowed during the year is evident from other parts of his preface, and no doubt he referred to the practice, founded on the legislation of St. Benedict's Rule, of assigning a special lenten book to each monk. Sometimes it would appear also that occasion was taken of this practice at the beginning of the lenten fast to cause all volumes then in use to be returned to the shelves of the aumbry; and in places, as at Barnwell Priory and elsewhere, the precentor at this time brought to

of the manuscript (Harl. MS. 4894) I had examined. I came to the conclusion, therefore, that this volume, now in the British Museum, was probably the identical book formerly at Durham. This conclusion was proved afterwards to be correct. On the first folio of the volume some words had evidently been erased, and were quite illegible. By the kindness of the authorities, however, acid was applied, and the words so carefully scratched out reappeared. They were, "Librarie Monachorum Dunelm."

[1] *Catalogue of the MSS. Materials relating to the History of Great Britain and Ireland* (Rolls series) iii., p. xiv.

the chapter those volumes which had been given to the church and monastery, and a special commemoration was made of the souls of those who had thus been benefactors, and of the souls of those of the brethren who had laboured in the writing of these books.

Care was taken that in the use of the volumes no unnecessary damage was done by the readers. The very mode of holding the manuscript was even apparently prescribed, if not by law, at least by general custom which subsequently passed into law. The *Traditio Generalis Capituli* of the Benedictine monks of England, given in a volume formerly belonging to St. Augustine's, Canterbury, orders that "when the religious are engaged in reading in cloister or church, if it be possible, they shall hold the books on their left hands, wrapped in the sleeve of their tunics and resting on their knees. Their right hands shall be uncovered with which to hold and turn the leaves of their books." It was by the constant exercise of care in the use of their precious volumes that such books as St. Aldhelm's Psalter at Malmesbury and St. Cuthbert's Gospels at Durham were preserved till the dissolution of the monasteries,[1] and that Leland could say in the 16th century that he found in the library at Bath several books given to the abbey by King Athelstan.[2]

One circumstance connected with monastic libraries is often forgotten. The great price of books

---

[1] Leland, *De Scriptoribus*, p. 100.   [2] Ibid., p. 160.

made it almost impossible for poor clerics to get the volumes necessary for their studies, and their need was often supplied by the loan of a volume from some conventual library. "The services rendered by the monastic houses in these circumstances," writes M. Léopold Delisle, "have not been sufficiently recognised. The lending of books was then considered as one of the most meritorious works of charity." The same authority notes that although the practice of placing books under *anathema* grew common, it was condemned as contrary to due Christian charity to the needy. Speaking specially of certain notes of a librarian of St. Ouen in the 14th century, he declares that even bishops and archbishops are found among the borrowers of books. At this monastery the greatest care was taken that no book should be lost. Before any volume was lent it was registered, and a note made in the catalogue, with the name of the borrower. At times, in the case of some special volume, it is mentioned that the loan was made by order of the abbot, and when it is sent far away the name of the messenger to whom it is entrusted is entered on the register.[1]

Some such system existed in every monastic house. Thus Hunter has printed[2] a list of some twenty volumes lent by the Carthusian convent of

---

[1] *Documents sur les Livres et les Bibliothèques du Moyen Age* in *Bibl. de l'Ecole des Chartes*, 3è serie i., p. 225.

[2] *English Monastic Libraries*, pp. 16, 17.

Hinton in Somerset to a neighbouring monastery in
A.D. 1343. The engagement to restore these books
was formally drawn and sealed.[1] The chronicle of
Ingulph, whether authentic or not, represents the
practice of Croyland in the later middle ages. "Our
books," the author says, "as well the smaller
unbound volumes as the larger ones which are
bound, we altogether forbid, and under anathema
prohibit, to be lent to any far distant schools,
without the leave of the Abbot, and a distinct
understanding as to the time when they shall be
returned. As to the lending of lesser books, however, such as Psalters, copies of Donatus, Cato and
the like poetical works, and the singing lesson-books to children and the relations of the monks,
we strictly forbid the Cantor, or anyone who shall
act as librarian, under pain of disobedience, to
allow them to be lent for a longer time than one
day without leave of the Prior."[2]

Caution was necessary lest the practice of charity
to others should make havoc in the monastic library.

---

[1] The following is an instance of this. In 1281 Archbishop John de Peckham stayed at Itchel, and amongst other business transacted at the time, gave a receipt, dated December 16, for a *Biblia Glosata*, in two volumes, lent to him by the executors of Nicholas de Ely, late Bishop of Winchester. The Bible in question seems to have been much valued on account of its annotations, and was bequeathed by the Bishop to the Prior and Convent of Winchester Cathedral. It was borrowed by Bishop John de Pontissara on April 26, 1299, who gave a formal bond for its safe return, which is entered in his Episcopal Register, fol. 139. (F. J. Baigent, *Crondal Records*, p. 408.)

[2] Ingulph, quoted in Maitland's *Dark Ages*, p. 265.

In a Constitution of Abbot Curteys, it is seen that at Bury St. Edmund's in the 15th century, so many books had been lent, sold, and lost to the house, that special attention had to be paid to the matter. Some of the books, the Abbot says, he has been able to get back " by begging for them, some by payment, some with great trouble only, and at great expense, and sometimes even at the great indignation of those who held them." And not only was all further lending, pledging or selling forbidden, but all were ordered within fifteen days " to bring, carry, and produce " (to the Abbot) " all and each book belonging to our said monastery yet remaining" in their custody.[1] One instance of what must be abundantly evident without it—namely, how easily books so lent by a religious house might go astray and be lost—may be here given. In the middle of the 12th century, Nicholas Sandwich, Prior of Christchurch, Canterbury, appointed two of his monks to receive back from the convent of Anglesey, Cambridge, a book which had been lent

[1] Monasticon iii., pp. 114-5. At the end of the library catalogue of the Convent of St. Anthony at Padua, in 1396 (ed. W. von Göthe (?), p. 161 seqq.; see note 1, p. 10, ante) is a careful list of those who had borrowed books from the library. The list includes the name of a Pope and many strangers, besides various friars. One of these latter is "Friar David, *Anglicus*." The first list is supplemented by one of books lent but not returned up to 1423. A note says that most of the borrowers here named " are dead," though still marked as having various volumes in their keeping. At the end there is a record that "a fine decretal " and other books were pledged to one Andrew, a miller, on July 14, 1407, " to secure payment for flour supplied to the community."

Master Lawrence de St. Nicholas, Rector of Terrington, which book, on the death of Master Lawrence, had remained in the possession of the convent in Cambridgeshire.[1]

The truth is that books in the middle ages, in spite of all the possible care of their owners, disappeared, were lost and destroyed quite as easily as in the present day. The fires which brought disaster to so many monasteries, and the civil disturbances which swept over England, were the worst enemies to the monastic libraries. Hereward and the Danes burnt the library of Peterborough; Owen Glendower that of the Franciscans of Cardiff, which had been put into the castle for safety. The books of the library of Norwich were either burnt

---

[1] *Notes and Queries*, i., Ser. i. 20. The book was "Johannes Crisostomus de laude Apostoli. In quo etiam volumine continentur Hystoria vetus Britonum quæ Brutus appellatur et tractatus Roberti Episcopi Herfordie de compoto." The volume is found, two centuries later, in Prior H. Eastry's catalogue. In the *Literæ Cantuarienses* (Rolls Series ii., pp. 146—152) is printed a list of books found to be absent from the library shelves at Christchurch, Canterbury, on the feast of St. Gregory (March 12th), 1337. Some are noted as having been registered to various brethren of the house, and they are called upon to account for them. Others, some seventeen in number, are registered as lent to seculars. In fact, to whatever country one turns, whether to France, Italy, or England, the same quasi-public character of the monastic library is found to exist, and scholars, even at considerable distances from a monastic centre, were able to obtain the loan of a volume required for their studies. It is worth recording that the last volume entered in the list printed in the *Literæ Cantuarienses* is "liber qui dicitur *Johannes Crisostomus de laude Apostoli*," apparently the very same volume which we find lent from the Canterbury library more than a century before.

in the fire which destroyed the church, or carried off by the citizens in the consequent confusion.

A few words must now be said as to the presents of books made to monastic libraries. Throughout the monastic chronicles those who procured manuscripts for the house, or those who gave or made them, are duly commemorated. At St. Augustine's, Canterbury, as elsewhere, special prayers were yearly offered for such as had been benefactors to the library;[1] and as the obit of each abbot and monk whose zeal in this regard had been conspicuous came round, a special memorial was made in the chapter of his good deeds. It would be impossible, even if the reader's patience has not already been exhausted, to do more than touch upon this large subject. Two examples only may here be mentioned. One is that of Adam Easton, a cardinal of the holy Roman church.[2] He had been a monk of Norwich, and it is pleasing to find that he did not forget his old home when raised to his great dignity. The library of his monastery, as we have noted, had perished by fire, and hence Cardinal Easton's collections made in Italy would have been

---

[1] Thorne in Twysden's *Decem Scriptores*, col. 2008.

[2] Adam Easton had accompanied Simon de Langham, Cardinal Archbishop of Canterbury, to Avignon, and was present at his death there in 1375. The following year Easton writes to Nicholas Litlyngton, Abbot of Westminster, to say that the late Archbishop, formerly Abbot of that house, had left a large number of books and vestments, which he had collected as Cardinal, to his old monastery, and that they were then on their way to Bruges.

specially a benefaction, and we can imagine the joy of the convent on the reception of "ten barrels of books" from Rome, which in 1407 Henry IV. allowed to pass toll free through the port of London.[1]

The second example I take from a period close upon the dissolution of the monasteries, and it shows the anxiety of Prior Moore of Worcester to enrich the library of his convent in the last days of its existence. The details are taken from that excellent but little-known volume, "*The Monastery and Cathedral of Worcester*," by John Noake. In A.D. 1518 Prior Moore made his first journey to London after his election. On that occasion he says: "I redeemed a lyttell portuos (breviary) lying to pledge in Teames Street," 53s. 4d., which would be some £25 of our money. Then follows a list of books purchased, one of which, the *Speculum Spiritualium*, is said to have been "delyvered to ye cloister awmery" (*i.e.*, aumbry) and the "hoole work of Scynt Austen's in print delyvered to our library," 50s. In the following year the names of

[1] Rymer, *Fœdera* viii., 501. Visitors to Rome may perhaps be reminded of Cardinal Easton by the exquisite fragment of his tomb which still remains in the Church of Santa Cecilia. It would be interesting to know whether the sculptor was an Englishman or an Italian. Not unfrequently benefactors would make over books to some religious house with the proviso that they were to retain the use of them during life. Thus a Bishop of Torcelli in 1496 by Charter secured to the monastery of St. Justina of Padua his Pontifical and Book of Preparation for Mass, *usum vero istorum duorum librarum sibi retinuit in vita sua.*

some 20 books are given as added to the library, one of which is "a hoole co'sse of sevyll (? course of civil law) fyve volumes." In 1520 the Prior "Bought ye hoole worke of Abbott, 22s. 8d.," and "Paid for 3 books of Seynt Benett's rewle in Englishe, 2s. 7d." In the following year he paid for "a baggett of lether to bare my books in," 10d., and so on till the year 1523, when the Prior purchased "a great bucke of statutes of Ingland from first yere of Edward 3rd till ye parlyment holden after Crystmas, 25th Henry eygth, 10s.; a great boke of Councils, 8s. 4d.; Natura Brev. and Magna Charta, 2s.; a book of the Passion, 2s."[1]

To procure books for new religious houses was sometimes thought an occasion worthy of royal letters to neighbouring monasteries. Thus Henry III., in 1271, on the foundation of Dernhall, afterwards Vale Royal, issued his letters patent to the abbots and priors of England for this purpose.

---

[1] Among the other books bought are: St. Jerome's works, 5 vols., 40s.; St. Gregory's, 1 vol., 8s.; St. Ambrose, 3 vols., 13s. 4d.; Hugh of St. Victor, 3 vols., 15s.; Richard of St. Victor, De Trinitate, 16d.; Opera Ruparti (of Deutz), 3 vols, 15s.; Opera Bedæ, 1 vol., 6s. 8d.; Opera Hilarii, 1 vol., 6s.; Opera Basilii, 1 vol., 3s. 4d.; Opera Cypriani, 1 vol., 5s.; Opera Fulgentii, 1 vol., 16d.; Bedæ de Natura Rerum; Angelomus (who figured very soon after in the great Eucharist disputes), 2s.; Opera Laurentii Justiniani, 1 vol., 6s. 8d.; Opera Senecæ, 1 vol., 5s.; Philo Judæus, 2s.; Ludolphus De Vita Xpi, 4s.; Legenda Sanctorum Angliæ (evidently Capgrave), 16d.; St. Bernard's works; Legenda Sanctorum in English; English Cronacles, 2s. 8d. It is useless to continue the list, but it is evident that at this time the English Benedictines were perfectly alive to all the productions of the foreign, no less than the English book market.

Having recited how his son Edward had intended to establish this new Cistercian abbey, he begged them to assist the monks of the place with "any theological books" they could spare, asking them to inform one Thomas de Boulton what they could do in the matter, and promising them his thanks and those of his son for all they did in this way to meet his wishes.[1]

An account of the way in which the monastic libraries were enriched by the presents of single volumes and collections of books deserves separate treatment; but no notice of our monastic libraries would be even fairly complete without some mention of the subject. An example or two may be given at random:—Abbot Benedict of Peterborough, who was chosen in 1177, was a great lover of books, and enriched the library of his house with some fifty-three volumes. He had been

---

[1] Monasticon v., p. 709. An interesting example of the way books were collected on the continent and forwarded to England may be seen in the Register of Adam de Orlton, Bishop of Hereford. The following letter dated at Avignon, November 4, 1319, is entered on folio 33 of the Episcopal Register: Universis pateat per presentes quod nos Adam permissione Divina Heref. Eps. recepimus a Laurentio Bruton de Chepyn Norton Summam Fratris Thomæ de Aquino in quatuor voluminibus. Item scriptum ejusdem Fratris Thomæ super quartum librum Sententiarum. Librum de Similitudinibus. Librum Historiæ Scolasticæ, Librum Rethoricæ Aristotilis. Librum Rethoricæ Tullii. Librum Geometricæ cum Commento. Quos quidem libros bonâ fide promittimus eidem Laurentio in Anglia restituere vel justum pretium eorundem prout placuerit Religioso viro Fratri Johanni Abbati Monasterii de Hayles, avunculo dicti Laurentii et Laurentio antedicto."

Prior of Christchurch, Canterbury, and owing to the difficulties in which he found Peterborough involved, his health gave way, and for a time he retired to his old home at Christchurch. There, during his convalescence, he wrote a fine book (volumen egregium) on the passion and miracles of St. Thomas, and composed antiphons and music for his house. Among the collection of books which he gave to his abbey at Peterborough, were some twenty-one Bibles, glossed and simple texts, some works on Canon law, two arithmetics, a Seneca, a Martial and a Terence.[1]

Again, Abbot Marleberge of Evesham before becoming a monk had taught canon and civil law at Oxford. On entering the monastery he brought his collection of law books with him, and also added to the monastic library a Cicero, a Lucan, and a Juvenal. Both as Prior and as Abbot his literary tastes are shown in the many volumes he bought, or caused to be written, for his house.[2]

So, too, the various chronicles of monastic houses show that monks very frequently procured special books for their monasteries, or enriched the collections with volumes dealing with subjects in which they were specially interested. Thus Herveus, the sacrist of Bury St. Edmund's in the time of Abbot Anselm, through his brother Thalebot the Prior, gave " a great Bible written in two volumes for the

---

[1] Sparke, *Historiæ Anglicanæ Scriptores* ii., 98.
[2] *Chron. Abb. de Evesham*, ed. Macray (Rolls series), pp. 267 seqq.

Refectory," and Stephen, the "monk-doctor and infirmarian" (medico monacho), obtained and "gave to the convent three large and fine books on medicine."[1] In a word, it is impossible to examine monastic records without feeling that the special studies or tastes of individuals were very frequently the means whereby the general collection of books was increased.[2]

With this I conclude these somewhat rambling notes on mediæval monastic libraries. It is a large subject to which in England sufficient attention has hitherto not been paid. The suppression of the monasteries was accompanied by a ruthless destruction of priceless treasures in the shape of manuscripts. Of this it is not necessary to speak; but so completely were the hundreds of monastic libraries scattered to the winds, that their very memory has perished.[3] Perhaps it would have been as well had Bale's proposition been adopted,

[1] Copy of an Edmundsbury MS. in the town library at Douai in my possession, pp. 67-8.

[2] This of course applies to others beside those who entered the monastic state. Thus Richard de Haute, Rector of Westerham, in 1337 left by will to Christchurch, Canterbury, "*corpus juris civilis*. Item, *Decretalia et decreta una cum glossa Hostiensis in duobus voluminibus.* Item, *summa copiosa et speculum judiciale*" (*Literæ Cantuarienses*, Rolls Series, ii., p. 153).

[3] A pathetic instance of the endeavours of the monks to save some of their literary treasures is afforded in the case of Monk Bretton. At the dissolution of the house the prior and other monks managed to purchase the manuscripts. The Priory was granted by the King to William Blitheman who sold the buildings and church piecemeal to the highest bidder. The monks apparently remained together in the

that there should be established " in every shire of England one solemn library for the preservation of noble works and the preferment of good learning in our posterity." But this was not the genius of the times, for as the author of the *Essay on Sepulchres* says, the Reformation like the French Revolution " was signally a period in which a plot was laid to abolish the memory of the affairs which had been, and to begin the affairs of the human species afresh."

little village of Worsborough, a few miles from their old home, until 1558; at that date a list of books shows that the volumes of their former library were distributed about in the various small chambers of their refuge at Worsborough. (This catalogue has been printed by Hunter, *Monastic Libraries*.

II.

THE MONASTIC SCRIPTORIUM.[1]

BOOK-MAKING is commonly allowed to have been a work *par excellence* of the mediæval monk. So far at least as the mechanical labour of writing and embellishing the pages of a manuscript with illumination goes, even those who have least sympathy with monks and monasteries would perhaps be not disinclined to concede that, in this respect, they have deserved well of the world. Indeed it is difficult to see how less could be allowed, seeing that well-nigh all our manuscript treasures are, in one sense or another, the products of the monastic workshops. Sweep away these works of the cloister scribe, and destroy the printed volumes already copied from them, and it is little indeed that, even in this learned nineteenth century, we should know of the past ages of the world. And however much we may be inclined to agree with the ancient dame who objected to " history " on the

[1] Reprinted, with additions, from the *Downside Review*, vol. xi., p. 4 seqq.

ground that "bye-gones should be bye-gones," there are few who would not look upon total ignorance of the men and events of times that have gone by as a real misfortune. So it comes about that most people are inclined to look even favourably upon the labours of the mediæval writers, by which so much that is precious has been preserved to our age. And even if they are not, they might perchance be interested in some brief account of the process of mediæval book-making.

It may perhaps be thought, from much that has been written about the *Scriptoria* of ancient religious houses, that every well-regulated monastery had its special place or room in which the writing of manuscripts was performed. This is hardly correct. No doubt in some of the greater houses this was the case; but in most instances the work formed part of the daily exercises conducted by the monks chosen for the purpose, in the cloister of the monastery, or at most in the little studies or carells, partially screened off from the common walks of the cloister, in the window recesses. Sometimes, too, there would have been small writing places or cells made to contain only one person, which, because the general occupation of students in those ages was writing, were *Scriptoria*.

One of these private studies, belonging to a secretary of St. Bernard, who was afterwards an abbot, is thus described for us by himself:—" Its door opens into the apartment of the novices, where commonly a great number of persons, distinguished by rank as well as by literature, put on the new man in the newness of life. On the right runs the cloister of the monks, in which the more advanced part of the community walk. There, under the strictest discipline, they individually open the books of Divine eloquence. From the left projects the infirmary and the place of exercise for the sick. And do not suppose that my little tenement is to be despised; for it is a place to be desired and pleasant to look upon, and comfortable for retirement. It is filled with most choice and divine books, at the delightful view of which I feel contempt for the vanity of this world. This place is assigned to me for reading and writing, and composing, and meditating, and praying, and adoring the Lord of Majesty."[1]

Such private cells or *Scriptoria* as these, however, were probably only assigned to the more learned members of the community, or those whose special work made it important that they should be more free from distractions than they would be in the common cloister. And it was very possibly in such studies, as Sir Thomas Hardy has remarked, that the old English monastic historiographers, William of Malmesbury, Matthew Paris, and the rest, compiled their annals.[2]

Of the work of writing carried on in the cloister

---

[1] Maitland, *The Dark Ages*, p. 401.
[2] Hardy, *Descriptive Catalogue*, iii., p. 21.

there are numerous instances. Abbot Herimann, speaking about Ralph, the Prior of his monastery of St. Martin at Tournay, under his predecessor Abbot Odo (*circa* A.D. 1093), says:—" Frequently he did not go out of the monastery for a month together, but, being devoted to reading, he took the utmost pains to promote the writing of books. He used, in fact, to exult in the number of writers which the Lord had given him; for if you had gone into the cloister you would have generally seen a dozen young monks sitting on chairs, writing at tables, diligently, artistically, and in silence."[1]

As to the *Scriptorium* proper, that is, a set place for the work of writing,[2] there is evidence, for example, that such a room existed at an early date at St. Alban's. Abbot Thomas de la Mare (1349-96) not only himself formed " a study, or library," but encouraged Dom Thomas, of Walsingham, the cantor and *Scriptorarius*, to construct a " *domus Scriptoriæ*," which was completed at the Abbot's expense.[3] This, of course, refers to the place merely; for when three hundred years before the nephew of Archbishop Lanfranc, Abbot Paul (1077-93), by the introduction of Lanfranc's *Consuetudinary* made St. Alban's a *quasi-schola* re-

---

[1] Herimannus, *De Restit. S. Martini Tornacensis*, cap. 79, in D'Achery, *Spicilegium*, ii., 913.

[2] The assignment of a special place for writing called the Scriptorium, seems to have been rather Cistercian as a general practice, although there was one at the Monastery of St. Gall.

[3] Walsingham's *Gesta Abbatum*, iii., 389.

ligionis, and established there the writing school afterwards so famous,[1] he was perhaps doing no more than restoring an older institution.

Wherever the scribes sat at work, whether in the cloister, scriptorium, or private studies, there the strictest silence was enjoined. Conversation or noise of any kind, it was recognised, would probably lead to slips of the pen; and accurate copying was the chief point at which the old monastic writers were taught to aim. " Fixed places for this work " (of writing), says one consuetudinary, " are to be arranged apart from the community, but within the cloister, where the writers may pursue their labours without disturbance or noise. There sitting at work they ought to keep silence most carefully. . . . . No one must go to them except the Abbot, Prior, Sub-Prior, and Librarian."[2] To the same necessity of silence and quiet for the work of transcribing Alcuin refers in the lines :—

> " Hic sedeant sacrae scribentes famina legis
> Necnon Sanctorum dicta sacrata Patrum.
> Hic interserere caveant sua frivola verbis
> Frivola nec propter erret et ipsa manus.
> Correctosque sibi quærant studiose libellos,
> Tramite quo recto penna volantis eat
> Est decus egregium sacrorum scribere libros
> Nec mercede sua scriptor et ipse caret."[3]

Besides being a place of silence for the purpose of writing, the Scriptorium, where there was one,

[1] Ibid., Walsingham's *Gesta Abbatum*, i., 58.
[2] *Liber Ordinis S. Victoris Parisiensis*, Ducange, s.v. *Scriptores*.
[3] Alcuin, Poem 126 et apud Canisium.

was used sometimes for other purposes, for which quiet was equally necessary. Amongst these are mentioned in one rule "reading, meditating, studying, or hearing confessions."[1]

Like the Library, the writing school of the monastery was under the charge of the cantor. The case of St. Albans has already been mentioned. There Dom Thomas Walsingham, whose literary labours are so well known to us through the *Gesta Abbatum* and other works, held the office of "Cantor and Scriptorarius," during which office he constructed, or rather rebuilt, the *domus scriptoriæ* of the abbey. So at Abingdon it is ordered, that "from the rents assigned to the cantor, the cantor shall find parchment, ink, and everything necessary for the production of the books of the community."[2] Instances of this could be easily multiplied; but perhaps the most interesting, as it is the most particular instruction on this point, is to be found in the Consuetudinary of the Canons Regular of St. Victor's of Paris, from which a short extract has just been given. As it is a very full account of the cantor's office so far as its literary aspect is concerned, another and a longer quotation may perhaps be allowed. "All writings which are in the church either within or without pertain to his (*i.e.*, the cantor's) office, so that he shall provide parchment, *et cetera*, needful for writing, and hire those who

[1] Martene, *Anecd. Col.* iii., 1292.
[2] *Chron. Mon. de Abingdon* (Rolls series), ii., 371.

write for money. For the brethren of the cloister who are scribes and on whom the duty of writing has been imposed by the Abbot, let the Librarian arrange what they shall write, and provide whatever is necessary for their work. Let none write except as he is ordered, nor otherwise than at his will and disposition. The Librarian shall not appoint the brethren, who know how to write but on whom the Abbot has not imposed the work, to any such work, but if he has need of their assistance he should first point it out to the Abbot, and so by his leave and order do what has to be done. Let no one presume to write anything except what has been enjoined him.

"To all writers in the cloister, whether those who are ordered or those who are permitted to write, let the librarian furnish everything necessary, so that no one chose at his pleasure this or that, neither writing place, inkhorn, knife, nor parchment, nor anything else, but let all take without refusal or objection what he shall give as proper for the work.

"All documents which are written in the cloister, whether notices (breves) of the dead or other public and common business, even (the document) which is fastened to the paschal candle, belong to his office, and to write these, no one who knows how to write and whom he has appointed, should refuse, save that he who so writes cannot be absent from the regular hours, nor be dispensed from community observance without the leave of the Abbot. Whenever the work of scribe is enjoined to anyone in the cloister, it should be imposed in the common chapter. And there the Abbot will settle for them the times they are to spend in writing, and when he wishes them to return to the community life, and they must observe afterwards what is so settled for them.

"When parchment has to be cut or scraped, or books mended or bound, or anything of this kind, which pertains to the office of librarian in which he requires the aid of brethren, he shall take anyone to do this if he is unoccupied. That is, if other obedience does not hinder he must not excuse himself."[1]

From the work of the Master of the Scriptorium, who also held the important office of Librarian, or *armarius*, and Cantor, it is natural to pass on to speak of the scribes. These were of course, generally speaking, in monasteries the monks themselves. In fact, it was held to be the special and proper work of the monk that he should be able to fulfil the office of a scribe. Among the Carthusians it was enjoined as the best possible way in which they could labour. "Diligently labour at this work," writes Prior Guigo; "this ought to be the special work of enclosed Carthusians. . . This work in a certain sense is an

[1] Martene, *De Antiq. Eccl. Ritibus.*, iii., p. 253 *seqq.*

immortal work, if one may say it, not passing away, but ever remaining; a work, so to speak, that is not a work; a work which above all others is most proper for educated religious men."[1] So, too, the *statuta* of the Benedictines in England in the 13th and 14th centuries make it clear that this was looked upon as no less a part of the English monastic work. "By this constitution we order," says the Chapter of 1343, "that every monk not otherwise reasonably prevented at the time and place (appointed) be occupied in the study of reading, or in writing, correcting, illuminating, and likewise in binding books."[2] The direction of the Benedictine general Chapter of Canterbury in A.D. 1277 was that:—"In place of manual labour the Abbots shall appoint other occupations for their claustral monks according to their capabilities (namely) study, writing, correcting, illuminating, and binding books."[3] Such work, however, was to be done only by permission of their superior, and for the use of their monastery. This is clear from a direction of the Chapter of 1388, in which it is directed that "no one shall write or illuminate a book, either great or small, without the permission of his prelate and except it may be turned to the use of his monastery."[4]

[1] *Lib. de quadripertito Exercitio Cellæ*, cap. 36 (ed. Migne, vol. cliii., col. 883).
[2] Reyner, *Apostolatus*, iii., p. 160. The direction of the Chapter of 1444 (Ibid., p. 129) is the same.
[3] MS. Twyne (Oxon) 8, p. 272.
[4] B. Mus. Cott. MS., Faust, D. II., f. 96.

Of course, as it was so important to secure careful and accurate copying, only those who were known and tried scribes were allowed to take their part in the regular work of the *Scriptorium*. At Westminster, for example, although the novice master, when he considered his novices sufficiently instructed, could allow them to sit apart from the other students and read books from the aumbry of the seniors, still they were "not yet to write or have carrels, even if they were priests, unless the master should find that their writing can be of service to the church."

Nor was it the monk alone who worked at copying in the cloister. Many an abbot found time, in the midst of the heavy labours imposed by the management of a large establishment, to take his share in this special monastic employment. St. David, it is said, had his own writing-place, and with his own hands began the Gospel of St. John in golden letters. Even so great and busy a man as St. Dunstan did not consider it beneath his dignity to practise the art of a scribe, and by William of Malmesbury we are informed that the skill of this great archbishop in writing and illuminating was most remarkable. More than one Anglo-Saxon charter is said to be in his own hand, and in one work a picture, representing the Saint upon his knees at the feet of the Saviour, is attributed by some lines above it to him. Several of the abbots of St. Alban's are supposed to have actually taken part in the work of the renowned scriptorium of that house; and Abbot Marleberge of Evesham, who, before becoming a monk, had taught canon law at Oxford and Exeter, not only brought with him to Worcestershire his collection of books, but "found everything necessary for four noted antiphonals," which the brethren wrote under his supervision.[1]

One small point regarding the labours of scribes and copyists deserves to be noted. The work of the monastic copyist was looked upon as the common work of the house, and the individual was sunk in the work itself. If the hand of one held the pen, that of another was occupied in some other equally necessary, if perchance not so lasting, a work for the common good of the establishment. So although now we would fain know the names of some of those scribes whose manuscript work in our days forms the most precious treasure of our national libraries, it is seldom that our curiosity is satisfied. However carefully we may examine the folios, which have come from some great writing-school, such as Corbie, or Tours, or St. Alban's, we shall in vain look for any indication of the names of those monks who have written them, and indeed each manuscript was the joint work of many hands and heads. When the first scribe had done his part with the body of the work, the sheet had to pass under the eye of the "corrector," to

[1] *Chron. Abb. de Evesham* (Rolls Series), p. 267.

receive the finishing touches from some master hand and to have its initials and titles written in fair red-lettering by the "rubricator," or illuminated by the monastic artist.

In speaking of those occupied in book-making it is necessary to remember that besides the monks engaged upon the work, there was a class—and in later times a large class—of professional scribes. In most of the larger monasteries provision was made for the employment of one or more of these to aid in the labours of the scriptorium. Among the Augustinians, for example, at Barnwell Priory, the cantor is directed "to provide the writers with parchment, ink, and everything else necessary for writing, and to hire those who write for money." So at Abingdon:—"If there be an extern scribe writing at the disposition of the abbot and cantor, the abbot shall find his food, the cantor his wages."[1] Abbot Simon, of St. Alban's, too (1168-83), who in the latter half of the 12th century did so much for the resuscitation of this school of writing, so endowed it that succeeding abbots could have one scribe always kept at work. In some instances it seems not unlikely that these professional writers worked at home, whilst they were much employed on non-monastic work by such ecclesiastical lovers of books as Bishop Richard of Bury, and such patrons of learning as Humphrey, Duke of Gloucester, and the Regent Duke of Bedford. Richard of

[1] *Chron. Mon. de Abingdon* (Rolls series), ii., 371.

Bury says that in his "hall there was no small number of *antiquarii*, scribes, binders, correctors, illuminators, and generally of all who could usefully work in the service of books."[1] Of course, this learned cleric's library was not all made up of copies made by his own writers. The story how Abbot Richard II. of St. Alban's (1326-35) gave him a Terence, Virgil, and two other books from the monastic library, and agreed to sell thirty-two more volumes for £50, is well known. This gift Walsingham considered "altogether abominable," since it deprived "the cloistered monks of their best and only comfort." When made Bishop of Durham in A.D. 1333, be it added, Richard of Bury restored several of these precious volumes, and the next abbot, Michael de Mentmore, purchased others from his executors after his death.[2]

The great religious houses formed so many schools of writing in mediæval times, and the work of many of these scriptoria can be distinctly recognised by characteristic peculiarities initiated by some great writer and continued by his disciples. To these schools students repaired for instruction and information. Thus a monastery like St. Denis near Paris was renowned for its classical volumes like the Vatican Virgil, and the Carolingian Terence.[3]

[1] *Philobiblion*, cap. ix. *Antiquarii*, the author says in another place, are " transcriptores veterum."
[2] Walsingham, *Gesta Abbatum* (Rolls series), ii., 200.
[3] Hunter (*Monastic Libraries*, p. 23) considers that from the "frequent application of *vetus* to the manuscripts of the classics" in the catalogues

The religious evidently knew and studied Greek, Armenian, and Runic. During the 13th, 14th, and 15th centuries they were the historians, and to them all went for information on literary matters. In the special work of the scriptorium, it is certain that there existed at St. Denis an excellent school of writing and painting.[1]

There is evidence of the existence of monastic writing schools in England from the earliest times. St. Benet Biscop, who was a traveller and collector of books from his youth, had not only enriched the monasteries he founded with well-furnished libraries, but in A.D. 678, on his return from his fourth journey to Rome, he brought back with him the Abbot John, the Roman Archcantor, to teach them the annual order of singing and saying the office as it was done in the Church of St. Peter in Rome. Besides this there is little doubt that at

of the old English Monastery libraries, it may be suspected "that most of the manuscripts of that class in England were really of very high antiquity;" at St. Edmundsbury, for example, there was a Sallust described as "*vetustissimus.*" In another place (Monk Bretton Catalogue, p. 7.) the same authority notes that only one known Hebrew codex of the Scriptures has been traced to any of the English monastic libraries. He adds (p.11), "It is, perhaps, fortunate for Biblical literature that scarcely any manuscript of the Christian Scriptures in the original tongue, the most important of all, had found their way to England. But we cannot but regret that so many copies of the Latin version perished; some of which were of the highest antiquity, and had an additional value from the circumstance of their connection with some venerable name in the early history of Christianity in Britain. The *Red Book of Eye* was the very copy of the Gospels which had belonged to Felix."

[1] Delisle, *Cabinet des Manuscrits*, i., 204.

the same time he established teachers of writing in his houses of Wearmouth and Jarrow. This is something more than a mere conjecture, for Venerable Bede tells us that amongst other matters the Archcantor John was charged by the Pope to find out and relate upon his return the belief of the English on certain matters. He brought with him the acts of a Synod held by Pope Martin, "and gave them to be transcribed in the aforesaid monastery of the most religious Abbot Benedict."[1] Ceolfrid, the successor of St. Benet Biscop, certainly had three copies made of the Latin translation of the Holy Scriptures, one of which, when going to Rome as an old man, he took with him to present to the Pope. In recent times this identical copy made at Wearmouth, and taken thence by Ceolfrid in the 8th century, has been recognised in the celebrated *Codex Amiatinus*.

This codex is in handwriting like the 7th century Durham Gospel of St. John, the Stonyhurst St. John of the 6th or 7th century found in the coffin of St. Cuthbert, and the Lindisfarne gospels in the British Museum, which manuscript most resembles the *Codex Amiatinus*. Further, two fragments of manuscripts bound up with the *Utrecht Psalter* are very similar to the writing of Ceolfrid's Codex, and a fragment of the Gospel of St. Luke in one of the Durham MSS. is said to be identical in text and practically the same in writing as this *Codex Amiatinus*.

[1] *Historia*, Bk. iv., c. 18.

"There was then," says a recent writer, "a large and flourishing school of caligraphy at Wearmouth or Jarrow in the 7th and 8th centuries, of which till lately we had no knowledge at all. It produced manuscripts such as the *Codex Amiatinus*, which have never been equalled for grandeur, and such as the *Stonyhurst* St. John, which have never been equalled for delicacy and grace; and we have to thank the Commendatore de Rossi for fixing a date and a place for one of the most important Vulgate MSS., and for giving to England the credit of a writing school which more than rivals that of Tours."[1]

One point as to the schools of writing it is of interest to notice. It is by no means impossible to recognise the work of a special school of writing by means of some marked and characteristic handwriting, or some peculiarly shaped letter which, once introduced into the scriptorium of a great abbey, was continued through many generations of scribes. The handwriting, for example, in the St. Alban's school of writers is very characteristic. The broken back *h*, for instance, which is a noted feature of the works from the pen of Matthew Paris, can be seen in much subsequent manuscript work from the St. Alban's scriptorium. The same scribe, possibly the great historian himself, must have taught many to write and copy their master's

[1] H. J. White in the *Studia Biblica*, ii., p. 287. But Alcuin's influence at Tours is not to be forgotten.

peculiarity so exactly that it is possible to say with tolerable certainty that this or that manuscript must have been made in that workshop.[1]

With regard to the kind of books which were copied, it may be said that they embraced works of all sorts and subjects. Church books and copies of the Holy Scripture and commentaries upon it were the chief care of the monastic scribes, and time, labour and all that was best in art and design were ungrudgingly bestowed upon these sacred volumes. There was no manifestation of hurry, or desire to see the completion of a work once commenced, in the workers in the mediæval writing schools. The labourer toiled at his task for a day, or a year, or a life-time, knowing that if when the pen dropped from his fingers the work was not completed, there would be another hand ready to carry it on to the desired end. In those days men did not live for themselves or their age, but they were and they regarded themselves as parts of one great and lasting whole. So whether they built churches, or tilled and cultivated the soil, or worked in the monastic scriptorium, the individual was lost in the community, and the grave was not the end of a work.

Besides the strictly ecclesiastical works there

---

[1] The acute and patient investigation of M. Delisle (a very model of such research) into the work of the Tours school is well known. The existence also of a great and flourishing school at Rheims is now becoming recognised.

was apparently in most of the monastic houses some kind of historiographer whose duty it was to take note of the chief events and digest them into annals. Fordun in his *Scotichronicon* says:— "It is properly ordered in most countries, and as I have heard in England, that every monastery of royal foundation should have in that place an appointed scribe or writer who might note all remarkable matters which happened in the time of each king as he believed it to be, with the dates. At the next general assembly after a king's death, all these chronicle writers were to assemble and produce their writings." These were to be submitted to certain chosen judges in order that one reliable chronicle should be formed, "which might be placed in the monastic archives as authentic chronicles to which credit might be given, lest by lapse of time the memory of the acts of a reign might perish."[1]

However exaggerated this account may be as regards England and English monasteries, it is certainly true that the great abbeys were regarded as the natural national archives, and were often selected to preserve documents of importance to the country. The charter of Liberties, for instance, granted by Henry I. was sent to the principal monasteries in each district; and the great Magna Charta, although not recorded in the Royal Chancery, was freely copied into the records of numerous

[1] Fordun, *Scotichronicon*, iv., p. 1343 (ed. Hearne).

religious houses. Thus in A.D. 1207, documents about the marriage of Louis Count of Los and the daughter of Adelheid, Countess of Holland, were placed for safe keeping in the Abbey of Reading. In A.D. 1291, writs were directed to the cathedrals and monasteries of England, commanding a search to be made in the chronicles to be found in their libraries and in their other archives for all matters relating to Scotland; the information obtained to be transmitted to the king, under the common seal of the house, without delay. From these returns, which may be found in Rymer, several matters of interest may be gathered. That of Bath is endorsed, "that it contains nothing to the purpose." Contrary to what might be expected, Burton-on-Trent appears to have possessed some channel through which a good number of state documents came into its archives. Several important papers about the revolutionary proceedings in the reign of Henry III. were to be found there and nowhere else. Croyland sends no excerpts from Ingulph; "a strong evidence," says Palgrave, "that it did not exist" at that time.[1] Norwich—to give but one more instance—excused itself for the smallness of its return, because all the chronicles containing the memorials of ancient times had been destroyed when the church was burnt, or carried off by the citizens in the consequent disorder.

[1] Palgrave, Introduction to *Documents, &c., illustrating the Hist. of England,* page 102.

In the same way, under A.D. 1291, Walsingham gives two letters in reference to the transactions about the Scottish crown, and notes that "these two letters the King of England sent to different monasteries, to preserve the record of the fact."[1] In the same way the record of the submission of the Scotch competitors was sent to be enrolled in the chronicles of monasteries "in perpetuam rei memoriam." The originals of the writs ordering them still remain in the Treasury addressed to Lewes, Ely and York, whilst pursuant to these writs the submissions were entered in a ledger of Evesham, in the chronicles of Waverley, the Register of the Dean and Chapter of St. Paul's and elsewhere.[2] To the above may be added the instance recorded by Matthew Paris, one of our most important writers in connection with English history in the middle ages. This writer received the Benedictine habit at St. Alban's on January 21, 1217. In 1236 he accompanied his prior, John of Hertford, to London, to represent St. Alban's at the nuptials of Henry III. with Queen Eleanor; and in October, 1247, he went with many others to witness the celebration of the feast of Edward the Confessor at Westminster. King Henry, seeing the chronicler, commanded him to come and sit "on the step midway between his throne and the altar," and to take a particular account

[1] *Ypodigma Neustriæ*, pp. 183—185.
[2] Palgrave, op. cit., *ibid.*

of the proceedings. Matthew Paris thus records King Henry's commands: "I therefore beg you, and in begging order you to write a special and full account, and record all these proceedings in fair writing indelibly in a book, that the memory of them be not lost by any length of time." As Matthew Paris' history had not then been seen beyond the walls of St. Alban's, it is clear that the King, in recognising the monk in the crowd at Westminster, must have known that he was the historiographer or Scriptorarius of the great Hertfordshire abbey.

Other incidents in the life of the monk, Matthew Paris, show us that he was present on other public occasions. For example, he was present at Winchester in July, 1251, at the royal court, and at York for the marriage of the King of Scotland with Henry's daughter. In the March of 1257 the king himself visited the abbey of St. Alban's and remained there a week, and during this time not only did Matthew Paris converse with him and sit at his table, but Henry communicated to him as he relates, historical facts[1] and details which had come within his own royal experience. On reading the history of Matthew Paris and what he calls his *Additamenta*, or collection of documents, we find that papers of the utmost importance and even secret state documents relating to England were known at St. Alban's. Moreover, to our surprise

[1] See the article in *Encyclopædia Britannica*, Ed. 9th.

we find also that the workers in the Scriptorium of that abbey were acquainted with state documents of equal importance relating to the Empire and the East, some of which are known to us only by this means. At a later date the St. Alban's Chronicles had obtained a general fame, and the monk of St. Benet Holme, Oxenedes, finishes his account of A.D. 1250 with the words: "If any one desire to further examine into these matters let him look into the chronicle of Matthew Paris at St. Alban's for the year 1250. At this date the said monk, Matthew Paris, of St. Alban's, finished his chronicle." On the following page, speaking of the council held by Otto, the Pope's legate, he says: "In this council he deprived of their benefices all who had immediately succeeded their fathers. The rest of what was settled in this council is written in the Chronicles of St. Alban's."

Finally the same author, in relation to a document as big "as a Psalter" called *De Vita et Moribus Tartarorum*, speaks as if Matthew Paris' work was open to inspection at St. Alban's to all who might wish to inspect it. "If any one wishes to see it," he says, "he can find it at St. Alban's in the book of *Additamenta*."[1]

---

[1] *Chron. Johannis de Oxenedes*, ed. Sir H. Ellis (Rolls series) preface, pp. ix., x.

III.

A FORGOTTEN ENGLISH PREACHER.

HOW very little, indeed, do we know about Mediæval Preaching in England! Possibly few would be disposed to regard this lack of information, upon a subject in itself presumably dull and likely to interest none but the dry-as-dust specialist, as a matter of much regret. To most people, probably, it is sufficient that the modern sermon has at times to be endured as a necessary evil, but the very notion of, say, a fourteenth-century discourse, with its crude methods and quaint expressions, with its endless divisions and subdivisions, its marshalling of texts of Scripture and expressions from the Fathers, and even with its lighter illustrations and stories, is sufficient to conjure up in the imagination a vision of something inexpressibly dreary—a very Sahara of unmitigated dryness. There is, it must be confessed, something to be said for this view; and from a vague dread of finding themselves overwhelmed by ponderous and wholly uninteresting masses of material,

English students have so far allowed the oratorical efforts of mediæval English preachers to remain undisturbed under the dust of centuries. Indeed, so far has this neglect gone that the very names of those, who, in their days, must have stirred, and often deeply stirred, the hearts of our English ancestors by their exhortations, are now for the most part forgotten.

There is, however, another point of view. History now welcomes every side light, however dim, which may help to illustrate the origin, course or issue of events, and anything, however insignificant, which may go to explain the causes of popular movements, the growth of popular institutions, and the popular characteristics of nations. In considerations of this kind, it is obvious that pulpit literature may afford considerable help to the historian. The preacher in the middle ages, as well as in our own days, had occasion sometimes to raise his voice against the abuses, social and religious, which stood in need of correction, or in defence of the usages and institutions of Church and State; and in these, and similar utterances, it is not unlikely that from the point of view of the historian, there may be found, not mere chance references to passing events only, but useful and even necessary illustrations of popular morals and time-honoured customs. To some extent, indeed, this has been recognised in regard to later preachers, and Latimer's Sermons of the Plough, for example, have long been one of the chief sources from which writers on the times of Henry VIII. have drawn abundant illustrations of sixteenth century manners.

It would, of course, be incorrect to suppose that mediæval discourses of this kind are very numerous. In those days, as in our own, parochial sermons were, for the most part, simple explanations of the Creed, or moral exhortations founded upon some Biblical passage, and prones upon the Scripture lessons proper for the special Sundays upon which they were preached. But an attentive examination even of these would probably prove to be not unprofitable to anyone interested in the history of the English people. What has been done by French scholars to illustrate the history of the French pulpit in the later middle ages is amply sufficient to show what a thorough examination of English sources might do for the history of our own people. The study of the methods and style of the French preachers, the examination of the sources whence they drew their material, and the consideration of the effect produced on their hearers by their eloquence or even more by their homely instructions, has contributed not a little to a better knowledge of the domestic, no less than the literary, history of France. In Germany scholars have been not a whit behindhand; indeed they have if anything been more active in this branch of literature.

But, leaving altogether out of consideration the more simple prones and familiar instructions of our

English mediæval preachers, there exist not a few collections of set discourses which deserve to be better known, both for their own merits and for the light they throw upon the history of the times in which they were delivered. Not to speak of the sermons of so distinguished a man as Bishop Grosseteste, of Lincoln; there are numerous fourteenth century discourses by the learned Archbishop of Armagh, Richard Fitz-Ralph, still lying unnoticed among our literary treasures in the British Museum and elsewhere. This great orator was born in Ireland, passed his early life in the household of that lover of books, Richard de Bury, Bishop of Durham, and then became Dean of Lichfield. Here, or at St. Paul's Cross, in London, or subsequently in his Cathedral church of Armagh, most of his best known sermons were delivered. He is chiefly regarded as an uncompromising opponent of the mendicant friars, and in the eight English sermons he preached at the Cross in St. Paul's churchyard, in 1356, at the request of the English Bishops, he attacked their privileges in bold and vigorous language.

Full of interest and learning as these sermons of Archbishop Fitz-Ralph are, they cannot compare, in my estimation, with those of another English preacher who often occupied the pulpit at St. Paul's a few years later, but whose name is now all but forgotten, and whose discourses apparently are entirely unknown. This was Thomas Brunton, who filled the See of Rochester from 1372 to 1389, and was called upon under difficult circumstances, on several occasions, to act as spokesman for the English episcopate. In early life Brunton became a Benedictine monk of Norwich, and is said to have studied both at Oxford and Cambridge, becoming a Bachelor of Theology and a Doctor of Canon law. At Norwich he had for a contemporary the monk, Adam Easton, who was afterwards made Cardinal by Pope Urban VI. When, in 1368, Archbishop Langham, who had previously been abbot of Westminster, resigned the See of Canterbury, and went to Rome to be created Cardinal he took with him probably his two Benedictine brethren from Norwich, Thomas Brunton and Adam Easton. In the Eternal city the former for a time held the office of papal Penitentiary, and upon the death of the Bishop of Rochester, in 1372, Pope Gregory appointed him to the vacant See, as the election of John Hertley, the Prior of Rochester, had been put aside by the Pope, for reasons which do not appear.

Thomas Brunton ruled the diocese of Rochester for some seventeen years, during a disturbed and critical period. When he came to his see, Edward III. had already fallen partially under the influence of the nobility hostile to the Church, and, enfeebled by a premature old age, had commenced his disgraceful liaison with Alice Perrers. Edward the Black Prince had returned to England with the seeds of the disease which a year or two later was to send him to a premature grave, and was using his failing strength to check the unfortunate influence exercised by John of Gaunt on the affairs of the nation. Already the popular voice proclaimed the reverses experienced by the English arms abroad a manifestation of God's wrath at the shameless life which was being publicly lived by some of the highest in the land, and this open degradation of the upper classes was giving strength and meaning to the socialistic movements among the masses, which culminated in the popular rising of 1381.

It was a time eminently suited to inspire the utterances of a fearless ecclesiastic and an accomplished orator, such as the sermons of Thomas Brunton prove him to have been. These discourses, written in free and elegant Latin, were for the most part preached in English, and they contain many historical and topical allusions which make them an interesting and valuable addition to our knowledge of the period. It will be seen from the extracts I purpose to give, that Bishop Brunton did not hesitate at times to speak out, and with a manly vigour to attack abuses, even in the highest places of the land, with a boldness that astonishes the reader as it must have done the men who heard him. He spared no one when he thought it his duty to reprove. All, from the King to the peasant, come in for their share of condemnation, whilst he does not hesitate to blame the silence and worldly motives of his fellow bishops. To a great extent his sympathies are engaged on the side of the people, as distinguished from that of the nobility, and he indulged in some very plain speaking about the unchristian way in which the territorial magnates treated their poorer brethren. Still, though his utterances often sound very democratic, it is clear enough that his preferences are really given to the lower classes because he looks upon their betters as being very generally a disgrace to the christian name. There can be no doubt left in the mind of anyone who may take the trouble to read these sermons of the day, delivered in London and elsewhere by Bishop Brunton between the years 1373 and 1389, that the reign of Edward III. closed, and that of Richard II. began, in very evil times indeed. Making all due allowance for oratorical exaggeration, and for the words of one feeling upon himself the responsibility of the Episcopal office, it is impossible not to see that the moral state of the upper classes at this time was deplorable. This, indeed, is only what we may gather from the account of Walsingham, and still more clearly from the pages of the suppressed Chronicle of St. Albans, which was discovered and published in the Rolls series not very long ago, by Sir E. Maunde Thompson. This latter is a curious instance of the way in which, even before Tudor times, history was toned down, and unpleasing facts smoothed over, for fear of offending the ruling powers, since there seems little doubt that it was the writer's strong condemnation of John of Gaunt, on moral as well as religious grounds, that led to its disappearance from the Chronicles of St. Albans. It was no doubt considered unwise for the abbey to court the displeasure of the Lancastrians by any display of animosity, however justified, against the father of Henry IV.

It is, however, time to allow Bishop Brunton to speak for himself, and I take the liberty of translating his words once more into the language in which they were originally spoken. Speaking of the state of England, we may suppose, sometime about 1375, he declares that the many misfortunes that have fallen upon the country must not be attributed to the stars fighting in their courses against the land, nor to the influence of Saturn or the other planets, but "altogether to our sins." Hence he urges the need of public prayer to avert God's wrath. To public prayer enjoined for the purpose, he has no wish to compel people to come, "but," he adds, "does it not seem to you a thing to be deplored and condemned, that when a procession is ordered in London to pray for the King, or for the peace of the realm, or for any other possible need, there can be found to follow it hardly a hundred men? It seems to me that in such processions, the presence of the king, the princes and lords would be both pleasing to God and honourable to themselves, even from a worldly point of view" (p. 66).

It was probably about the same time—that is, about the time of the meeting of "The Good Parliament" of 1376, to which he plainly refers—that the Bishop passes a sweeping condemnation upon those who had the conduct of State affairs in England at this period. He is again addressing a London audience, and in the discharge of his duty he does not hesitate to speak as follows:—

"Amongst other English institutions established in the past, one practice, of great renown and most excellent, is still in vogue: the Lords and Commons are called together to Parliament to discuss and legislate for the good estate of the country. Of what use, however, is it to treat of affairs in Parliament, and publicly to denounce transgressors of the law unless due correction follows upon such denunciation? Laws are worthless except they be rightly enforced. But is it not known, and almost everywhere publicly acknowledged, that it is not those who incline to virtue, but they who lead vicious and scandalous lives who long have had the chief share in the government of this Kingdom. Against the rule of such men, though, we universally murmur and protest; still, we have not the courage to speak the truth as to the proper remedy."

"Saint Augustine states what is the real reason of our silence in the following:—'When the Egyptians desired, in spite of considerable opposition, to deify

Iris and Serapis, they, in the first place, ordered that anyone who called them men, or discussed their existence, should be put to death. And that no one should be ignorant of this law, in every place where the images of these gods were set up they erected a statue with its finger to its mouth, so that by this token of silence all who entered the temple might know that the truth was to be concealed.'"

"In the same way, our modern rulers—those overthrowers of truth and justice — wishing to raise their lords to the altars, as they know how, have proclaimed the coward a hero, the weak man strong, the fool a wise man, the adulterer and the pursuer of luxury a man chaste and holy. And in order to turn all interests to their own advantage they encourage their king in notorious crimes, whilst, so as to be seen by all coming to court, they set up the idol of worldly fear in order to prevent anyone, of whatsoever rank and condition he may be, from daring to stand up against, or castigate, the evil doers."

"But whose duty is it to speak of these matters? Most certainly an obligation lies upon the Bishops, lords temporal, confessors, and even on the preachers. As to the Bishops, why do they, who like columns ought to support the Church on their shoulders, and even lay down their lives in defence of its liberties, remain silent when they see Christ daily crucified in their presence? Why are they silent when they see the innocent condemned as guilty, poor ecclesiastics deprived of their benefices, and their rights so outraged that to-day the Holy Church of God is in greater slavery than it was under Pharaoh, who knew not the divine law? By such conduct they prove themselves mere hirelings, and not shepherds, and the reason is that they are only seeking for higher preferment and aspiring to be translated to richer Sees."

"The lords temporal are silent because they shrink in dread from offending their King; whereas in truth there is no place for fear, since it may well be believed that if the truth were once told him, he is so yielding and easily led that he would by no means suffer such things to go unchecked in the realm."

"Confessors hold their peace, because, whilst they can easily have their own comforts, conveniences and honours, they care not for souls. Therefore, they ought to be called not confessors, but confusers; not teachers, but rather traitors—traitors firstly to Our Lord, whose authority and commission they notoriously abuse; secondly, to their temporal lords, to whom they ought not to hesitate to speak the truth, that they may reclaim them from their errors."

"Preachers hold their tongues, because many of those who, before this time, at the Cross of St. Paul's, have touched upon the vices of the lords, have been at once arrested and taken before the king's Council as malefactors. There, after being examined, they have been condemned and banished, or suspended from further exercise of their office of preaching."

"But some will say, leave the Commons, who, like the foundations of the republic, effectually support the king and the Parliament (to look to it). Not so, Reverend sirs, lest our Parliament be compared to the Parliament of rats and mice in the fable. About this, we read that, in their assembly, they had strictly ordained that every cat should have a bell attached to its neck, so that, warned by the sound, the mice might have sufficient time to escape in safety to their holes. An ancient rat, meeting a certain mouse returning from the Parliament, inquired what was the news. When the mouse had explained to him the gist of the business, the rat remarked: 'This law is most excellent, provided someone is appointed by your Parliament to carry it into execution.' The mouse replied that no such order had been made by Parliament; and so the law remained consequently useless and inoperative."

"For the love of Christ, and in defence of our country brought to straits such as this, let us be not merely talkers, but doers. Let us cast off the works of darkness, and put on the armour of light, so that our lives may be amended, and our king directed in the way of justice."[1]

This is plain speaking enough about the state to

[1] Harl. MS. 3760, f. 186, *seqq*.

which the country had been reduced by the influence of those who ruled the kingdom, and encouraged the king in the excesses to which he devoted the closing years of his life. It is most probable, as I have said, that the sermon was preached during the time when the sitting of the "Good Parliament" had led men of honesty and uprightness to hope, through the powerful support of the Black Prince, for an improvement in the government, and to insist on the removal of the king's evil counsellors, and the wretched courtesan, Alice Perrers, who had obtained supreme influence over him. It is even possible that the discourse, spoken evidently to the clergy, may have been delivered at the meeting of Convocation, which at this time insisted that William of Wykeham must be allowed to take his place at their deliberations, although he had been disgraced and deprived of the revenues of his See of Winchester, through the influence and misrepresentations of those who held the old king in their power.

But to continue the Bishop's sermon: "It is patent to all men," he says, "that the kingdom of England, which of old abounded in riches, is now poor and needy: which of old was radiant with God's grace is now graceless and despicable: which of old regulated all things according to justice, is now without law of any sort." Then, after speaking of the three sins of adultery, luxury and simony, which polluted England at the time, he continues:—

"Nor need we wonder, since, if one of the people fall, he falls as if he were alone, but if a Prince or Prelate fall, as many seem to fall as he rules over. And indeed this sin (of luxury) has so scandalously prevailed among the temporal lords, that I can conclude what the Psalmist says, 'The earth is contaminated by their works.'"

He then goes on to declare that England is being punished for the sins of the upper classes. "Greater," he says, "are the iniquities of the rich, and the nobles than are those of the middle class and the poor. For, whereas the latter commonly live honestly on their own earnings, the former live, for the most part, upon the goods of other people —as, for example, by violent seizures, exactions, extortions, and the rest. It is truly against all rules of justice and equity that when processions are ordered to avert common tribulations there should be present at them ecclesiastics and religious only, and some few of the middle class, who, in comparison, have but slightly offended God by their sins, whilst the rich people and the nobility, who are the main cause of these afflictions, neither come, nor pray, nor do penance for their iniquities, but lie in their beds and enjoy their other luxuries to their heart's content."

He then proceeds to urge his ecclesiastical brethren not to suffer the power of the kingdom to remain in the hands of those who were using it solely to advance their own interests. "Does it seem to you right," he says, "that the king and his sons should be so led by their counsellors that they are ever poor and needy in respect to their rank, whilst their advisers are rolling in riches to such a degree that they could buy up a fourth part of the entire wealth of the kingdom? Moreover, though the king ought to reward in a princely way those who serve him, who should be nobles and the sons of nobles, still this should be done with measure, so that he pass not over his own children for the sake of his servants. It is neither fitting nor just that the servants become lords, and their lords remain in poverty. Unless the king and his children are provided with plenty they will think it necessary to spoil the Church and to devour the people. Does it seem right that low-born and unworthy people should have access to the king for furthering their affairs when the nobles and prelates, who come to the Court for necessary business, and for the needs of their churches, are not allowed an audience? Is it right that they be forced to remain outside in the courtyard among the poor, and after being catechised by people not really sent to them by the king, be compelled to go away without any proper reply? Alas! that the king of France thrice each week should grant audience to his people, and personally give full justice to all who ask it, whilst the nobles of England cannot get their rights, though they try their best. Moreover, should it be possible that when foreigners and above all the lords of Acquitaine, who in behalf of the rights of England have suffered the loss of property and birthright, come to this country, they be not received with honour—that they be not consoled nor assisted with presents? Yea, hardly do they meet with even a favourable reception, or a kindly word."

"Further, is it fitting that the king of France should have for his Privy Council seventy men chosen from every position of life, by whose advice all difficult matters are settled, and that our English king, though he has prudent and faithful counsellors, should act in like difficulties by the counsel of one only? Upon us that saying of the Holy Scripture has come, 'Operatus unus.'"

"Nor is it proper or safe that all the keys of the kingdom should hang at the girdle of a woman. It is well that Councillors should be men—not boys, youths, and lewd people. Roboam, rejecting the advice of the aged and following that of the young, lost his kingdom. Neither is it well that they should be women, shrewd in looking after their own advantages; but men of uprightness, experience, and holiness."

If Bishop Brunton could bring himself to use such vigorous language with regard to those who had obtained the mastery over the old king, and managed the affairs of State to further their own advantage, he did not hesitate, when the occasion demanded, even in public, to speak his mind about the duties of the clergy and bishops. In a sermon preached in his Cathedral of Rochester at the time of his visitation, for example, after quoting Valerius to the effect that a certain king of the Jews had set watch dogs in the city of Jerusalem, he goes on to tell his clergy what bishops should be and what they should do. "They should be ever going about their dioceses," he says, "visiting, preaching, making enquiries, correcting, and, in a word, by every means protecting their sheepfolds from the wolves." In this way, in the canons of the Church, bishops who do not preach and instruct their people, he declares, "are called 'dumb dogs.'"

Again, preaching to his clergy on the feast of St. Louis of France, he sketches for them the qualities which should distinguish the christian teacher, and laments the want of them in so many of the Church's ministers at that time. "The Church to-day," he says, "is afflicted with great interior sadness. To the guardianship of the Temple are appointed so many unfit and unworthy ministers, that is, the blind, the dumb, the deaf, the halt, the weak, and the sick. For they are blind who have no knowledge; they are dumb who have no eloquence; deaf who have no pity; halt who give no alms; weak and sickly, yea, even dead, who have no conscience."

At another time, speaking specially about the bishop's office, he says:—"In the Lord's vineyard a bishop should labour above all others. He ought to receive the canonical summons to mount to the prelate's office only on account of the merit of his life, and his sufficient discipline. In these days, however, I see bishops rise to it from other causes, and so impudently intrude themselves into the vineyard, that were it asked of them *What are you doing here?* (John vi.); or 'Who hath brought you in hither?' they, for the most part, could only reply, as it is written, *By chance I came to the mountain.* For, just as, according to grammarians, there are six cases . . . so some have thrust themselves into office in the nominative case of pomp, like the proud and presumptuous; others in the genitive case of family, like those of noble and gentle birth; others with the desire of money, like the simoniacal and ambitious; others in the accusative of calumny, like the envious and the cunning; others in the ablative of violence, like the hard and impecunious; few, or even, I might say, none, in the vocative of divine or canonical election, like those of fitting and virtuous lives, who alone are lawfully called by the Lord to the honour of the pastoral office."

Again Bishop Brunton speaks of the great need that there was at the time of bishops who would strive to walk in the footsteps and imitate the example of those who had gone before. They should be always at work " now praying, now visiting their churches, now preaching, and in particular, after their own dioceses, should they preach in London, the chief city of England, according to the example of Christ, who was daily teaching in the Temple at Jerusalem; and as in London there is greater devotion and the people are more intelligent, so greater fruit may be expected from their preaching. Moreover, every bishop has in London some of his subjects, and so when preaching there he is instructing his own church as well as the other churches of England."

"We prelates," he says in another place, "are called by Christ the salt of the earth and the light of the world. From the dignity of our office we have the primacy of Abel, the patriarchate of Abraham, the government of Noah, the orders of Melchisedech, the dignity of Aaron, the authority of Moses and the power of Peter. What, if when we should be correctors of souls we be but mere extortioners of money; and when we should be columns of strength we be in reality but reeds and straws?"

It is not very difficult to connect the foregoing with the circumstances of the time. The author of the suppressed Chronicle of St. Albans makes use of very similar expressions with regard to the general attitude of the episcopate towards the scandalous liaison of Edward with Alice Perrers. The "Good Parliament" had insisted upon the removal of this mistress of the dying king, who had risen from mean birth to almost supreme power, and who had abused her influence to the full. In her greed she had maintained false causes, and, if we are to believe Walsingham and the anonymous chronicle, had by her presence on the bench terrorised the judges into giving wrongful judgments. At length, after long lamenting the king's infatuation, the Commons " determined to risk offending their king rather than God," and insisted upon Alice Perrers' removal from Court, and bound her by oath never to return. The arrangement did not, however, last long. The " Good Parliament " after appointing a permanent council of twelve to advise the king, was dissolved in 1376. Forthwith John of Gaunt came again into full power, the provisions of the " Good Parliament " were set aside, and Alice Perrers again appeared and took possession of the king. Loud were the murmurs of the people, and they in vain looked to the ecclesiastical authorities to take action against her for this public violation of her oath. " But," says the Chronicle, " the Archbishop and his suffragans—became as dumb dogs, not daring to bark; and, to speak the truth, they were in this not shepherds, but scatterers of the flock, and hirelings, who for fear of the wolf, deserted their sheep. I do not," the writer adds, " include all, for the Lord left Himself some few, who did not bow their knees to Baal. But those who had received the sword of Peter to cut off such disease elected to soothe rather than to probe the sores of the sinner; and so, through the negligence of the bishops the scars reappeared on the erring sheep, and the said Alice returned (like the dog) to the vomit."[1]

In more than one sermon our preacher refers to the notorious maladministration of justice above recorded from the contemporary but subsequently suppressed Chronicle of St. Albans. "Our modern judges and jurors who can be bought, condemn to death the innocent if they be prosecuted by a great or malicious person. As an example take that of the youth hanged for the theft of a few pears. And though judges and jurors of this kind excuse themselves for shedding innocent blood because they fear the power of the Lords, they cannot thus be held guiltless of the crime, since they ought rather to die than shed innocent blood. . . . On the other hand, if there is brought before them a murderer or a manifest robber, whose blood justice demands, he is allowed to escape without punishment, if a plentiful money bribe be offered by him or his friends."

"False witnesses," he proceeds, " can be readily procured, by whose testimony one man is deprived of property, which is his by law and birthright, and another unjustly gets it; another man obtains a benefice before the legal time because he makes oath that he is of proper age; another obtains a benefice by a fictitious title, to which he has sworn, when in reality he has no such title."

[1] Chronicon (Rolls Series) p. 104-5.

In the same sermon from which this passage is taken the Bishop raises the burning question in ecclesiastical circles at the time, of the powers of the mendicant orders to act as confessors, &c., by virtue of their special privileges. He points out "that although by virtue of ordination every priest has the keys of the church, they can be used ordinarily in three ways only. First, by the gift of the cure of souls; for all such, whether they hold greater offices or lesser, are properly priests (having the charge of those under them). Thus the Pope and his Penitentiary, the Bishop and his Vicar, the Archbishop at the time of the visitation of his Province, the Rector and his Vicar, &c., &c., permanent or temporary, are properly priests, having charge of souls. They are the ordinary, and consequently necessary, judges in the domain of conscience. From their hands, if they be negligent in their office, the blood of their subjects will be required."

"Secondly, the keys of the church are in the possession of the mendicant friars by virtue of special licence or by privilege. They are voluntary judges, and when admitted they have the same power as curates and parish priests unless more ample faculties be given to them by the prelates."

"Thirdly, the keys are granted by licences bestowed by the (Roman) curia. Of this kind are the *tricenales*, which I do not condemn, though I do blame those who unjustly abuse the privileges. For, in such licences people are warned as a duty to look for proper confessors, and those only can be considered such who can discreetly judge between cause and cause, &c. But what are they who are chosen in these days? I see that anyone wanting for the sake of his bodily health to be blooded, calls to himself the most skilful, the most expert, and the surgeon best known for his discretion; but when he wishes to purify his soul from the blood of sin he does not make choice of him who is most instructed in the science of the soul and most holy, but of him who is the most run after; not of him who is most discreet and straightforward, but of him who is the most easy; not of him who is the most expert and has best knowledge of him, but of the stranger and of him who is ignorant of his wants, &c."

"Confessors, too, can be unfaithful to their duty if they do not tell the plain truth to their penitents, and so turn them from their evil ways. How many great men are there not now in this kingdom of England living in infamy? Some of them are extortioners and destroyers of their tenants, retaining for their own uses tithes and oblations, violating the rights of the church, and ever acting most ungratefully against it; still it is unheard of that such by the advice of their confessors ever restore or make good what they have wrongfully taken or kept back."

"Others again are publicly defamed for adultery and incest—so much so that there is not a nation under heaven with such an evil reputation for adultery as the English nation at this day." "Others are scandalously defamed for simple fornication, which can be seen in the case of so high a person of such exalted dignity. . . . Tell me, for instance, too, why in England so many robberies remain unpunished when in other countries murderers and thieves are commonly hanged? . . In England the land is inundated by homicides, so that '*veloces sint pedes hominum ad effudendum sanguinem*,' so that there is no conscience in killing a man. For this I fear that the blood of the slain cries to the Lord for vengeance."

To many people the most instructive and interesting portions of the sermons of this fourteenth century preacher will probably be those in which he touches upon the great social movement which was then in full progress in England. Up to the middle of the century the ancient order of inequality passed unquestioned as the divine law of the universe. The verses of *Piers Ploughman* and *The Canterbury Tales* help us to realise the social chasm which still divided, as it so long had done, the upper from the lower classes—the small but powerful rich nobility from the numerous but subject masses of the population. The old principles of feudalism were no longer able to assert their supremacy over the agricultural classes, and the endeavour to re-assert ancient rights and privileges by high-handed measures provoked open and determined resistance.

The gospel of equality preached in Longland's verses and John Ball's sermons is eagerly welcomed as the Gospel of justice and Christianity, and for the first time in our history there appears "a fierce hatred of nobles and gentlemen, and a startling assertion of levelling principles and social equality as bold as any which were taught four centuries" later in France. With much of the legitimate aspirations of the people in this social movement Bishop Brunton evidently sympathised, and his pulpit utterances echo the prevailing demand for fair and considerate treatment of the poorer population by the upper classes. It is of interest to remember that many of his sermons were preached in his own diocese of Rochester at a time when the leader of the advanced socialistic party, John Ball, was addressing his audiences of yeomen in the village churchyards of the same county of Kent.

Preaching, for instance, on the text *Simul in unum dives et pauper*, the Bishop takes up the bitter cry of the poor in almost the same words in which it is expressed by the "mad preacher," as the courtly Froissart nicknames the Kentish clerical leader, John Ball. All, both rich and poor, Bishop Brunton reminds his audience, are descended from the common parents of all, Adam and Eve; and he emphasises the blessedness of almsdeeds by referring to the story of St. Oswald giving away the silver dish and St. Aidan's prophecy that the hand that had given it should never corrupt. Poverty leads to begging and to theft. We ought consequently, he declares, "to feed and support the poor, and this for two reasons: Firstly, because of the similarity of nature in all mankind. Every animal loves its life, and so great a similarity is there between rich and poor that *unus est introitus omnibus ad vitam* (Sap. 7). For God in the beginning of the world has not created a gold man and a silver man to be the progenitors of the rich and the gentlefolk, and another of clay, from whom have descended the poor and the needy. With a spade Adam cultivated the earth.[1] So, too, in death all, both rich and poor, find the like end; as hired actors on a stage when their parts in the play are over, all return to the position from which they had been raised, and so *Simul in unum dives et pauper.*"

"The princes of India collect from the rich wherewith to minister to the wants of the poor; but Christian princes extort from the poor the money necessary to maintain the rich in their proud position. Among Christians no one ever hears of an ecclesiastical tithe, or a tax on the people at large, being levied in aid of the poor who are dying of hunger; but it is well nigh a daily occurrence that both the church and the lay folk are asked to contribute to the rich and to princes. The very Saracens are scandalised that we treat the poor,

---

[1] This forcibly reminds us of John Ball's well-known saying: "When Adam delved and Eve span Who was then the gentleman."

whom we call the servants of Christ, so mercilessly and inhumanly. This is evidenced in the life of Charles the Great; for, whilst fighting against the Infidels there came to him one who had thoughts of becoming a Christian. Seeing some people eating their food on the ground he asked: 'Who are they that clad in such poor garments eat upon the floor?' To this the king answered, saying: 'They are our serfs, whom we feed for the love of our Lord Jesus Christ.' Upon which the Saracen Prince exclaimed: 'Your servants are splendidly clothed, they feed and drink luxuriously, whilst the servants of your Christ are left naked and hungry. I will join no sect which loves its Lord so slightly.'"

In several passages in his sermons, Bishop Brunton laments the great rift which was, seemingly, only too patent in his day between those "who had" and those "who had not." "Nowadays," he says, for example, in one discourse, "there is such a hopeless division between the people and the burgesses that the rich take all the advantages of their wealth, and if there be any burden to be borne or loss to be endured, it must all fall upon the poor."

Again he laments loudly that there was one law for the rich and another for the poor; that a man of position was able to avoid the penalties of his transgressions, whilst they fell heavily upon the shoulders of a man of the lower class, and that ecclesiastics were by no means blameless in making this unjust distinction. "If they find" he says "that a poor man or a rustic has but slightly fallen away from his duty, they at once cite him, excommunicate him, and judge him in the most rigid manner so that his punishment may be a warning to the rest. But if they find a precious stone, that is, a man that is rich or of position among the nobility, no matter how vicious his life may be, they treat him with all gentleness. They punish a poor man accused of simple fornication more rigorously than they do a rich man for adultery and incest. This is not justice, my brethren: this is not justice."

"Temporal lords," he says again in another place, "hardly pay their servants their proper and appointed wages. In this way the masters frequently are false to God's law by keeping back the just payment due to their servants, and the servants are thieves by appropriating at will what belongs to their masters." Again and again he bids his hearers remember that all Christians are members of one body, no matter what their state and condition of life may be. "We, though many," he says, "form but one body. Of this mystical body indeed there are many members: for the kings, princes and prelates are the head; judges and the wise and true counsellors are the eyes, religious are the ears, good teachers the tongue, soldiers ready to defend it from attack are its right hand, its left being merchants and faithful artisans;

the citizens and burgesses, as the middle class, are its heart, and, firmly supporting the whole body as its feet, come the husbandmen and labourers."

If the sympathies of the Bishop are clearly engaged on the side of the suffering poor, he does not, on the other hand, hesitate to speak out plainly about the duties of servants to their masters and to blame with all the force of his powerful rhetoric the popular risings which at that time led to much destruction of life and property. In two of these sermons we have his declaration against those who took part in the events which in 1381 led to the mob seizing Archbishop Sudbury and putting him to death on Tower Hill. Preaching on the 4th Sunday in Lent he reminds his hearers that the absolution of those who have maliciously set fire to churches is reserved to the Pope, and the same in the case of those who have made an insurrection with the design of killing, or of destroying churches. "The absolving, however, of such as have taken part in the insurrection," he continues, "but who have not had a hand in killing, or in the destruction of churches, is reserved to the bishops, since they are traitors and in many things fall under the ban of the Canons of the Church, and," he adds, "let the friars take heed that they do not absolve them."

"As to the Archbishop," he continues, "all who have treated him infamously or who have struck or killed him, or have ordered or ratified the deed, or were associated with those who did it, or counselled or favoured it, or knowingly shall have protected the doers of it, are excommunicated, and except in the danger of death, can be absolved by the Supreme Pontiff only. And even if they be absolved *in articulo mortis*, should they recover they are bound, under pain of incurring *ipso facto* the excommunication again, to present themselves personally before the Roman Pontiff. And if the blood of Abel slain by his brother in secret cry from the earth to God for vengeance, much more loudly does the blood of such a prelate so cruelly slain without cause call loudly for the punishment of those concerned. The rest of those who, compelled to take part in the insurrection, have not been guilty of incendiarism and have not killed anyone, but with the rest of the insurgents have perchance in many ways hurt their neighbours and their masters, can be absolved by those having cure of their souls provided they shall have made due satisfaction to those whom they have injured."

"But how are they to make satisfaction? I reply that two things render that insurrection most abominable, and worthy of all condemnation. First, on account of sin servitude was introduced, and hence justice ever requires that masters should rule their servants, and servants be in subjection to their masters. The apostle proclaims this law in saying *servi subdite*, and 'Servants be subject to your masters with all fear' (1 Peter ii.). Now, since those who have taken part in the insurrection, proposed to lord it as masters, and to have put their masters to death, their act is most worthy of condemnation, and in no wise to be borne. Secondly, the servants knew not, as their acts show, how to govern themselves, and hence they are bound to make restitution, not alone for the injury done to property and person, but to the rights and liberties of their masters. The Scripture calls to us *Reddite quæ sunt Cæsaris Cæsari*—'Render to Cæsar the things that are Cæsar's.'"

Later in the same year, in a sermon preached on the Sunday after the Feast of the Ascension, our preacher again declaims against those who have had any part in the murder of the Archbishop. He says that "this horrible and abominable deed is covered up, excused, and until this present time has remained unpunished," and he prophesies God's punishment upon the kingdom if "those who are excommunicated are allowed publicly to despise the power of the Church's keys."

In one sermon, preached at Cobham on the Feast of St. Mary Magdalene about the year 1383, Bishop Brunton laments the state of the country. "If of old," he said, "anyone had preached and prophesied the evils which have happened to England, the evident vengeance of the Lord, in the murders even of the highest, in the famines, in the mortality, in the storms, in the internal commotions and external wars, who would have believed him? Or, had they done so, who would not have done penance with Nineveh?"

"For myself, I say it with tears, I have preached for ten years continuously against the sins rife in my diocese, and still I cannot see that any one has risen effectually from his evil life. For the most part they are like to the dead man whom Simon Magus pretended to have raised to life, but who, by his incantations, only appeared to move his head. For, when they hear good exhortations, they move their heads, but do not cast off their sins. For, tell me, where is the adulterer who has got rid of his mistress and returned to his lawful spouse? Where is the usurer who has repaid what he has wickedly acquired? Where is the unjust maintainer of causes? Where the false swearer, who restrains himself from his evil courses? Where is the man that by the use of false measures had deceived his neighbours and poor strangers, who now has broken and burnt them? Where is he who from his heart has renounced an old enmity, and does not wait to avenge himself when he sees his opportunity? Yea, which of those accursed insurgents, whose dangerous position I have so often pointed out in my sermons, is contrite, or truly confessed, or has in any point made satisfaction? and yet the sin is not forgiven unless what was taken away is restored. For these reasons I fear that in many things we to-day are worse than the inhabitants of Nineveh. They humbled themselves under God's chastisements, whilst we are presumptuous and proud beyond all bounds. They clothed themselves in sackcloth, but we deck ourselves in precious stuffs, so much so that there is to-day no difference between a knight and a squire, a clerk and a priest, between the wife of an earl and that of a citizen. They (the inhabitants of Nineveh) fasted, whilst we violate the appointed fasts, and indulge in our pleasures. Their king and his magnates were filled with fear, and through fear ceased to sin, whilst our nobles and lords neither fear God nor reverence man. Yea, those who ought to defend the Church and its rights and privileges are foremost in attacking them."

The Bishop then went on at some length to warn the people against the false teachers who were going about England at this time propagating their erroneous doctrines. In these we have no difficulty in recognising the followers of John Wyclif, especially as he indicates the nature of the Lollard teaching against which he protests. These unauthorised preachers declare, he says, that when a priest or bishop baptizes whilst in a state of sin the sacrament is not conferred, that auricular confession is superfluous for those who are contrite, and that in the Mass the bread and wine are not changed into our Lord's Body at the words of consecration. "To-day," he says in another place, referring evidently to the alliance between the

Wycliffite agents and the party of John of Gaunt—"To-day the temporal lords seek to resist ecclesiastical censures, however just and reasonable, and to escape from the orders and just counsels of their ordinaries. They bring to their aid extraordinary teachers skilled in tickling the ears of the people, by whose means false doctrine and numerous errors are instilled into the popular mind; so much so that if the laity make any attack against the liberty of the Church, however grave it may be, and however much condemned and disapproved of by all, these new doctors against conscience and justice accept, approve, and justify the deed. Wherefore it happens that the Church (which ought to be the mistress) is in these days in England trodden under foot, a thousand rumours are set on foot to the prejudice of the clergy; the law, in itself just, is perverted; reason is lulled to sleep; justice is oppressed and equity is buried."

In this fourteenth century, as in most other ages of the world, as Bishop Brunton points out, a preacher's audience liked to fit the cap upon every head but their own; and they were best pleased when they could point the moral of a sermon by making it apply to others. If this could be done the stronger the language the orator used the better satisfied were those who listened to his words. "It is nowadays a common failing" he says, "that most people are better pleased to hear preaching directed against the vices of others than against their own. Clerics, for example, desire that sermons should be directed against laymen who neglect to pay their tithes: laymen like to hear preaching directed against clerics and ecclesiastics who set a bad example. Husbands are quite satisfied when the words of the preacher are directed against the ostentation and dress of their wives; wives when they condemn the superfluous expenses of the husbands. Prelates are pleased with sermons against the want of due obedience on the part of their subjects; subjects with those against the vices and neglect of the prelates. And so what one dislikes satisfies another."

On this principle the Bishop never hesitates to speak openly and in the strongest language about any abuses he desires to see corrected. He spares —when his subject requires him to speak plainly— neither king, nor prince, nor prelate; and whilst clearly a man of the people, he is uncompromising in his condemnation of what he holds to be wrong in popular aspirations and methods. At the same time his own order—the bishops and clergy— receive perhaps the most plain-spoken measure of admonition which is to be found in this volume of sermons.

To pass to another subject of interest. On the festival of the Holy Trinity, 1376, there died in London, Edward the Black Prince. He was, as the monk of St. Albans tells us, "a devout client of the Holy Trinity, and his spirit, as amidst enemies and wars, remained unconquered by death. For he bade farewell to the world rather than died; he passed as it were to his own country as if from death to life, as if from a life of toil to glory."[1] He was buried according to his own request in Benedictine Canterbury, near to the shrine of the martyred St. Thomas. Bishop Brunton presided at the funeral service held for the repose of his soul at his cathedral in Rochester. Amongst these sermons we have the words which he spoke on the occasion. As clerks, he says, coming from the schools bring back with them letters of praise as a testimony of their work; "so this prince in the school of this world laboured to merit the grade of true princedom, and now by death, the finisher of all things, has returned to the earth from which he came. . . . Truly, the name of this prince is worthy of all praise, and this for three reasons. It is due first to his dignity; secondly to his uprightness and honesty; and thirdly to his strict integrity. As to the first, Cassiodorus in his Epistle says, 'It is proper for a king or a prince to display his honour in the cause of morality.' Every prince should excel his subjects in power, in wisdom, and in goodness, and thus present in himself a living image of the Holy Trinity; with his *power* he displays the attribute of the Father; with his *wisdom* that of the Son; and with his *goodness* that of the Holy Spirit. Our Lord prince excelled in all these

[1] Chronicon Angliæ (Rolls edition, p. 88).

three: his power appeared in his glorious victories, for which we all so greatly praise him, as the Scripture bids when it says: *Laudemus viros potentes et gloriosos.*

"In particular is this so in the victory of Poitiers, in which, by the help of the God of justice, the French army were scattered in a marvellous way by the English power, and the French king taken prisoner, although so great was the host of warriors with the king of France, that ten Frenchmen, fighting on their own soil, were opposed to every Englishman. Thus, for this one deed alone, might our Prince take to himself the saying of Malachy: *Magnum fuit nomen meum in gentibus*—My name was great among the nations."

"His wisdom has been manifested in the regulation of his life, and in the prudence of his utterances. He was no mere speaker of words, like the lords of this time, but a doer of deeds, and he never put his hand to any work that he did not finish it in a praiseworthy manner. . . .

"His goodness chiefly rests upon these three points: where temporal lords commonly oppress their tenants and disturb their dependents, this prince ever assisted, and in numberless ways sustained his followers. Where other lords are commonly so ungrateful to their servants, and others who toil with them in the wars, that they take from them or otherwise extort what they have lawfully obtained, this prince was so liberal to all who worked with him or served him, that he enriched them and made himself correspondingly poor. So, also, where the temporal lords are commonly so indevout that they hear Mass and divine service only for form's sake, this prince was so devoted to the Divine mysteries, that at the time of their celebration he could be seen upon no business. And because power without wisdom is like a sword in the hands of a madman, and wisdom without goodness should be counted as mere cunning, this prince is worthy to be praised. He excelled in power, in wisdom and in goodness so evidently as to display in himself an image of the Holy Trinity, whilst he loved the Holy Trinity above all things. Born, as it is said, on the feast of the Trinity, he paid the debt of nature on the same holy festival, and chose as his burial place the church of the Holy Trinity (at Canterbury), where his memory and his praises shall be celebrated for ever and ever."

The following year (1377), Bishop Brunton was the spokesman of the clergy, at the coronation of Richard II. The day following the ceremony, July 17th, was appointed for a solemn procession to pray for the king and the peace of the kingdom. At this there were present all the prelates and magnates who had been at the ceremony the previous day. The historian, Walsingham, has left us a brief account of the sermon which the bishop of Rochester addressed to the populace of London on that occasion. In this short note we can recognise the same earnest speaker who appeals to us even to-day so forcibly in the manuscript sermons to which I have introduced the reader. He spoke of the dissensions and discords which had so long existed between the upper and lower classes, and he showed, by many arguments, that such disagreements must be displeasing to God, and hurtful to the kingdom. "He exhorted the lords," the chronicler tells us, "not in the future to levy such unreasonable taxes on the people. He warned the latter that when there was a reasonable cause in which they ought to help their King and their country in every way, they should do so patiently and without murmuring, and that they should look upon sedition as a matter of conscience."

It has been here possible to give merely examples of the interesting and important sermons of this eloquent fourteenth century preacher. In view of the very many less important works, even from an historical point of view, which have found their way into the publications of our learned societies, and even into the national historical series of the *Chronicles and Memorials*, published under the direction of the Master of the Rolls, I may, perhaps, be allowed to express a regret that these discourses have not long ago been rescued from the oblivion into which, apparently, they have fallen. Bishop Brunton was an orator and an Englishman who most certainly deserved to be better remembered among his people than he has been.

IV.

THE PRE-REFORMATION ENGLISH BIBLE.[1]

FOR some years duty has taken me almost daily through the King's Library at the British Museum. There—reposing on cushions of purple velvet, in a spacious shrine of polished oak, marked "number 1"—is a large and handsome manuscript volume written in the fourteenth century,[2] which rightly attracts the attention of many visitors. I have frequently stopped on my way past this case to admire the well-written page with its painted border, and again and again I have read and re-read this legend, inscribed on a card below: *The English Bible, Wycliffe's translation.* Passing this interesting book, as I did often many times a day, I conceived a desire to know something more about it. One afternoon, therefore, taking advantage of an hour free from other occupations, I

---

[1] Reprinted from the *Dublin Review*, July, 1895.
[2] Egerton MS., 617.

wrote a request for a personal interview in the students' room, and a few minutes later had the pleasure of finding the manuscript at my desk there. The present paper is really the result of a train of researches and considerations started at that interview.

I suppose most of us have been taught to regard with feelings of some awe, although hardly perhaps with much reverence, the strange personality of Wyclif. Whatever we may hold as Catholics as to his unsound theological opinions, about which there can be no doubt; or as peace-loving citizens about his wild and revolutionary social theories, on which there can be, if possible, still less, few of us I fancy would venture to grudge him the credit which rightly attaches to what is known *par excellence* as his work—the translation of the Bible into the English language—or to deny him the title of " Father of English prose " thereby so justly earned. Why should he not have all his due, morning star though he be of the glorious " Reformation " ? Is it not written in all our school books and taught to every child that the first vernacular translation of God's Word was conceived and carried into execution by this same John Wyclif in the fourteenth century ? As an instance of what is believed on all hands upon this matter, we may conveniently take the account given by Mr. F. D. Matthew in his Preface to the *English Works of Wyclif*, published by the *Early English Text Society :*

"Of Wyclif's other religious task, the translation of the Bible, I need say little; its consequences to English religion and to the English tongue are generally recognised. We have but to look at the long list of MSS., given at the beginning of Forshall and Madden's great edition (170), and to remember that these are but the gleanings, after time, neglect and the zeal of the inquisitor have gathered in their harvests, and we see how widely the translation was disseminated and how eagerly men caught at the opportunity of reading the Bible in their mother tongue."[1]

Moreover, beyond the fact of Wyclif's connection with this great work, as here stated, the actual circumstances under which the task was in the end accomplished are not unfrequently related with considerable detail. Take, for example, the following, given in a book on the Bible placed on the shelves of the reference library in the Museum: Wyclif's

"translation, which was finished in the year 1380, is supposed to have occupied him amidst various interruptions for many years. Some have imagined that this great work employed the translator for ten years only, but Mr. Barber with far greater probability has said: 'From an early period

[1] P. xvii. "As regards the general question of the supposed hostility of the Church to the reading of Scripture, it may be useful to quote the authority of Maitland: 'I have not found about it the arts and engines of hostility, the blind hatred of half-barbarian kings, the fanatical fury of their subjects, or the reckless antipathy of the Popes. I do not recollect any instance in which it is recorded that the Scriptures or any part of them were treated with indignity, or with less than profound respect. I know of no case in which they were intentionally defaced or destroyed (except, as I have just stated, for their rich covers), though I have met with and hope to produce several instances in some of which they were the only, and in others almost the only, books which were preserved through the revolutions of the monasteries to which they belonged, and all the ravages of

of his life he had devoted his various learning and all the powerful energies of his mind to effect this, and at length by intense application on his own part, and with some assistance from a few of the most learned of his followers, he had the glory to complete a book, which alone would have been sufficient (or at least ought) to have procured him the veneration of his own age and the commendations of posterity.'"[1]

The same story is told by our masters in the literature of this country:

"We hear of it in the fourteenth century, this grand Word of God (writes M. Taine). It quitted the learned schools, the dead languages, the dusty shelves on which the clergy suffered it to sleep, covered with a confusion of commentators and fathers. Wyclif appeared and translated it like Luther and in a spirit similar to Luther's."[2]

Nor is this implicit belief in the intimate connection between the pre-Reformation translation of the Bible and Wyclif, the so-called "Reformer" of the fourteenth century, confined to non-catholic writers. Whatever may have been the case with our earlier chroniclers and historians, in modern days it is generally accepted. Lingard, for example, in his *History* under the reign of Richard II., states that:

fire, pillage, carelessness, or whatever else had swept away all the others. I know (and in saying this I do not mean anything but to profess my ignorance, for did I suppress such knowledge I might well be charged with gross dishonesty) of nothing which would lead me to suppose that any human craft or power was exercised to prevent the reading, the multiplication, the diffusion of the Word of God'" (*Dark Ages*, p. 252).

[1] Christopher Anderson, *Annals of the English Bible*, Introduction, p. xxxvii.

[2] Taine, *History of English Literature*, i., p. 166.

Wycliff made a new translation (of the sacred writings), multiplied the copies with the aid of transcribers, and by his poor priests recommended it to the perusal of their hearers. In their hands it became an engine of wonderful power.

A similar statement will also be found in that useful book, "The Catholic Dictionary."

We may take it then that the *fact* of Wyclif's connection with the first translation of the Holy Bible into English is generally, if not universally, accepted as true. I wonder how many out of the hundreds that annually visit the old parish church of Lutterworth, venture to criticise even the evidence which is offered to them there? At the west end of Wyclif's old parish church may still be seen a venerable oaken table, supported by heraldic lions holding scrolls, which the credulous visitor is told represent the Scriptures. At this table sat Wyclif, when now more than five centuries ago, he was engaged in the great work of popularising the Word of God—at least, so said the venerable verger, and I have little doubt that on his testimony thousands of eyes have regarded this relic with becoming awe and reverence.

Over and above this full and implicit belief in Wyclif's connection with the English Bible, there can be no doubt that most people are inclined to think, with my friend the Lutterworth parish clerk, that so determined were the English ecclesiastical authorities to prevent the laity having the Scripture in the vernacular, that Wyclif's troubles were entirely due to his determination to furnish his countrymen with God's Word at all costs; and that during the next century or more his Lollard followers were hunted down and done to death chiefly, if not altogether, for endeavouring to spread their master's translated Scriptures.

Now, what are we to believe on the matter? My purpose in this paper is simply to examine into what we really know on this question. To some the very existence of the numerous manuscript copies of the English Scriptures will be accounted sufficient evidence of Wyclif's handiwork, just as the rocks in the valley were to Herodotus proofs of the truth of the legend that the Gods had hurled them from the heights above. But "I know it to be true, for I have seen the rocks," is evidence of a character which, let us hope, is likely to satisfy few in these days of scientific investigation.

The chief points for our consideration then may be stated thus:

1. On what evidence is the first English translation of the Bible, or any part of it, ascribed to Wyclif?

2. What had Wyclif's immediate followers or later adherents to say to the composition of the work, or to its spread among the people generally?

3. What prohibitions, if any, existed against the vernacular translations of the Sacred Scriptures in England?

4. Is there any evidence for thinking that an orthodox catholic vernacular version ever existed?

At the outset of any inquiry into the connection between Wyclif and the first English Bible, it is not unimportant to recall the warning given by Professor Shirley not too readily to credit the Reformer with any English work of the period. "Half the English religious tracts of the fourteenth and fifteenth centuries," he writes, in the Introduction to the *Fasciculus Zizaniorum*, " have been assigned to him in the absence of all external, and in defiance of all internal evidence."[1] That this is really the case cannot for a moment be doubted by any one who has made a personal examination of the tracts written at this period. For a very long time past it has been quite sufficient that a pious tract of that age be in English, for it to be at once and unhesitatingly ascribed to Wyclif or one of his followers. It is perhaps hardly wonderful that this should be the case when the position occupied by Wyclif at this period in the history of England be taken into account. His was perhaps the most striking figure at a time when English began to be the language of the nation. We are apt to forget the fact that till past the middle of the fourteenth century French was actually the tongue of the Court and of the educated classes generally. Only in 1363, for the first time, was the sitting of Parlia-

---

[1] Introduction, p. xiii. Blunt, in his *Plain Account of the English Bible* (p. 17), says: "The name of John Wycliffe has been used as a peg to hang many a work upon with which the owner of the name had nothing whatever to do."

ment opened by an English speech, and in the previous year only had it been enacted that the pleadings in the courts of law might be in English in place of the French which had hitherto been the legal language; but even then the record of the proceedings was still to be in Latin. French, however, continued for almost a century longer to be the language of the upper classes, and in it were written the rolls of Parliament, and such wills and deeds as were not in Latin. An explanation of this retention of the French language is of course to be found in the circumstances of the time. Before the era of Wyclif consequently, the reading public, that is to say, the higher classes or the clergy, found in the Latin version of the Holy Scriptures, or in such French versions as existed in England, what they required.

Such, then, is the very simple explanation of the non-existence of any English translation of the entire Bible before the time when Wyclif came upon the scene. In the first half of the fourteenth century probably the only entire book of Scripture which had appeared in English prose was the book of Psalms translated by Richard Rolle, who died in 1349. This work he undertook at the request of Dame Margaret Kirby, a recluse at Hampole. At the same time, probably about 1320, another translation of the Psalms was made by William de Schorham, a priest of Chart Sutton, near Leeds, in the county of Kent.

Besides these, however, there were the metrical paraphrases of Genesis and Exodus, the *Ormulum*, or poetical version of the Gospels and Acts of the Apostles, the work of an Augustinian canon called Orm, and more than one metrical translation of the Psalms, approaching almost to a literal translation, all productions of the thirteenth century. It is, moreover, of interest to remark that after the Norman Conquest, whilst the wants of the educated class were satisfied by the Norman-French translations, " the Anglo-Saxon version of the Gospels was copied as late as the twelfth century."[1]

Meagre as is the evidence, then, of vernacular versions of the Sacred Scriptures in England previous to the close of the first half of the fourteenth century, it is sufficient to show that the idea did not originate with Wyclif, and was not the outcome of his movement. The simple fact being that it was not until his era that the need for vernacular versions became pressing; or, indeed, that the undoubted establishment of the supremacy of English as the national language became assured. The so-called Reformer of the fourteenth century was fortunate in the time in which he lived, so far as this is concerned; and, if to have ascribed to one much that does not of right belong, is to be accounted as good fortune, then Wyclif was indeed greatly blessed in being a great personality in an age when pens began to be busy

[1] E. M. Thompson, Wycliffe Exhibition (British Museum), p. xvii.

on English tracts and English translations, because on this account alone, as Sir E. Maunde Thompson, the principal librarian of the British Museum, well observes, "it is not surprising that much has been ascribed to him which is due to writers whose names have died."

It will perhaps be thought that this can hardly with any possibility be the case in respect to so important a matter as the translation of the Bible into English. Yet what as a fact do we know about it? In the first place, the tendency to ascribe to Wyclif what clearly is not his is directly illustrated in regard to Biblical literature. The Commentary on the Apocalypse, which probably dates from the middle of the fourteenth century, and those on the Gospels of SS. Matthew, Luke, and John, were all believed to be the works of his pen, "although recent criticism has rejected his claim to the authorship."[1] It is also, I believe, very questionable whether the translation of Clement of Lanthony's Harmony of the Gospels, known as *One of Four*, was Wyclif's work at all, as is often asserted. The version differs from the received Wyclifite text, and the only reason apparently for ascribing it to him is the existence in one copy of an Introduction, in which the practice of reading the Scripture used in the Church services in English after the Latin is defended. The most that can be said is that *possibly*

---

[1] Thompson, *ut sup.* p. xvii.

Wyclif may have been the translator, although there exists no evidence that such was the case.

Passing now to the translation of the Bible itself, it will probably be a surprise to many to learn that only "the New Testament portion," as Sir E. Maunde Thompson has pointed out, can be said even "probably" to be due "to the hand of Wyclif himself." The rest it is tolerably certain owes nothing to his pen. Of the second, or revised version of the whole Scriptures, the same high authority says: "Wyclif himself, who above others would be conscious of defects, *may* have commenced the work of revision. He did not, however, live to see it accomplished."[1] So far, then, as Wyclif personally is concerned, the New Testament portion of the version, which goes under his name, is all that can be said to be even probably his work. The part taken by Wyclif's immediate followers will be treated of later; but first it is well to understand precisely upon what evidence even the probability of Wyclif's having had anything to do with the translation of the New Testament is based.

The introduction to the edition of the Wyclifite

---

[1] Thompson, *ut sup.* p. **xix**. Blunt, *Plain Account of the English Bible* (pp. 17-19) says: "There is scarcely any contemporary evidence, except that of his bitterest opponent, that Wyclife was really the author of this translation, but there can be no doubt that tradition is to be believed when it associates his name with it. . . . The popular idea of Wyclife sitting alone in his study at Lutterworth, and making a complete new translation of the whole Bible with his own hands is one of those many popular ideals which will not stand the test of historical inquiry."

Scriptures by Messrs. Forshall and Madden may be taken as gathering together every particle of evidence on the matter. The learned editors, by the way, hold, like Sir E. M. Thompson, that only the Gospels can with any probability be assigned to Wyclif himself. The evidence for this conclusion is practically the following:

1. John Hus, writing in Bohemia against the Carmelite John Stokes, about 1411, says: "It is reported among the English that he (*i.e.*, Wyclif) translated the whole Bible from Latin into English."[1] It is now allowed by all that there is not even a probability that he did anything of the kind.

2. Henry Knyghton, the Canon of Leicester, complains that Wyclif had made the Gospel cheap and common "by translating it from Latin into English tongue."

3. In a letter addressed by Archbishop Arundel and his suffragans of the Province of Canterbury to Pope John XXIII. it is certainly implied that Wyclif at least propagated his errors against the Christian faith by the aid of a new translation of Holy Writ.

On the other hand, it is difficult to account for the silence of Wyclif himself, who in none of his undoubted writings, so far as I am aware, lays any stress on, or, indeed, in any way advocates having the Scriptures in the vernacular, except so far as is implied in the claim that the Bible is the sole guide in faith and practice for all. This claim is

---

[1] Hus, *Historia et Monumenta*, ed. 1558, p. cvii.

advanced, it must be remembered, when copies could not be multiplied by the printing press and when the vast majority of the people would not have been able to read them in any case.

Equally difficult is it to explain the silence of contemporaries generally; for with the exceptions given, though many have written very fully about Wyclif and his errors, only one has noticed any connection between him and any Scriptural translations. This is true even of his chief adversaries who attack him so freely, and whose works against him are so full, so complete, and so voluminous. Neither Woodford, nor Walden, nor Whethamstede so much as refer to Wyclif's translations, or to any special desire upon his part to circulate God's Word in English among the people. The ground, I must confess, is not very firm or certain, and from what we know of Wyclif's active, restless, and combative disposition, and of his particularly speculative turn of mind, we should hardly have been disposed to assign to him so tedious a task as that of mere translation.

We can now pass to the second point to be considered in regard to this matter—namely, What had Wyclif's immediate followers to say to the translation of the Bible? We may conveniently again take Sir E. Maunde Thompson's account as expressing what is known, or rather conjectured, on this subject. It will be noticed how extremely vague and uncertain the information at hand really is:

THE PRE-REFORMATION ENGLISH BIBLE. 115

"In this (*i.e.*, the translation of the Old Testament into English), which was probably the work of Nicholas Hereford, one of Wyclif's most ardent followers at Oxford, the Latin was rendered too literally, to the disadvantage of the English translation. Two MSS. of the old Testament which are preserved in the Bodleian Library are of the greatest value for the history of the Wyclifite version. For one of these is the original MS. of the translator; and the other, which is transcribed from it, has a note at the end assigning the work to Hereford. It is remarkable that both MSS. break off abruptly in Baruch iii. 20. Hence it may be inferred that the translator was interrupted in his work and never resumed it. When we remember that Hereford was summoned before the Synod in 1382, and that soon after he left England to appeal to Rome we may fairly conjecture that it was at that date that he suddenly ceased from his labours. The remaining portion of the Old Testament may have been finished by Wyclif himself. The whole of the Bible therefore (?) was probably completed by the end of the year 1382."

This so far regards the earlier of the two translations which now go under the name of the Wyclifite Scriptures. If the note ascribing the version to Nicholas Hereford is, as Forshall and Madden testify, practically contemporary, it certainly furnishes us with strong evidence that Hereford had a main hand in the translation of the Old Testament. The English version of the Psalms, it may be remarked, was certainly founded on that of Hampole. It is of interest, consequently, to know something more of this Nicholas Hereford. He was a Doctor of Divinity at Queen's College, Oxford, and with many other members of the University, in the beginning of the Wyclifite movement, he took the side of the Reformer, and was cited to appear before the London Synod in 1382. Having been excommunicated for holding dangerous opinions, he appealed to the Pope; but in 1391 he received letters of protection from the King, and three years later his character as a true son of the Church was so clearly established that he received the office of Chancellor of the diocese of Hereford, and subsequently also became Treasurer. In 1417, however, he resigned his dignities and became a Carthusian monk in the Coventry Charterhouse, where he died. So far, then, and no further does the evidence take us as to the first translation.

Of the second or revised version, Sir E. M. Thompson gives the following account:—

"A revised version was undertaken probably soon after. The difference in style between the Old and New Testaments was unsatisfactory, and Wyclif himself, who above others would be conscious of defects, may have commenced the work of revision. He did not, however, live to see it accomplished. It was carried to a successful issue by John Purvey, his disciple and the friend of his last days, and was given to the world probably about the year 1388."[1]

Now I believe that practically the only direct evidence to connect Purvey with this translation is the fact that his name appears in a single copy of the revision as a former owner. Like Hereford, Purvey was an ardent follower of Wyclif, and lived with him at Lutterworth during the later years of

[1] Thompson, *ut. sup.* p. xix.

his life.[1] In 1400 Purvey made a public recantation of his opinions at St. Paul's, and he subsequently seems to have held ecclesiastical preferment. He was a man, apparently, of great ability, and Walden, the chief English opponent of the Wyclifites, speaks of him as "illustrious doctor of great authority."

There is one circumstance about this second translation which, according to the received idea, was inspired by Wyclif, even if he did not actively assist in the commencement of it, that requires notice. In some few copies there exists a lengthy prologue, which gives an account of the method employed by the translator. Whatever the author says of these methods is borne out in the actual version; and there is thus no room for doubting, as Henry Wharton long ago observed, that the prologues and the translation are by the same hand.

---

[1] The position of Wyclif during his stay at Lutterworth has been much misunderstood. Dean Hook says : "The modern biographers of Wycliffe are diligent in attempting to prove that he was not guilty of inconsistency, and that he did not recant. It is sufficient for us to know that he certainly explained himself so as to render it possible for the Archbishop and the other prelates, who did not like to deal harshly with him, to permit him to depart in peace." (*Lives of the Archbishops of Cant.*, ii., p. 365.)

Collier (*Eccl. Hist.*, ed. 1846, iii., p. 143) says that Wyclif must have given " the Synod some sort of satisfaction. To mention some particulars of his apology, he owns himself willing to retract any error that he may have been guilty of, and submit to the correction of Holy Church."

"For these reasons and other (wrote the author of the preface), with common charity to save all men in our realm which God will have saved,[1] a simple creature has translated the Bible out of Latin into English. First, the simple creature had much travail with divers fellows and helpers to gather many old Bibles, and other doctors and common glosses, and to make one Latin Bible some deal true; and then to study it off the new text with the gloss and other doctors as he might get, and specially Lyra[2] on the Old Testament that helped him full much in this work; the third time to counsel with old grammarians and old divines of hard words and hard senses how they might best be understood and translated; the fourth time to translate as clearly as he could to the sense and to have many good fellows and cunning at the correcting of the translation."

It would seem tolerably certain from the above extract that the writer had no knowledge of any previous translation, and this is quite inconsistent with the idea that it was the work of one so intimately connected with Wyclif as Purvey was; that is, always supposing that Wyclif had any part in the first version. It is hardly likely, moreover, that the author of the second version, were he an ardent follower of Wyclif, would have manifested such scrupulous care to give the meaning of Holy Writ according to the interpretation of approved "doctors and common glosses."

We may now turn our attention to a brief

---

[1] These words must of course be understood in the sense in which they were used in those days, not according to the mind of the modern Bible Society in these days of printing.

[2] At the top of fol. 1, Royal MSS., 1 C., ix., is the note "Here beginneth ye bible playnly the text: and where that eny maner clause is set in ye text and is not thereof Lire certificth it plainly."

consideration of the attitude of the English ecclesiastical authorities of the fourteenth and fifteenth centuries towards a vernacular translation. It might seem unnecessary, perhaps, in these enlightened days to say much upon this; but the same old stories are being repeated almost daily, and writers of various kinds still indulge themselves in the congenial task of embellishing cherished traditions without caring to inquire too particularly, or for that matter at all, into the grounds of their belief. I have already referred to this attitude of mind, and I may here take as an example the writer of an article in the latest edition of the "Encyclopædia Britannica":

> The work of translating the Holy Scriptures (he says) assumed important dimensions mainly in connection with the spirit of revolt against the Church of Rome, which rose in the twelfth and thirteenth centuries. The study of the Bible in the vulgar tongue was a characteristic of the Cathari and Waldenses, and the whole weight of the Church's authority was turned against the use of the Scriptures by the laity. The prohibition of the Bible in the vulgar tongue, put forth at the Council of Toulouse in A.D. 1229, was repeated by other councils in various parts of the Church, but failed to quell the rising interest in the Scriptures. In England and in Bohemia the Bible was translated by the reforming parties of Wyclif and Hus; and the early presses of the fifteenth century sent forth Bibles not only in Latin, but in French, Spanish, Italian, German and Dutch.[1]

[1] A writer has shown that in the collection of Bibles in the British Museum, according to the Catalogue of 1892, there are eleven German editions of the Bible, ranging from 1466 to 1518; three Bohemian editions between 1488 and 1506; one Dutch dated 1477; five French

We are, of course, concerned chiefly with England: but it may be useful to remark upon the misleading tendency of this passage from the "Encyclopædia." It has been shown beyond the possibility of doubt that in Germany there existed in the Middle Ages some seventy-two partial versions of the vernacular Scriptures and fifty complete translations, all emanating from Catholic sources. The same numerous translations existed also in France, with this difference, that, whilst most of the French manuscripts are *livres de luxe*, in Germany they appear to be small volumes, which point to their use as aids to personal piety rather than as books for mere library use. The same may also be said of the printed editions. France, Spain, and even Italy, each had editions of the vernacular Scriptures in the fifteenth century, as some of the earliest efforts of their national printing presses. In Germany, indeed, no fewer than seventeen such editions existed before the time of Luther, and still people may yet be found who cling to the old fable of the accidental finding of the Bible by the German reformer;[1] the truth being that there is

---

from 1510 to 1531; seven Italian between 1471 and 1532. These, be it remembered, are all Catholic in their origin and execution, and they by no means represent all the editions published, but only such as the English nation has secured for the British Museum collection (cf. *The Church and the Bible*. Melbourne, 1896).

[1] Luther's providential discovery of the Bible chained up to the wall of his monastery is still, I fear, believed in very generally. "There are no lies that die so hard as lies that have a controversial

ample evidence to show that in making his translation of the Scriptures he had before him and was actually using one of these Catholic versions.[1]

If England did not possess a pre-Reformation printed Bible this was due to circumstances to which I shall have to refer later. It should, moreover, be borne in mind that its place was supplied by the extremely popular "Golden Legend," which contained nearly the whole of the Pentateuch and the Gospel narrative in English, and which was issued from the press by Caxton before the close of the fifteenth century.

As to the attitude of the ecclesiastical authorities in England towards the translated Scriptures, it is believed on all hands, apparently, that it was uncompromisingly hostile. To judge from our ordinary history books we should certainly conclude that what Mr. Matthew calls "the zeal of the inquisitor" prevented any large circulation of the

importance," says a writer in the *Saturday Review* (July 25, 1874). And, he adds that "the whole history of the Blessed Reformation, from whatever side it is told, is a conspicuous illustration of this." D'Aubigné, in his still popular *History of the Reformation*, boldly states that Luther, after having studied two years in the University of Erfurt, where "he had read the Philosophy of the Middle Ages in the writing of Occam, Scotus, Bonaventura, and Thomas Aquinas," had not known that there was such a book as the Bible in existence! Mr. Ward's so-called great historical (?) picture representing this fable of Luther and the discovery of the Bible, has done much to perpetuate the legend in this country. If report be correct, it was purchased for some £3,000, and presented to the British and Foreign Bible Society.

[1] Cf. *Athenæum*, December 22, 1883.

newly translated Word of God.¹ Yet a strange fact confronts us at the outset; the number of manuscript copies of English Bibles extant, hardly falls short of that of the German and French vernacular translations, which it is admitted were allowed. It has, I believe, been hitherto taken for granted without sufficient examination that the authority of the Church in this country was directed not merely to discourage the reading of the Bible in English, but absolutely to forbid the making of any translation whatever. But what, again, are the facts? As a proof of this distinct prohibition of the English Church, a constitution of the Council of Oxford, in A.D. 1408, under Archbishop Arundel is usually relied upon. This is what the Council has to say upon the matter (Wilkins, iii., p. 317):

"It is dangerous, as Saint Jerome declares, to translate the text of Holy Scripture out of one idiom into another, since it is not easy in translations to preserve exactly the same meaning in all things. . . We therefore command and ordain that henceforth no one translate any text of Holy Scripture into

[1] A writer in the *Academy* (August 7, 1886), Mr. Karl Pearson, remarks thus on the attitude of the Church towards the Vernacular Bible: "The Catholic Church has quite enough to answer for . . . but in the fifteenth century it certainly did not hold back the Bible from the folk, and it gave them in the Vernacular a long series of devotional works, which for language and religious sentiment have never been surpassed. Indeed, we are inclined to think it made a mistake in allowing the masses such ready access to the Bible. It ought to have recognised the Bible once for all as a work absolutely unintelligible without a long course of historical study; and, so far as it was supposed to be inspired, very dangerous in the hands of the ignorant."

English or any other language in a book (*per viam libri*), booklet or tract, and that no one read any book, booklet or tract of this kind lately made in the time of the said John Wyclif or since, or that hereafter may be made either in part or wholly, either publicly or privately, under pain of excommunication until *such translation shall have been approved and allowed by the diocesan of the place,* or (if need be), *by the Provincial Council.* He who shall act otherwise let him be punished as an abettor of heresy and error."[1]

Now it is obvious from the words of the decree that in this there is no such absolute prohibition as is generally represented. All that the fathers of the Synod of Oxford forbade was unauthorised translations. The fact that no mention is made of any Wyclifite translation of the entire Bible is not without its significance, and in view of the Lollard errors then prevalent, and of the ease with which the text of Holy Scripture could be modified in the translation in any and every MS., so as apparently to be made to support those views, the ordinance appears not only prudent and just, but necessary. Even when the introduction of printing at last rendered it possible to secure that all copies should be identical, the version had still to be authorised.

---

[1] *The heading is* VII. CONSTITUTIO, *Ne quis texta S. Scripturæ transferat in linguam Anglicanam.* In *Ms. Lamb,* it runs, *Ne textus aliquis S. Scrip. in linguam A. de cetero transferatur per viam libri aut tractatus. Statuimus igitur et ordinamus, ut nemo deinceps aliquem textum sacræ Scripturæ auctoritate sua in linguam Anglicanam vel aliam transferat, per viam libri, libelli aut tractatus, nec legatur aliquis hujusmodi, liber libellus aut tractatus jam noviter tempore dicti Johannis Wycliff, sive citra compositus, sive in posterum componendus in parte vel in toto, publice vel occulte, sub,* &c. (Wilkins, iii., p. 317.)

Beyond this safeguarding of the text the words of the decree seem to imply that proper authorisation might be obtained, and even that an official vernacular version of the Bible was seriously contemplated.

In this sense, there can be no doubt, the Constitution of Oxford was understood by those whom at the time it concerned. The great canonist Lyndewode in his gloss upon this passage says that the prohibition does not extend to translations of the Scripture made before the time of Wyclif, and he assigns the following as a reason why more recent translations must be approved, that:

> "Although it be the plain text of Sacred Scripture that is so translated, the translator may yet err in his translation, or if he compose a book, booklet, or tract, he may, as in fact frequently happens, intermingle false and erroneous teaching with the truth."

Sir Thomas More takes the same view, and specially denies that the church authorities in England had ever prohibited the making of English translations of the Bible or the reading of such when made.

> "For as much (he writes) as it is dangerous to translate the text of Scripture out of one tongue into another, as holy St. Jerome testifieth, for as much as in translation it is hard always to keep the same sentence (*i.e.*, sense) whole. It is, I say, for these causes at a council holden at Oxenford provided upon great pain, that no man should from thenceforth translate into the English tongue, or any other language, of his own authority, by way of book, libellus or treatise, nor no man openly, or secretly, read any such book, &c., *newly made* in the time of the said John Wyclif or since, &c., until such

should be approved. And this is a law that so many so long have spoken of, and so few have in all this while sought to seek (or find out) whether they say the truth or no. For I trow that in this law you see nothing unreasonable. For it neither forbiddeth the translations to be read that were *already well done of old before* Wyclif's days, nor damneth his because it was new, but because it was naught; nor prohibiteth new to be made, but provideth that they shall not be read if they be made amiss, till they be by good examination amended."

In a subsequent place the same authority says again that:

" When the clergy, in the Constitution Provincial before mentioned, agreed that the English Bibles should remain, which were translated afore Wyclif's days, they consequently did agree that to have the Bible in English was no hurt." [1]

Of course the further question arises as to the action of the ecclesiastical authorities subsequent to the Council of Oxford. On this matter one writer says that:

"It appears by our Bishop's Registers, that by virtue of it (*i.e.*, the Constitution passed in the Council of Oxford) several men and women were afterwards condemned to be burnt, and forced to abjure, for the reading of the New Testament and learning the Ten Commandments, the Lord's Prayer, &c., and teaching

---

[1] Canon Dixon (*Hist. of Church of England from the Abolition of the Roman Jurisdiction*, vol. i., p. 451) writes about the attitude of the Ecclesiastical authorities to the vernacular Scriptures thus: " From the earliest times the English Church or nation was possessed of the sacred writings through the labours of monks and bishops. . . At length, however, at the beginning of the fifteenth century, the resolute prelate Arundel passed his famous Constitution to forbid any man making new translations on his own account, or reading those that had been made in or since the time of the lately deceased Wicliffe. He thus proclaimed the war of authority against private versions,

them to others, of Dr. Wicklif's translation. This (the writer adds) one of our Church historians (namely Fuller) called in question the truth of, and argued against the facts, but, according to our author, quite wrongly."

Yet what—as far as they can be ascertained—are the facts? In the first place let us confine our attention to the manuscript versions of the English Scriptures, before the question was complicated by the attempted dissemination of the printed copies of Tyndale's English Testament in 1526.

During the fifteenth century the examinations of Lollards and those who were in any way suspected of a leaning towards Wyclifite doctrines were numerous and were conducted upon well recognised and well understood principles. The articles upon which the suspected were to be questioned are well known. In a copy to be seen among the Harleian MSS.[1] at the British Museum, the interrogatories number thirty-four and embrace a great variety of points of Christian faith and practice. The subject

though certainly he neither forbade the ancient versions to be used, nor denied that an authorised version might be made." Dean Hook had previously expressed the same opinion (*Lives of the Archbishops of Canterbury*, iii., p. 83). "It was not from hostility to a translated Bible, considered abstractedly, that the conduct of Wicliff in translating it, was condemned. Long before his time there had been translators of Holy Writ. There is no reason to suppose that any objection would have been offered to the circulation of the Bible, if the object of the translator had only been the edification and sanctification of the reader. It was not till the designs of the Lollards were discovered, that Wicliff's version was proscribed."

[1] Harl. MS. 2179, fol. 157.

of the vernacular Scriptures is, however, not so much as raised in any of them. Further, in the very large number of recorded examinations of people charged with holding Lollard opinions, and in the various abjurations made by all classes of people condemned for their heretical opinions, which I have been able personally to examine, I have met with but one or at most two references to the Sacred Scriptures in English. Take an example. In 1469 one John Turner of Sydney abjured, amongst other errors of which he had been convicted, the following: "that religious people from mere envy prevent lay persons having the Holy Scripture translated into the English language."[1] As John Turner retracted this opinion, we may take it that in some sense or other the assertion was untrue. For the rest, the many examinations, the records of which exist, reveal the fact that the followers of Wyclif could never have made any very special point of their determination at all costs to have the Sacred Scriptures in English. Had they done so some evidence would have been forthcoming in their examinations before the ecclesiastical courts. This is, moreover, exactly what we should expect, since in no well recognised work of Wyclif is any stress laid upon the Bible in the vernacular, beyond what some may consider to be implied in his general claim to have

---

[1] Foxe, "Acts and Monuments" (ed. Townsend), iii., 539, records an instance of Ralph Mungin, in 1416, being charged with having "The Gospels of John Wyclif," whatever that may mean.

the Scripture as his sole rule of faith, as I have before pointed out.

It is frequently asserted that all copies of the English Scriptures that fell into the hands of the ecclesiastical authorities were destroyed. Sir Thomas More says that "if this were done so, it were not well done; but," he continues in reply to one who had asserted this, "I believe that ye mistake it." And taking up one case objected against him in which the Bible of a Lollard prisoner named Richard Hun, a London merchant, was said to have been burnt in the Bishop of London's prison, he says:

"This I remember well, that besides other things framed for the favour of divers other heresies there were in the prologue of that Bible such words touching the Blessed Sacrament as good Christian men did abhor to hear and that gave the readers undoubted occasion to think that the book was written after Wyclif's copy and by him translated into our tongue, and that this Bible was destroyed consequently not because it was in English, but because it contained gross and manifest heresy."

This is borne out by the account given by Foxe, who has printed from the Register of Fitzjames, Bishop of London, thirteen articles extracted from "the prologue" of Hun's "Great Book of the Bible." These were read to the people from the pulpit at Paul's Cross, and they were invited to come and examine the Bible for themselves in order to see that it contained these errors.[1] If this list of

---

[1] Foxe, *Acts and Monuments*, iv. p. 186.

articles can be relied upon, and there is no reason to distrust the account, it bears out Sir Thomas More's contention that this "great Bible" must have been a Lollard production, although we shall look in vain in the edition of Wyclifite Scriptures published by Forshall and Madden for any trace of these errors.

Turning now from ecclesiastical to State records, we find no mention whatever of the Bible, or indeed of any part of the Scriptures, among the fairly numerous entries regarding the works of Wyclif and his Lollard followers recorded on the Patent and Close Rolls. In the period from Richard II. to Henry VII. searches were frequently directed to be made for the works of these reforming spirits, but no mention whatever is made in the orders for such quests of any translation of the Holy Scriptures. The usual form is much as follows: The king directs his sheriffs and other officers to search out and seize "all books, booklets, *cedulæ* and *quaterni*, compiled either in English or Latin, containing conclusions or wicked opinions contrary to the teaching of Holy Church." So careful were the authorities to carry out these instructions, that on the first intimation of any suspected centre of Lollard opinions the house was to be thoroughly searched to see "whether any English book, the reading of which was forbidden, could be found."[1]

From the absolute silence of all records, both

[1] Harl. MS., 2179, f. 158.

ecclesiastical and lay, as to any Wyclifite version of the Bible, it may be fairly argued that the determination at all costs to spread the Scriptures in English formed no part of the practical politics of the Wyclifites. After this it need perhaps hardly be added that the rigour with which they were treated by Church and State authorities was in no sense caused by this lofty aspiration to propagate the gospel or any peculiar zeal manifested by them for the written word of God. The misunderstanding—to call it by its least objectionable name—is probably caused by certain circumstances relating to the first prints of the English Bible in the sixteenth century, upon which it is well here to make some brief remarks.

The difficulty first arose about 1526, when the translation of the New Testament, which had been made on the Continent by Tyndale, assisted by an ex-friar, named William Roye, was first brought into England. Their object, as described by the learned Cochlæus, who professes to have first-hand information, was that they "entertained hopes that in a short time, through the New Testament, which they had translated into English, all the people of England would become Lutherans, whether the king would or no."[1] Whether this was the case

---

[1] Green in his *History* (vol. ii., pp. 127-8), though by no means unfriendly to Tyndale on this point, writes as follows:—" We can only fairly judge their action by viewing it in the light of the time. What Warham and More saw over the sea might well have turned

or not does not greatly matter, since it is allowed on all hands that the version so printed was gravely, if not grossly, corrupt. "In some editions of Tyndale's *New Testament*," writes the Protestant historian Blunt, "there is what must be regarded as a wilful omission of the gravest possible character, for it appears in several editions, and has no shadow of justification in the Greek or Latin of the passage (1 Peter ii. 13, 14). Such an error was quite enough"[1] to justify the suppression of Tyndale's translation.[2] That this infidelity was in truth the real reason for its condemnation clearly appears in the monition addressed by

them from a movement which seemed breaking down the very foundations of religion and society. Not only was the fabric of the Church rent asunder, and the centre of Christian unity denounced as 'Babylon,' but the reform itself seemed passing into anarchy. Luther was steadily moving onward from the denial of one Christian dogma to that of another; and what Luther still clung to, his followers were ready to fling away. Meanwhile the religious excitement was kindling wild dreams of social revolution, and men stood aghast at the horrors of a peasant war which broke out in Germany. It was not, therefore, as a mere translation of the Bible that Tyndale's work reached England. It came as part of the Lutheran movement, and it bore the Lutheran stamp in its version of ecclesiastical words. 'Church' became 'congregation'; 'priest' was changed into 'elder.' We can hardly wonder that More denounced the book as heretical, or that Warham ordered it to be given up by all who possessed it."

[1] Blunt, *History of the Reformation*, p. 514.

[2] The passage was "Submit yourselves unto all manner of ordinance of man for the Lord's sake, whether it be unto rulers as unto them that are sent of him," &c. The words "whether it be unto the king as chief head" are left out. (See ed. of 1531 and 1534, Douce B., 226, 227, Bodl. Lib.)

Tunstall, at that time Bishop of London, to the archdeacons of his diocese:—

"Some sons of iniquity and ministers of the Lutheran faction (he writes) have craftily translated the Holy Gospels of God into our vulgar English, and intermingled with their translation articles gravely heretical and opinions that are erroneous, pernicious, pestilent, scandalous, and tending to seduce persons of simple and unwary dispositions."

For this reason he orders that every copy of the translation that could be found or detected should be forthwith delivered up to his officers.[1]

For some years after this ecclesiastical prohibition of Tyndale's translation, demands were from time to time made for an authorised printed version. It is open to us in these days, perhaps, to regret that no measure to satisfy this want was taken in due time by the Catholic bishops; but their reason for delaying the production was the substantial fear that it would only tend further to spread the ever-increasing flood of erroneous opinions. As the royal proclamation "against translating the Bible in English, French, or Dutch," issued in 1530, says:—

"Having respect to the malignity of this present time, with the inclination of the people to erroneous opinions, (it is thought) that the translation of the New Testament and the Old into the vulgar tongue of England would rather be the occasion of continuance or increase of errors among the said people than any benefit or commodity towards the weal of

Commission dated October 24th, 1526.

their souls, and that it shall be now more convenient that the same people have the Holy Scriptures expounded to them by preachers in their sermons as it hath been of old time accustomed."

For these reasons all are ordered to deliver up the copies of the printed Testament " corruptly translated into the English tongue," the king promising " to provide that the Holy Scripture shall be, by great learned and Catholique persons, translated into the English tongue, if it shall then seem to his Grace convenient to be." [1]

The postponement of this promised issue was not decided upon without due consideration, and those who lived at the time and may be considered as likely best to understand the circumstances, imputed no blame to Archbishop Warham and the English ecclesiastical authorities generally for their continued opposition to the scheme. Even Cranmer himself says: "I can wel think them worthie pardon, which at the comming abrode of the

---

[1] Wilkins, *Concilia*, iii. 741. Canon Dixon says of this prohibition of Tyndale's Scriptures: "If the clergy had acted thus, simply because they would have kept the people ignorant of the Word of God, they would have been without excuse. But it was not so. Every one of the little volumes containing portions of the Sacred Text that was issued by Tyndale, contained also a prologue and notes, written with such a hot fury of vituperation against the prelates and clergy, the monks and friars, the rites and ceremonies of the Church as . . . . was hardly likely to commend it to the favour of those who were attacked. Moreover, the persons themselves were held to be hostile to the Catholic Faith, as it was then understood, and to convey the sense unskilfully or maliciously."—*History of the Church of England*, i. pp. 451-2.

Scripture doubted and drew backe." On this point it has been well remarked, by the way, that there was no such general desire to have a vernacular Bible in England, as is commonly represented. Except among a small minority of interested persons, who saw in these translations a possible means of spreading their "new doctrines," England was certainly not a Bible-thirsty land.[1]

After this brief digression, which was necessary to explain the attitude of the English bishops in the early part of the sixteenth century towards the printed vernacular Scriptures, we may return to the question of the manuscript versions. We are now in a position to consider the fourth point in our inquiry, namely: What evidence, if any, is there for the existence of a catholic and orthodox version? So far as I am aware, every one who has dealt with the subject of the English Scriptures has taken for granted that none existed. But in the first place we are confronted with the distinct assertion made by Sir Thomas More. Besides expressly denying that there was any general prohibition of the English Bible, he asserts that there was an undoubted catholic edition well known in his days.

"As for old translations, before Wyclif's time (he writes), they remain lawful and be in some folks hands. Myself have seen and can show you, Bibles, fair and old, in English

[1] J. R. Dore, *Old Bibles*, p. 13.

which have been known and seen by the Bishop of the Diocese and left in laymans hands and womens."

Again, in another place he says :—

"The whole Bible was long before his (*i.e.*, Wyclif's) days by virtuous and well learned men, translated into the English tongue and by good and godly people with devotion, and soberness, well and reverendly read."[1]

It may, I think, be justly argued that, whether Sir Thomas More may have been wrong or not in assigning the manuscript copies of the version he knew as the authorised catholic one, to a date prior to the age of Wyclif, he cannot have been wrong as to the *fact* of the existence in his days of well-known and approved copies of the Bible in English.

This evidence is corroborated by Archbishop Cranmer himself, who, in the prologue to the second edition of the Great Bible, writes in defence of the Scriptures in English thus :—

"If the matter should be tried by custom, we might also allege custom for the reading of the Scripture in the vulgar tongue, and prescribe the more ancient custom. For it is not much above one hundred years ago, since Scripture hath not been accustomed to be read in the vulgar tongue within this realm, and many hundred years before that, it was translated and read in the Saxon's tongue, which at that time was our mother tongue, and when this language waxed old and out of common usage, because folk should not lack the fruit of reading, it was again translated into the newer language whereof yet also many copies remain and be daily found."

[1] *Dyalogues* (ed. 1530), p. 138.

These copies, it is hardly necessary to remark, the writer must have regarded as authorised translations, and it must have been one of these that he took as the basis of his projected print of the Bible in 1535, dividing it into nine or ten parts, which he submitted to various bishops for their correction.[1]

The same testimony—so far, at least, as regards the existence of vernacular versions of the Scriptures independent of John Wyclif's—is given by Foxe, the martyrologist. In his dedication to Archbishop Parker of his edition of the Saxon Gospels he writes:

"If histories be well examined we shall find both before the Conquest and after, as well before John Wickliffe was born as since, the whole body of the Scriptures was by sundry men translated into our country tongue."

In the face, then, of so much distinct evidence, it is extremely difficult not to admit the existence in pre-Reformation days of some well-recognised and perfectly orthodox version or versions of the Holy Scriptures in English.[2]

Now the question at once arises, What has become of the catholic version known to Sir Thomas More, Archbishop Cranmer, and John Foxe? If we are to accept the conclusions of those

---

[1] Strype, *Memorials of Archbishop Cranmer* (ed. 1812), i., p. 42.

[2] The writer of the article on the "Vernacular Bible" in the *Encyclopædia Britannica* (9th ed.), viii., p. 381, *seqq.*, suggests that "the many copies spoken of by Cranmer disappeared in the destruction of the monastic libraries."

who have hitherto written on the subject, we know of but two English manuscript versions of the entire Bible, those which are now called the Lollard Scriptures, and as such they are printed in Forshall and Madden's great edition. Of any other—that is, any catholic version—we are asked to believe that there is now no trace whatever. But, I would ask, may it not be possible that under the influence of a preconceived idea, people have gone off on a wrong scent altogether? If we start with a foregone conclusion, we can have little hope that we shall read facts rightly, even though they be as plain as the proverbial pikestaff, and in this instance it appears to me that it has been assumed altogether too hastily that the extant pre-Reformation Scriptures could not have been catholic, and must have been and were the outcome of the Wyclifite movement. For myself, I may say, that after much consideration, I have been led to the belief that facts cannot be made to square with this theory as to the origin of these versions of the English Bible. Startling as the assertion may seem to many, I have come to the conclusion that the versions, now known as the Wyclifite Scriptures, are, in reality, only authorised catholic translations of the Bible. Every circumstance that can be gleaned regarding these manuscripts strengthens this belief. Whether Hereford, or Purvey possibly (for at best we are, so far as this is concerned, dealing with possibilities), may have had any part in the translation does not, after all, so much concern us. Our chief interest is not with the translator, but with the work itself, and with the question whether it may fairly be claimed as the semi-official and certainly perfectly orthodox translation of the English Church; or whether, on the other hand, it must be regarded as a version secretly executed, clandestinely circulated, and still more stealthily studied, by the Lollard followers of Wyclif. This is the main point of interest.

Now, I hardly think it can be questioned that if we were to rely upon the testimony of our writers of history, and our so-called masters of English literature, we must accept the latter alternative, and regard the English Bible as the book which the Lollard followers of Wyclif made, multiplied and studied, and for which they died. Take the description in Taine's *History of English Literature:*

"Fancy (he writes) these brave spirits, simple and strong souls, who began to read at night in their shops, by candle-light, for they were shopkeepers, tailors, skinners and bakers, who with some men of letters began to read and then to believe, and finally got themselves burned." [1]

So far as I have been able to discover, however, from an examination of the two texts, there is nothing inconsistent with their having been the work of perfectly orthodox sons of Holy Church. In no place where (had the version been the work of Lollard pens) we might have looked for texts

[1] Taine, *History of English Literature*, i. p. 167.

strained or glossed to suit their well-known conclusions, do any such appear. Sir Thomas More indeed, as we have already seen, speaks of a Bible that was destroyed because it contained "such words touching the Blessed Sacrament" that people took it for a Lollard Bible. This is quite what we should have expected, seeing that some verses, written about the reign of Henry VI., are inserted into a copy of Hampole's Psalter, charging the Lollards with having interpolated their special teaching into this work so as to claim for it the authority of the holy hermit. Apparently all such garbled Scriptures must have fallen into the hands of those officials, who rigorously sought for any scrap of Wyclifite writing, since such Bibles are not now known to exist.

I cannot but think that an unbiassed mind which will reflect upon the matter must see how impossible it was for a poor persecuted sect like the Lollards, for the writings of which frequent and rigid searches were made, to produce the Bibles now ascribed to them. Many of these copies, as we may see for ourselves, are written with great care and exactness, and illuminated with coloured borders executed by skilful artists. These must surely have been the productions of freer hands than the followers of Wyclif ever were allowed to have in England. The learned editors of the so-called Wyclifite Scriptures, Messrs. Forshall and Madden, apparently hardly appreciated the force of this when they wrote:

"The new copies passed into the hands of all classes of the people. Even the Sovereign himself and the princes of the blood royal did not disdain to possess them. The volumes were in many instances executed in a costly manner, and were usually written upon vellum by experienced scribes. This implies not merely the value which was set upon the Word of God, but also that the scribes found a reward for their labours among the wealthier part of the community."[1]

This is undoubtedly the case, and it is to be explained only on the supposition that the English Bible thus widely circulated was in truth the authorised catholic version, and was in the possession of its various owners with the thorough approval of the ecclesiastical authorities. Is it likely that men of position, of unquestioned orthodoxy and of undoubted hostility to Lollard aims and opinions, would have cherished the possession of copies of a Wyclifite Bible? When we find, for example, that a finely-executed vellum folio copy of the Scriptures, with illuminated borders, was not only the property of King Henry VI.—a monarch, by the way, of saintly life and "enthusiastic in the cause of religion"—but that he bestowed it upon the monks of the London Charterhouse, we cannot but acknowledge that this must have been known as the perfectly orthodox translation of the English Church.

The same version is found to have had a place in the royal library of Henry VII. In this copy not

[1] Introduction, p. xxxii.

only is the excellent character of the workmanship altogether inconsistent with the notion that it is from the pen of some poor hunted adherent of Wyclif, but a leaf supplied at the beginning, in a late fifteenth century hand, is illuminated with the royal arms, the portcullis and red and white Tudor roses. Moreover, curiously enough, this border surrounds the prologue, "Five and Twenty Books" so freely attributed to Wyclif.

A third copy of the English Scriptures—the very manuscript now displayed in the British Museum as Wyclif's translation, to which I referred at the commencement of this paper—formerly belonged to Thomas of Woodstock, Duke of Gloucester, the firm friend and ally of that uncompromising opponent of Lollard opinions, Archbishop Arundel. Indeed, the inventory of the Duke of Gloucester's goods, now in the Record Office, shows that, besides "the Bible in English in two big volumes bound in red leather," he possessed in his by no means extensive library an English Psalter and two books of the Gospels in English.[1] Another copy of this version of the New Testament was the property, and has

---

[1] R. O. Exch. Q. R. Escheator's Accts. $\frac{7}{4}\frac{7}{}$. The celebrated biblical scholar, Dr. Adam Clarke, who formerly possessed this manuscript, considered that it was certainly not Wyclifite in origin. The Thomas of Woodstock for whom the book was illuminated was the youngest son of Edward III., and was murdered at Calais in 1397. "How long before 1397 this work was written is uncertain," writes Dr. Clarke, "but it must have been in the very nature of things several years before this time." (Townley, *Biblical Literature*, ii., p. 44.)

the autograph, of Humphrey—"the good Duke Humphrey"—of Gloucester, the generous benefactor of St. Albans, and the constant friend of its abbot, Whethamstede, whose hostility to Lollard doctrines is well known.

Another point which must not be overlooked is the good catholic company in which this version of the Scriptures, or parts of it, are occasionally found. Thus, in a volume in the Museum collection we find not only the lessons from the Old Testament read in the Mass book, together with the table of Epistles and Gospels, but a tract by Richard Rolle, "of amendinge of mannes life, or 'the rule of lifing,'" and another on contemplative life and love of God.[1] Another copy of *The Book of Tobit*, in the later version, which is followed by the translated *Magnificat* and *Benedictus*, has also in the volume some tracts or meditations, and what is called the "Pistle of the Holy Sussanne." With this is bound, possibly at a later date, Richard Rolle of Hampole's *Craft of Deying*. The catholic origin of this volume is borne out fully by the fact that it belonged to the abbey of Barking in Essex. Indeed, it appears to have been written by one of the nuns named Matilda Hayle, as the note *Iste liber constat Matilde Hayle de Berkinge* is in the same hand as the body of the book, which, by the way, subsequently belonged to another nun named Mary Hastynges.[2]

A copy of the English Bible, now at Lambeth,

---

[1] Lansdowne MS., 455.   [2] Add. MS., 10,596.

formerly belonged to Bishop Bonner, that *Malleus hereticorum*, and another, now at Cambridge, to William Weston, the Prior of St. John's, Clerkenwell.

In like manner a copy of the English translation of the New Testament, now attributed to Wyclif, among the manuscripts of the Duke of Northumberland at Alnwick, was originally, and probably not long after the volume was written, the property of another religious house. On the last page is the name of Katerina Methwold, *Monacha*, Katherine Methwold, the nun.

There are, moreover, instances of the English Bible—the production, the secret production, of the Lollard scribes—that perilous piece of property to possess, as we are asked to believe—there are instances of this being bequeathed by wills publicly proved in the public courts of the Bishop. Others, not less publicly, are bestowed upon churches or given to religious houses. It is, of course, obvious that this could never have been done had the volume so left been the work of Wyclif or of his followers, for it would then indeed have been, as a modern writer describes the Wyclifite books, "a perilous piece of property." Thus, before the close of the fourteenth century, namely, in 1394, a copy of the Gospels in English was bequeathed to the chantry of St. Nicholas, in the Church of Holy Trinity, York, by John Hopton, Chaplain there.[1] Fancy

---

[1] *Testamenta Ebor*, Surtees Soc., i., 196.

what this means on the theory that the English Scriptures were the work of Wycliffite hands! It means nothing less than that a catholic priest publicly bequeaths, in a will proved in his Bishop's court, to a catholic church, for the use of catholic people, the proscribed work of some member of an heretical sect.

Again, in 1404, Philip Baunt, a Bristol merchant, leaves by will a copy of the Gospels in English to a priest named John Canterbury, attached to St. Mary Redcliffe's Church. And—not to mention many cases in wills of the period, where it is probable that the Bible left was an English copy—there is an instance of a bequest of such a Bible in the will of a priest, William Revetour, of York, in 1446. The most interesting gift of an English New Testament, as a precious and pious donation to the Church, is that of the copy now in the possession of Lord Ashburnham,[1] which in 1517 was given to the Convent of our Lady of Syon by Lady Danvers. On the last page is the following dedication:—

"Good .... Mr. Confessor of Sion with his brethren. Dame Anne Danvers widowe, sometyme wyffe to Sir William Danvers, knyght (whose soul God assoyle) hathe gevyn this present Booke unto Mastre Confessor and his Brethren enclosed in Syon, entendyng therby not oonly the honor laude and preyse to Almighty God but also that she the moore tenderly may be committed unto the mercy of God.

[1] Ashburnham MS., Appendix xix. (No. 156 in Forshall and Madden). The text of this MS. was printed for Mr. Lea Wilson by Pickering, in 1848.

The aforseid Dame Anne Danvers hathe delyvered this booke by the hands of her son Thomas Danvers on Mydde Lent Sunday in the 8th yere of our lord King Henry VIII. and in the yere of our Lord God a M. fyve hundred and seventeene. Deo gracias."

To all who know what Syon was: how for a century past it had represented the very pink of pious orthodoxy and was the centre of the devotional life of the period; how the practical piety of its sisters was fostered by the highest ascetical teaching of Richard Whytford and others; to all who understand this it must appear as nothing less than the height of absurdity to suppose that any lady would insult its inmates by offering for their acceptance an heretical version of the English Bible.

And, whilst on the subject of Syon, attention must be called to another very important piece of evidence for the existence of a Catholic version of the Scriptures. It is contained in a devotional book, written probably not later than the year 1450 for the use of these sisters of Syon, and printed "at the desyre and instaunce of the worshypfull and devoute lady abbesse [1] of the worshypful Monastery of Syon and the revendre fadre in God [2] general confessowre of the same" about the year 1530. It is called *The Myrroure of our Lady very necessary for religious persons*, and it is practically a translation of their Church services into English to enable the nuns the

---

[1] Dame Agnes Jordan, the last abbess.
[2] John Fewterer, who also survived the Dissolution.

better to understand their daily ecclesiastical duties. The point to which attention is directed is the following paragraph in the "first prologue," written, remember, not later than the middle of the fifteenth century: "Of psalms I have drawn (*i.e.*, translated) but fewe," says the author, "for ye may have them of Richard Hampoules drawinge, and out of *Englysshe bibles* if ye have lysence thereto."[1] It is not very likely that these pious sisters would have been able to get their psalms from Wyclifite versions.

It is clear that the compiler of this book of devotions did in fact obtain them on *imprimatur* of authority for the translations of various quotations from Scripture in the volume. He writes :—

"And for as much as it is forbidden under pain of cursing that any man should have or translate any text of Holy Scripture into English without licence of the Bishop diocesan ; and in diverse places of your service are such texts of Holy Scripture. Therefore I asked and have licence of our Bishop to translate such things into English to your ghostly comfort and profit, so both our conscience in translating and yours in the having may be more sure and clear in our Lord's worship, which may it keep us in His grace and bring us to His bliss." Amen.[2]

[1] "The Myrroure of oure Ladye" (ed. J. H. Blunt), E. Eng. Text Soc., p. 3.

[2] Ibid., p. 71. The editor of *The Myrroure* upon this passage notes : "This reference to English Bibles seems to imply that they were very common in the middle of the fifteenth century. These may have been the copies of the Wyclifite version, but it seems unlikely that the Sisters would have received 'licence' to read these, especially as 'de quibus cavendum est' is written against some works of Wyclif in the Library Catalogue preserved at C.C. Coll. Cambridge." After quoting

To pass to another point—it has been remarked upon as somewhat strange that in Wyclif's sermons, which seem to have been written at the close of his life, the Scripture quotations are in no case made from the version now declared to be his. A preacher, of course, may have turned the Latin into English at the moment, but in his case this is hardly likely, if, as we are given to understand, the popularising of his reputed version was the great object of his life. Moreover, what may well have been the case in spoken discourses would scarcely have been adhered to in written and formal sermons. Beyond this the same is true of every work reputed to be Wyclif's. In no instance does he quote his own supposed version. On the other hand it is at least most remarkable that the Commentary upon the Apocalypse, formerly attributed to Wyclif, but which is now acknowledged not to be from his pen, has the ordinary version for its text.

Further, it is not without significance that Bishop Pecock in his "Repressor," a work written ostensibly against the position of the Lollards, and their claim to make the Sacred Scripture their sole and sufficient guide in all things, not only uses what is now called the Wyclifite version of the Bible in all his quotations, but throughout his work evidently

the Oxford Constitution of 1408, and Lyndewood's Gloss, Mr. Blunt adds: "As his words were written about the same time as those to which the note refers, they seem to corroborate the evidence given in the *Mirror*, that in the earlier half of the fifteenth century English Bibles were freely used by the people." (Notes on *The Myrroure*, p. 310).

takes for granted that the lay-folk generally had the Scriptures with authority, and nowhere blames the fact. Moreover, he is careful to explain that he only speaks of the Lollards as "Biblemen," because of their wish to found every law of faith and morals on the Written Word.

"This what I have now said (he concludes) of and to Bible men I have not said under this intent and meaning that I should feel to be unlawful (for) laymen for to read in the Bible and for to study and learn therein, with help and counsel of wise and well learned clerks and with licence of their governor and bishop."[1]

And here we may note that this authorisation of the Scriptures, to which several references have been made, was in fact sometimes at least given. The Council of Oxford had laid down the law that the version must be "approved and allowed" by those in authority. Bishop Pecock, in the passage above quoted, speaks of this "licence of their governor and bishop," and Sir Thomas More declares that such approbation might be obtained without difficulty. When the Hours B. V. M., which were printed before A.D. 1500, were first translated about thirty years previously, the translator informs us that for his version of the Psalms he "asked and obtained the necessary permission from his bishop."[2] Another example of what apparently is an approbation is to be seen in one of

---

[1] R. Pecock, *The Repressor of over much Blaming of the Clergy* (ed. Rolls Series), i. p. 37.

[2] "Speculum B. Virginis," in Wharton, *Auctarium*, p. 448.

Lord Ashburnham's manuscript copies of the New Testament. The writing I refer to is unfortunately hardly legible. It is, however, certainly to be dated in the fifteenth century, and probably is hardly much later than the writing in the main part of the book. What can be read runs as follows: "A lytel boke of—£8. 6s. 8d., and it (was written by) a holy man (and) was overseyne and read by Dr. Thomas Ebb-all and Dr. Ryve .... my modir bought it." We have here then a mere chance record of the fact that this particular copy of the New Testament had been "overseen and read" by two learned doctors, deputed, it is hardly too much to conclude, by rightful authority for the purpose. This, by the way, is of course a copy of the later of the two versions now known as Wyclifite Scriptures.

To this instance we may add that the historian Strype records of Archbishop Arundel that he "was for the translation of the Scriptures into the vulgar tongue, and for the laity's use thereof." This he deduces from the testimony of an old manuscript written apparently at the time of the death of Anne of Bohemia, the consort of King Richard the II. in 1392.

"Also the Archbishop of Canterbury, Thomas of Arundel, that now is (runs the record), preached a sermon at Westminster, whereat there were many hundred people, at the burying of Queen Anne (on whose soul God have mercy), and in his commendation of her he said that it was more joy of her than of any woman that he knew. For notwithstanding that she was an alien born she had in English all the four Gospels, with the doctors upon them. And he said that she sent them unto him, and he said that they were good and true and commended her, in that she was so great a Lady and also an alien and would study such holy, such virtuous books." [1]

There is one curious piece of evidence which seems to point to the conclusion that the archbishops and clergy of England at one time actually proposed that Parliament should sanction an approved vernacular translation. The point in question is referred to in a strange old contemporary tract printed by John Foxe. The writer there says:—

"Also it is known to many men that into a Parliament, in the time of King Richard II., there was put a Bible, by the assent of the archbishops and of the clergy, to annul the Bible at that time translated into English with other English books of the exposition of the Gospel."

Apparently this project was opposed by John of Gaunt, and it came to nothing. I am, of course, aware that Foxe and subsequent writers have spoken of this as a Bill introduced by Archbishop Arundel to put down the newly-translated English Bible, but the tract clearly says it was a "Bible" proposed by the clergy to take the place of some unauthorised version, and the whole argument of the writer of the tract requires that this should be his meaning.[2]

Another not unimportant point in the evidence which goes to show that the vernacular versions,

---

[1] Strype, *Memorials of Cranmer* (ed. 1812), i. p 3.
[2] Foxe, *Acts and Monuments* (ed. Townsend), iv. p. 674.

now known as Wyclifite, are in reality perfectly orthodox and authorised, is the fact that most of the copies now extant are intended for use in the church.

Lewis long ago noticed[1] that the Anglo-Saxon translation was divided into sections over which was placed a rubric directing that it should be read. For instance, Matthew i. 18 is prefaced by the following in Anglo-Saxon: "This Gospel is to be read on Midwinter's mass eve." This, that writer says, "I think a good proof that at this time the Holy Scriptures were read in the public service of the Church in a language which the people understood." He failed, however, to remark that the same may be said of the English version. Most of the extant copies will be found marked for the Lessons, Epistles and Gospels, and a good many are prefaced by a table "or rule that telleth" in which chapters of the Bible "ye maye fynde the lessons, &c., that ben read in the chirche all the yeer aftir the use of Salisbirie."[2] Some of the manuscripts are in fact merely books of the Epistles and Gospels from the new Testament in this English version to which, that there might be no doubt about their use in connection with church purposes, there are added the portions of the Old Testament read at times in the mass. To some copies of the

---

[1] *History of the English Translations of the Bible*, p. 10.
[2] Harl. MS., 4890, f. 1.

entire New Testament these portions of the Old have been added. One copy of the older version (Harl. MS., 1710) is an excellent example of a fourteenth-century Gospel book, giving the parts of Scripture " as they ben red in the messe booke after ye use of Salisberi." Its actual connection with the Church services is further shown by its giving, on folio 15, "Ye Gospel at Matynes on twelfth day," and, on folio 9, a long rubric as to the chaunting of a portion of the office: 'Ye first verse and ye last by two togidere, but all ye myddel verse one syngeth only." This book belonged, by the way, to "Sir Roger Lyne, chantry prest of Saynt Swythyn's at London Stone." And this, says the maker of the Harleian Catalogue, "is a sort of proof that in times of Popery, the reading of God's Word in our mother tongue was not denied by authority."

I am aware that it is not generally considered probable that the Epistles and Gospels were read in the vernacular as well as in Latin at the mass. But I cannot myself doubt that this was done, frequently if not ordinarily. Such a course so obviously advantageous, was, as we know, advised by Bishop Grosseteste, not to mention others, and was at least sometimes done, as we know from specific instances. The existence of prones on the Gospels of Sundays and Feast days—some of them very early—in which the whole of the Gospel is translated and afterwards explained, is well known, and to me these marked copies of the English Scriptures and English Epistle and Gospel books are additional proof that the practice was more common than some writers are inclined to allow.

There is not even a shadow of probability in the suggestion that Wyclifite Scriptures would be marked for the Church Service for the use of his "poor priests." The truth is that these same "poor priests" had in fact little claim to any sacerdotal character. They are described by Professor Shirley as mere *lay* preachers, both "coarse and ignorant."[1] The few priests who were attracted at the beginning of the "Reformer's" career by his bold and withal brilliant attacks upon the ecclesiastical order, quickly returned to the bosom of the Church. "In this, therefore," writes the same author, "the most essential point of his whole system (independence of authority) he was unable to count on retaining the support of any but a few presumptuous fanatics, the 'fools who rushed in where angels fear to tread.'"[2] The assumption, then, that these copies of the vernacular Bible were marked with the passages of Holy Scripture used in the Sarum Missal, to assist the Lollard preachers is, in view of these laymen having no connection whatever with the Church or its services, of their having no special veneration, to put it mildly, for the mass in general, or "the use of Salisbury" in particular,

[1] *Fasciculus Zizaniorum*, Introduction, p. xl.
[2] *Ibid.*, p. lxvii.

without the slightest foundation in fact. Lechler, in his life of Wyclif, allows that the 'Reformer's' references to "Apostolic men," or "Evangelical men," in his later sermons is a proof that the term "priest" was no longer applicable to all the "itinerant preachers."[1]

Let me now sum up very briefly. I have no intention to deny that Wyclif *may* have had something to do with Biblical translations which we do not now possess. My concern is with the actual versions of the translated Scriptures now known to us. Two, and only two, such pre-Reformation vernacular versions are in existence. These have hitherto been ascribed unhesitatingly to Wyclif or his followers, and are known to all under the title of the Wyclifite Scriptures, as printed by Messrs. Forshall and Madden. It will be observed that the ascription of these translations to Wyclif is not based on positive testimony; but, when the case is looked into it really depends on the tacit assumption that there was no Catholic version at all. I desire, rather, to insist on this point, because to many it may seem more than strange that after the immense amount of labour that has been spent upon these manuscripts I should come forward with a theory that runs absolutely counter to the conclusions of many most learned and estimable men. But, if I mistake not, these same con-

[1] *Life of Wycliffe*, Eng. translation, vol. i., p. 309.

clusions have been formed without any consideration of an alternative. Accordingly, no practical need has been felt by writers who have dealt with the subject to consider a number of facts, which in themselves constitute grave difficulties against the theory of the Wyclifite origin of these versions, and they have, in the circumstances naturally, perhaps, been allowed to lie dormant. But, as I have pointed out, there seems no possibility of denying the existence in pre-Reformation times of a Catholic and allowed version of the English Bible. At once, therefore, all these difficulties rise into life, and must be faced honestly if the truth is to be reached. For my own part, having looked into the matter with some care, I do not see how it is possible to come to any other conclusion than this: that the versions of the Sacred Scriptures, edited by Messrs. Forshall and Madden, and commonly known as Wyclifite, are in reality the Catholic versions of our pre-Reformation forefathers.

V.

THE PRE-REFORMATION ENGLISH BIBLE.

II.

IN the *Dublin Review* for July, 1894, the article on *The Pre-Reformation English Bible*, now reprinted, appeared. In this I endeavoured briefly to examine four points connected with the history of the Early English translation of the Holy Scriptures, commonly known as *Wyclifite*. The four points were as follows :—

1. On what evidence is the English translation of the Bible, or any part of it, ascribed to Wyclif himself?

2. What had Wyclif's immediate followers, or later adherents, to say to the composition of the work, or to its spread among the people generally?

3. What prohibitions, if any, existed against the vernacular translations of the Sacred Scriptures in the Church of England? and

4. Is there any evidence for thinking that an

orthodox Catholic vernacular version of the Bible ever existed?

It is necessary to recall to the mind of the reader the previous position of the question. I believe that I am not overstating it in saying that it has been commonly, if not universally, held that all the known English versions of the Scriptures were directly or indirectly Wyclifite in origin; that the copies of this translated Scripture were multiplied and spread abroad by the followers of Wyclif, and by them alone; that the Church absolutely interdicted the translation of the Bible into English, and the ecclesiastical authorities exerted all their great power, and even invoked the secular arm of the State in their anxiety to prevent the spread of these Lollard versions among the people. Moreover, it is assumed that, as a consequence of this attitude of the ecclesiastical authorities, for a century and a half the adherents of Wyclif were persecuted and done to death for their noble determination to popularise the Word of God at all costs. Moreover, the common and concurrent teaching of writers of all classes certainly does not suggest that the Church in any way encouraged or, indeed, permitted, the use of the Bible in English among her children. The popular idea certainly was, and, I fear, still is, that it was the greatest glory of the Reformation to have first given the open Bible to the people of England, which up to that time had been denied to them, in spite of the noble efforts of the forerunner of the English Reformation—Wyclif, and his handful of earnest followers.

After a brief statement of the evidence upon which tradition has assigned the work of translating the Scriptures to Wyclif, or Wyclifite hands, I wrote in the previous essay: " My concern is with the actual versions of the translated Scriptures now known to us," and chiefly in the two versions printed in the great edition of Messrs. Forshall and Madden. These two versions must be held, I submit, upon evidence it is quite impossible to gainsay, to have been in general and public use by orthodox members of the Church, and in certain specific instances to have received ecclesiastical approbation. The real question at issue, consequently, is not whether Wyclif, or his adherents, had or had not anything to do with some vernacular translations, but whether the versions which have come down to us, and which are printed in this edition of Messrs. Forshall and Madden, are Wyclifite or orthodox in their origin.

In the *English Historical Review* of January, 1895, Mr. F. D. Matthew, an author well known for his studies in Wyclifite literature, criticised my conclusions. To this I had hoped to reply in the following number of the *Review*, but was told by the editor that he could only allow me space for a brief letter, if I wished to point out any error of fact into which Mr. Matthew had fallen. This rendered my reply, which of its nature must depend as much upon arguments deduced from facts and documents as upon the facts and documents themselves, impossible; subsequently other business necessitated two long absences from England, and prevented my again turning my attention to the subject. The delay, however, has so far proved fortunate, since it has given time for the appearance of a serious and courteous criticism of my conclusions as to the origin of the known pre-Reformation English version of the Scriptures by Mr. F. G. Kenyon, in his book, *Our Bible and the Ancient Manuscripts*. I now propose to consider together the points of objection raised by him, and those previously stated by Mr. Matthew.

The question of the origin of the Early English versions of the Scriptures has been hitherto complicated and its discussion prejudiced by what I may call the theological or controversial aspect of the matter. The assertion, so freely made and so generally believed, that there was no vernacular Bible in use among pre-Reformation Orthodox Catholics; moreover, the declaration that the English Scriptures were, in fact, prohibited by the highest ecclesiastical authority, and that men were punished with the gravest penalties for even the possession of an English Bible, not unnaturally imported into the consideration of the question a certain amount of the *odium theologicum* which, as in so many other cases, interfered with any calm and judicial consideration of the subject on its own merits. I may, I think, justly congratulate myself on at least eliminating this factor from the discussion. I understand both from Mr. Matthew's paper and from Mr. Kenyon's pages that they now agree with me in this: that the English Scriptures were certainly in the authorised possession of orthodox sons of the Church. "One is glad," writes Mr. Kenyon, " . . . that the leaders of the English Church should not have been hostile to an English Bible . . . nor need even those who most strongly opposed the socialistic and heretical opinions of Wycliffe have therefore refused to possess copies of his translation of the Scriptures, if the existence of such a translation formed no part of the cause of their hostility to him."[1] Mr. Matthew also allows as much. "That such (that is 'dutiful churchmen') did use an English version there is no doubt;"[2] and again: "No doubt Protestant writers have often exaggerated the hostility of the clergy to the vernacular Bible. There was no objection on their part to the devotional use of the Bible in English any more than in Latin."[3] Did Mr. Matthew, when he wrote this, forget that, speaking of these very copies of the English Scriptures, he

---

[1] *Our Bible and the Ancient Manuscripts*, p. 206. There is considerable ambiguity here: "those most strongly opposed," &c., certainly need not have refused to possess copies of Wyclif's translation if it had been approved by the authorities, but if it were disapproved the case would be the very opposite.

[2] *Authorship of the Wycliffite Bible.* English Hist. Rev., reprint, p. 4.

[3] Ibid., p. 6.

had previously described them as "but the gleanings after time, neglect and the zeal of *the Inquisition* have gathered in their harvests"?[1] I prefer to think that on consideration of the facts he has honourably changed his opinion, and now classes himself with "the Protestant writers who have often exaggerated the hostility of the clergy to the vernacular Bible."

Be this as it may, the main point of my previous paper was to establish the very fact now admitted, namely: that Catholics in pre-Reformation days had in England, as elsewhere, a recognised vernacular version of the Scriptures, and that these translations, now published under the name of "Wyclifite," were in pre-Reformation days uniformly regarded as perfectly orthodox by undoubtedly loyal sons of Mother Church. I am well pleased that in the opinion of my two chief critics I have made good this contention. Indeed, so certain does this part of my thesis seem to Mr. Kenyon, that he appears to doubt whether anyone has ever seriously questioned it. He dismisses the old pictures of poor Lollard followers of Wyclif persecuted for the possession and use of the English Bible as mere flourishes of rhetoric.[2] I need only,

---

[1] *The English Works of Wyclif* (Early Eng. Text Soc.), preface, p. xviii.

[2] I can only read this with amazement. As far as my studies go the consent of writers, both serious and popular, is practically unanimous that the Church suppressed the vernacular Bible altogether, and refused to recognise the existence of any authorised Catholic version.

on this matter, appeal to the recollection of my readers as to the opinion they had themselves formed by books read as sober history in their youth and since. It is not so long ago that the late Mr. Froude, with characteristic exaggeration, described in his *Erasmus* the ignorance of the sacred writings which prevailed among clergy and laity alike at the time of the publication of his hero's Greek Testament. "Of the Gospels and Epistles," he writes, "so much only was known by the laity as was read in the Church services, and that *intoned*, as if to be purposely unintelligible to the understanding. *Of the rest of the Bible nothing was known at all*, because nothing was supposed to be necessary."

The position of the question has thus, to my

As regards the particular versions edited by Messrs. Forshall and Madden—men who, from their eminent position and studies, were not given to rhetorical flourishes—this is what they say about the matter in question. After stating that 150 MSS. of Purvey's Bible had been examined for their edition, they continue: "Others are known to have existed within the last century, and more, there can be no doubt, have escaped inquiry; how many have perished it is impossible to calculate. But, when it is remembered that, from the first, the most active and powerful measures were taken to suppress the version—that strict inquisition was made for the writings and translations of Wyclif, Hereford, Ashton, and Purvey—that they were burnt and destroyed as most noxious and pernicious productions of heretical depravity—and that all who were known to possess them were exposed to severe persecution—and then if there be taken into account the number of MSS. which, in the course of four or five centuries, have been destroyed through accident or negligence, it is not too much to suppose that we have now but a small portion of those which were originally written." (*The Holy Bible, made from the Latin Vulgate by John Wyclif and his followers*, i., preface, p. xxxiii.)

mind, been greatly simplified by the ready admission now made that Catholics not only possessed the Bible in English, but that the only extant pre-Reformation English Scriptures have come down to us from Catholic sources. The further point of origin, of course, still remains to be settled, or at least discussed. On the face of the question it is difficult to believe that at a time when the writings of Wyclif and his followers were prohibited by civil and ecclesiastical law, and their possession punished, as unquestionably was the case, the Bible, which he or his immediate adherents had translated and circulated, should have been not only tolerated, but approved for the possession of English Churchmen. Mr. Kenyon, it is true, sees no difficulty in this. "The fact would seem to be," he writes, "that the Lollards were persecuted, but not their Bible. Such hostility as was shown to this was only temporary, and was confined to a few persons, such as Archbishop Arundel. Generally the translation was tolerated, and this is perfectly comprehensible, since the extant copies, which we have seen to be connected with Hereford and Purvey, show no traces of partisanship or of heretical doctrine. It is a plain translation of the Latin text of the Scriptures then current without bias to either side; and whatever Arundel might do, other Bishops, such as William of Wykeham (who was, moreover, a supporter of John of Gaunt), would not be likely to condemn it."[1]

[1] P. 207.

I confess that to me this explanation is not satisfactory. I could accept it only on the supposition that the fifteenth century possessors and users of the version were altogether without suspicion of its doubtful and heretical origin. Even as late as the time of Sir Thomas More it is evident from the description of the Bible, destroyed by order of Bishop Fitz-James, which belonged to Richard Hun, the London Lollard, that the Wyclifite Bible was not then considered the same as this version, which was reputed to be Catholic. For whilst Sir Thomas More strenuously maintains that the English Scriptures as such had not been destroyed ruthlessly by the ecclesiastical authorities, as was asserted, and that he could himself testify to the existence of what was regarded as an orthodox vernacular version, he declares that Hun's great Bible " gave the readers undoubted occasion to think that the book was written after Wyclif's copy, and by him translated into our tongue," and that this Bible was destroyed consequently, not because it was in English, but because it contained gross and manifest heresy. Sir Thomas More consequently, with the people of his day, believed that the translations of Wyclif were not the same as the vernacular Scriptures which they were authorised to read by their ecclesiastical authorities. These latter were the English Scriptures now commonly known as Wyclifite.

Mr. Kenyon, of course, holds that Sir Thomas

More was mistaken. He thinks that the version More, and we must suppose the rest of his contemporaries, held to be Catholic was in reality the work of Wyclif, or at any rate of his immediate followers. He indeed sees " no reason to doubt the personal responsibility of Wyclif" for the translation,[1] and declares that "his (*i.e.*, Wyclif's) championship of the common people led him to undertake a work which entitles him to honourable mention by men of all parties and all opinions, the preparation of an English Bible again." "After Hereford's departure the translation of the Old Testament was continued by Wyclif himself or his assistants." . . . "A marked difference in style distinguishes Hereford's work from that of Wyclif and his other assistants, if such they were. Wyclif's style is free and colloquial. There can be little doubt that he had in his mind the common people, for whom his version was specially intended."[2] Again, "we know that Wyclif and his adherents prepared a translation; we know that two of his most prominent supporters, Hereford and Purvey, had at least *some* connection with the translations which actually exist, and we can see no ground for refusing to take the further step and say that the Wyclif version and the existing translations are one and the same thing."[3]

With all due deference to my critic, I question

---

[1] *Our Bible and the Ancient Manuscripts*, p. 198.
[2] Ibid., p. 201.   [3] Ibid., p. 208.

whether anyone seriously reviewing the evidence will agree that "we *know* Wyclif and his adherents" did prepare any translation. To me it appears that it is exactly what we do not know, and my contention is that the evidence usually adduced does not bear out the assertion of Wyclif's own part in the work. Mr. Kenyon holds that I " seem to ignore the strength of the evidence which connects Wyclif and his supporters, not merely with *a* translation of the Bible, but with *these* translations." [1]

" That they were responsible for *a* translation," he continues, " is proved by the contemporary evidence of Archbishop Arundel, Knyghton, and a decree of the Council of Oxford, in 1408—all witnesses hostile to the Wyclifites." Do these witnesses on a careful examination prove anything of the kind? Let us take them one by one.

1. *Archbishop Arundel* is cited as an authority for the fact of Wyclif's translation on the strength of the letter which, conjointly with the English bishops, he wrote to Pope John XXIII. In 1412, in forwarding the list of grave errors which a Commission of twelve Oxford theologians had detected in the works of Wyclif, the Archbishop makes use of the passage relied upon. The errors referred to are stated in a series of 267 propositions[2] extracted from the various known works of the

---

[1] *Our Bible and the Ancient Manuscripts*, p. 205.
[2] Wilkins' *Concilia*, iii., *pp.* 339-349.

"Reformer," and it is at least remarkable that in the whole of this long list there is no mention whatever of the supposed translation. The passage upon which Mr. Kenyon relies to prove that Wyclif made *a* translation is as follows; after saying that Wyclif endeavoured to defame the ecclesiastical dignity, and to lower the good opinion of the sacred ministry in every way, Archbishop Arundel continues: "He even tried, by every means in his power, to undermine the very faith and teaching of Holy Church, filling up the measure of his malice by devising the expedient of a *new* translation of Scripture in the mother-tongue." Mr. Matthew, by the way, renders the passage into English, thus: "devising a plan of translation of the Holy Scriptures into the mother-tongue." It does not appear why, in his translation, he should have omitted to to give any English equivalent of the Latin word novæ,—*new*.[1] The letter, as it stands, certainly does not prove that Archbishop Arundel was "hostile" to any translation of the Scriptures into the vernacular, as writers have too hastily assumed.[2]

[1] Wilkins, iii., p. 350. The Latin is: "Novæ ad suæ malitiæ complementum Scripturarum in linguam maternam translationis practica adinventa."

[2] Mr. Kenyon (p. 207) says: "Such hostility as was shown to this (*i.e.*, the Lollard's Bible) was only temporary, and was confined to a few persons such as Archbishop Arundel. Generally the translation was tolerated . . . and whatever Arundel might do, other Bishops, such as William of Wykeham, who was moreover a supporter of John of Gaunt, would not be likely to condemn it, nor would the tendency to toleration be less as time went on, and when John of Gaunt's son had

It, however, on the face of it, indicates that the Archbishop knew of some recognised translation, which Wyclif, in order "to undermine the faith and teaching of Holy Church," tried to supersede by his own rendering—by suiting his translations to his heresies.

The ordinary and obvious meaning of the Archbishop's words is that the new translation of Wyclif was disfigured by the heretical colouring given to the text by the Reformer, its very purpose being to support his errors. It may be taken for granted, I think, that these readings do not exist in the versions now known as Wyclifite, and which were evidently an approved translation, as the manuscripts show, and common sense will, consequently, point to them as the recognised translations, implicitly referred to by Archbishop Arundel when he speaks of Wyclif's rendering as a "new translation."

Moreover, I do not myself believe that by this "new translation" is meant anything more than the vernacular rendering of passages of Holy Scripture, be they long or short.[1] The words must be inter-

---

succeeded to the throne." The very documents relied on as evidence of Archbishop Arundel's "hostility" proceed not from him alone but from all the bishops of the province of Canterbury. As to what Mr. Kenyon says about William of Wykeham, I neither understand his chronology nor his facts.

[1] It must be carefully noted that, even were I mistaken in this contention, Archbishop Arundel's letter does not bear out Mr. Kenyon's thesis. On the contrary, in my opinion it is fatal to it.

preted by other documents, and, as far as I can see, the provision of the Council of Oxford, which Mr. Kenyon also cites as a witness that Wyclif was responsible for *a* translation, makes it clear that this is the true meaning of Archbishop Arundel's letter. To this I now pass.

2. *The Council held at Oxford in* 1408 is generally adduced as distinct evidence that the ecclesiastical authorities forbade the use of the English Scriptures, and specifically condemned the version of John Wyclif. Did it do so? The passage in question is Article VII. of the Constitutions of the Provincial Synod of Oxford, and the material portion runs as follows:—

"We therefore command and ordain that henceforth no one of his own authority translate any passage (aliquem textum) of Holy Scripture into English in a book, booklet, or tract, and that no one read, wholly or in part, publicly or secretly, any such book, booklet, or tract lately written in the time of the said John Wyclif or since, or that may hereafter be made, under pain of excommunication until such translation has been approved and allowed by the diocesan of the place, or (if need be) by the Provincial Council.[1]

I cannot understand how this passage can be made to prove that Wyclif was the author of, or, at any rate responsible for, "a translation of the Bible" in the sense of a complete, or fairly complete, version. The expression is *aliquem textum*, which can only mean "any passage." This sense is borne out by the context, which states that the

[1] Wilkins, iii., p. 317.

translation may be "in a book, booklet, or tract." The title of this seventh constitution also shows conclusively, I think, that the Council referred merely to *passages* and not to any *complete* translation, for it uses the word in the plural; *Ne quis texta S. Scripturæ transferat in linguam Anglicanam* can only be translated: "That no one translate into English *passages* of Holy Scripture."[1] Or as the Lambeth Manuscript has it: "That no text of Holy Scripture be for the future translated into English." Moreover, the gloss of the great fifteenth century canonist Lyndewood accepts this sense as the correct one, where he says: "Although it be the plain text of Sacred Scripture that is translated, the translator may yet err in his translation, or, if he compose a book, booklet, or tract, he may, as, in fact, frequently happens, intermingle false and erroneous teaching with the truth." It seems, consequently, certain that not only does this provision of the Council of Oxford in no wise prove that Wyclif was the author, direct or indirect, of a vernacular version of the Bible, but it explains the meaning of Archbishop Arundel's letter when, a few years later, and as a distinct consequence of the Synod, he writes to the Pope that in order to undermine the very faith and teaching of the Church, Wyclif had "devised the expedient of a new translation of Scripture in the mother tongue."

[1] Wilkins, iii., p. 317.

So far, then, the witnesses relied upon by Mr. Kenyon to prove that Wyclif was responsible for a translation of the Bible, in my opinion entirely fail to do so. We have, however, still to consider the statement of the chronicle of Knyghton.

3. *Knyghton* was practically a contemporary writer, and his authority consequently is very weighty. Some scholars have expressed a doubt as to whether this portion of the chronicle is really to be attributed to Knyghton; but even on the supposition that the passage named is not really from the pen of the Canon of Leicester[1] it yet deserves the best attention; but it is necessary to understand clearly what it says. It runs as follows: " This Master John Wyclif translated from Latin into English the Gospel which Christ gave to clerks and teachers of the Church, so that they might sweetly minister to the lay folk and infirm, &c. In this way he made it vulgar and more open to lay men and women who know how to read than it is wont to be to learned and well instructed clerics. In this way the pearl of the

[1] The passage occurs in Book V. (Twysden, *Decem Scriptores*, col. 2644 seqq.). Dr. Shirley says that this book is not Knyghton's at all, but comes from a partisan of the Duke of Lancaster (*Fasciculus Zizaniorum*, p. 524 *note*). It should be noted that Book IV. ends ten years before Book V. begins. Mr. T. Arnold, *Works of Wyclif*, iii., pp. 525-6, argues that the 5th book is the work of Knyghton. But the latest editor, Professor Lumby (*Rolls Series*, ii., p. 96), agrees with the contention of Professor Shirley. It is worth noting as a matter needing elucidation that whilst the author of the 5th book is full of admiration for John of Gaunt, this passage as to Wyclif goes directly against a cardinal point of John of Gaunt's policy.

Gospel is scattered broadcast and trodden under foot by swine. And thus, what is wont to be esteemed by clerks and laity as precious is now become as it were the common joke of both; the jewel of clerics is turned to the sport of the lay people: so that what had before been the heavenly talent for clerks and teachers of the Church is now the *commune æternum* for the laity." Then, after quoting long passages from William de Saint Amour about the evils of that time when the Gospel should be made too cheap and common: when "some would labour to turn the Gospel of Christ into another Gospel, which they say is more perfect and better and more worthy, which they call the eternal Gospel or the Gospel of the Holy Spirit"— that is into what was known so well as the "*evangelium æternum*"—the author proceeds: "These things are most appropriate to the new Lollard folk, who have changed the Gospel of Christ into the *evangelium æternum*, that is the vulgar tongue, and *communem maternam* and so *æternam* since it is looked on by the laity as better and more worthy than the Latin language."[1]

Mr. Matthew (p. 2) holds that "it seems hard to imagine anything more clear and decisive than this contemporary evidence "that Wyclif was regarded as the person responsible for the English Bible." I fear that I cannot agree with him that it is either

---

[1] Knyghton (ed. Lumby), ii., p. 152-155.

"clear" or "decisive," and I am confident that the reader who will take the trouble to go through the whole of this section of the chronicle will agree with me. But what does the chronicler really mean? It seems natural to understand his language as referring not to the Scriptures in general or to the Gospels in particular; but to the Christian teaching and ministry so often then as now spoken of as "the Gospel." Writing in Leicestershire, where Lollardry was rife, the writer would have known more than enough of the unauthorised and vernacular teaching of Wyclifite lay ministers. That this is no fanciful explanation of the expressions used is sufficiently clear by the author's calling the result of Wyclif's work, the introduction of the "*æternum evangelium.*"

Mr. Matthew, in quoting the passage in which the chronicle says that the Lollards "have changed the Gospel of Christ into the *æternum evangelium,*" does not appear to have any suspicion of the meaning which the last words would convey to a contemporary of the writer. Even the long citations made in this connection by the author from the work of William de Saint Amour do not seem to have aroused in his mind any idea that the expression might mean something entirely different from the vernacular version of the Bible to which he supposes it to apply. One asks oneself whether he could have known that the *æternum evangelium,* so well understood by mediæval writers, had become a byeword for the reduction of religion to what was vile and unclean.

My belief is that anyone properly informed on the subject of the *æternum evangelium* on carefully reading the writer's own words in the entire passage (pp. 151-156) will come to the conclusion that by *evangelium* he means Gospel in the broader signification of Christian teaching. If this view is correct then on examination three of the witnesses upon whom Mr. Kenyon has relied to prove the personal connection of the Reformer with "a translation of the Bible," will have failed him. Neither Archbishop Arundel, nor the Bishops of the Council of Oxford, nor yet, in my opinion, the chronicler directly say, or even indirectly imply, anything of the kind. As far as I have been able to see, after much trouble, there is no proof of the personal connection of Wyclif with a translation except the rather vague and obviously incorrect statement of John Huss that "it is reported among the English that he (Wyclif) translated the whole Bible from Latin into English."

So much for the evidence upon which the connection of Wyclif personally with any vernacular translation of the Bible has been maintained. To me it appears that the tradition, for such it has now become, has been built up on a foundation of mistranslation and misunderstanding of Latin documents and misinterpretation of certain somewhat ambiguous expressions. Mr. Kenyon, it is true, goes further in the Wyclifite direction, and considers that the concluding words of the Prologue to what is called the revised or later text, "show that the author did not know how his work might be received by those in power, and looked forward to the possibility of being called upon to endure persecution for it." The words he quotes to substantiate this are: "God graunte to us alle grace to kunne well and kepe wel holi writ and suffer joiefully some peyne for it at the laste." I cannot accept Mr. Kenyon's gloss upon this passage, for the context makes it clear, I think, that the words "suffer joiefully some peyne for it," do not refer to possible persecution. After describing the minute care required by a translator to get the exact equivalent in English for a Latin word, the author of the Prologue writes: "By this manner, with good living and great travail, men moun come to true and clear translating and true understanding of Holy Writ seem it never so hard at the beginning. God graunt to us all grace to kunne well and keep well Holy Writ and suffer joyfully some pain for it at the last (to the pleasure and will of God, as one manuscript has it). Amen." I fancy that read with their context the words relied upon by Mr. Kenyon to show the Lollard fear of persecution and consequent Lollard origin, simply refer to the trouble which is necessary to fully understand the meaning of the Word of God and to keep it. Moreover, I can only repeat that it is hardly possible to read the Prologue referred to without seeing that the author of this translation had a filial reverence for the teaching of the approved doctors of the Church and was most scrupulous in his endeavour to translate the words exactly in accordance with the prevailing authoritative teaching. This is not what we should expect from a follower of Wyclif, whose renderings were expressly designed, as we are told on the contemporary authority of Archbishop Arundel " and the suffragans of the Province of Canterbury," " to undermine the faith and teaching of Holy Church."

To sum up the position of the question as far as I understand it: the ecclesiastical authorities in England so far from prohibiting the English Scriptures, most certainly approved of various copies of the actual versions now known as Wyclifite. This official, or quasi-official, approval of the version was given, be it remembered, at a time when there was a distinct prohibition, by ecclesiastical authority enforced vigorously by the civil power, of *all* Wyclifite literature. Moreover, these copies have in fact in many instances come down to us from Catholic sources, whilst in no single case, so far as I can discover, has any copy been traced to a possessor of distinct Lollard opinions. In the face of the evidence the fact that the known versions were regarded as orthodox by pre-Reformation Catholics, ecclesiastic and lay, cannot be questioned.

This we have also on the testimony of Sir Thomas More, and to his word as to the circulation of the vernacular Scriptures in pre-Reformation times, we may add that of Archbishop Cranmer himself. The whole force of the Archbishop's argument in favour of allowing the Bible in English rests on the well-known custom of the Church, and the fact that copies were in daily use.[1] Moreover, when the great Bible known as Cranmer's was in course of preparation, the Archbishop, as Morrice, his secretary, informs us, took an old English translation and, dividing it into nine or ten parts, sent it " to the best learned Bishops and others to the intent that they should make a perfect correction thereof."[2] This, when it appeared in 1541, " was overseen and perused at the command of the King's Highness, by the right reverend Father in God, Cuthbert (Tunstall), Bishop of Durham, and Nicholas (Heath), Bishop of Rochester." To those who know the character of the Bishops at this period it will be unnecessary to point out that Cranmer must have sent them for revision the recognised Catholic English version. To any Wyclifite version they would have been as opposed as to Tyndal's translation, which they considered as " tending to seduce persons of simple and unwary disposition," since with the rendering were intermingled " articles gravely heretical, and opinions that are erroneous,

---

[1] Preface to the Bible.
[2] Nichols, *Narratives of the Reformation* (Camden Soc.), p. 277.

pernicious, pestilent, scandalous." The passage of Archbishop Arundel adduced as evidence that Wyclif made a translation of the Bible is also, on the same ground, evidence that one previously existed. It would be interesting if Mr. Kenyon could explain how it came about that the version which was not objected to disappeared, and its place was taken by a version which not Archbishop Arundel alone, but all the Bishops of the province of Canterbury, told the Pope was made in order to undermine, or rather attack, the faith and teaching of holy Church! Further how it comes about that there are no traces of this intention in the extant "Wyclifite" versions. Taking the documents and the facts as documents and facts, they tell an intelligible story, but a story that runs counter to the thesis that the extant versions of the English Scriptures are Wyclif's. To maintain this seems to me to involve necessarily falling into inextricable contradictions and difficulties. I do not think that either Mr. Kenyon or Mr. Matthew has realised how completely the whole situation has been changed by the recognition that the Bible edited by Messrs. Forshall and Madden was actually authorised by the Church and so allowed free circulation.

VI.

RELIGIOUS INSTRUCTION IN ENGLAND DURING THE FOURTEENTH AND FIFTEENTH CENTURIES.[1]

THE history of the pre-Reformation Church in England has yet to be written. To many this may perhaps seem a somewhat startling statement in view of all that has hitherto appeared in print bearing on the ecclesiastical history of this country. Let me explain my precise meaning. For the most part, until quite recent times, the story of this England of ours has been made to consist mainly of a series of biographies of its rulers, intermingled with more or less detailed accounts of the wars and battles by which they mounted to power or rendered their names illustrious. Of the nation itself, as apart from the monarch, who honoured it by ruling over it, the historian in the past troubled his readers as little as possible; and thus, whilst he might learn to know the dates of many battles and the genealogies

[1] Reprinted from *The Dublin Review*, July, 1894.

of many royal houses, the inquirer remained practically ignorant of the English people. In the same way our Church annalists have not often thought it their duty to record much beyond the doings of illustrious English Churchmen, and the most conspicuous results which have flowed from their actions and their ecclesiastical policy.

Now, however, many are anxious to learn something more about the people who composed the nation, of the conditions under which they lived and acted, of their desires and aspirations, and of their struggles against difficulties external and internal. And in the same way the thoughts of all inquirers are turning more and more to a consideration of the religious side of our national life, an inquiry which promises to enlighten us at last as to the real history of the religion of the English people in the later Middle Ages and the century of the Reformation. What, for example, did our forefathers definitely believe? How were they affected by the religious system under which they lived? How were the services carried on in the churches, and what were the popular devotions of the time? Were the religious offices well frequented, and what was the general character of the behaviour of the people whilst present at them? How did the priests instruct their flocks, and what profit did they seemingly derive from their ministrations? What did the Church do for the great cause of education, and for the social and material welfare of the people at large? These and a hundred kindred questions are daily being proposed, but who is capable of giving any satisfactory reply to them? In order to form any judgment on these matters we should require to have placed fairly and dispassionately before us evidence still buried in our national archives beneath the dust of many centuries. For myself, I may perhaps be permitted to say that a familiarity of some years with original and much-neglected sources has taught me as a first lesson and condition of knowledge, that I know little—or what, when compared to all that yet remains to be done, is practically very little—about the social condition, the influence and the inner life of the Church of England previous to the sixteenth century. In spite of this, however, I venture here to propose for consideration an important question regarding the Church in this country during, say, the fourteenth and fifteenth centuries. It is a very simple point, but one, I think, which has not hitherto been sufficiently considered, and one the answer to which must seriously affect our judgment as to the character of the ecclesiastical system swept away by the so-called Reformation.

The first duty of the Church, after the ministration of the sacraments, is obviously to teach and direct its members in all matters of faith and practice, and to watch over the eternal interests of the Christian people. Was the pre-Reformation Church in England mindful of this obligation, or did it neglect so plain and essential a duty imposed upon all its ministers by its Divine Founder? This, then, is the plain question—Was there in Catholic days in England any systematic religious instruction? and if so, what was done in this important matter?

At the outset it must be admitted that the general opinion of Protestant writers has been, perhaps not unnaturally, that in Catholic England the people were allowed to grow up in profound religious ignorance, and that there was no systematic instruction whatever on points of belief and observance given by the clergy. I cannot, moreover, shut my eyes to the fact that in this verdict many Catholic writers have concurred. Conversation likewise with Catholics, as well ecclesiastics as laymen, has led me to conclude that at the present day the general opinion is, that this sad and very black view of the way in which the Catholic Church of this country neglected its obvious duty of instructing the people in religion cannot be gainsaid.

It should, however, in all fairness be borne in mind that up to the present time, so far as I am aware, no evidence whatever has been forthcoming, except the somewhat fervid declamations of those engaged in the destruction of the ancient faith, in support of this verdict; and one cannot but remember that barely ten years ago the English public generally implicitly believed in the traditional picture, drawn by non-Catholics in past centuries, of the appalling immoralities of monks and nuns, and the wholesale corruption of the clergy of England at the time of the suppression of the religious houses. We have lived to see a marvellous change follow upon the production of evidence. That unjust judgment after holding for many generations has now practically been reversed, and the unworthy stories originally "founded on ignorance and believed in only through the prejudice of subsequent generations have now," as the highest Protestant authority on the history of this period has declared, "gone for ever." This may well encourage a hope that an examination of evidence may lead to a similar rectification of what I firmly believe to be an equally false judgment passed upon the secular clergy of England in Catholic days, in regard to their neglect of the duty of instructing the people committed to their care.

I cannot help thinking that Chaucer's typical priest was not a mere creation of his poetical imagination, but that the picture must have had its counterpart in numberless parishes in England in the fourteenth century. This is how the poet's priest is described:

> A good man was ther of religioun,
> And was a poure parsoun of a town;
> But riche he was of holy thought and werk.
> He was also a lerned man, a clerk,
> That Christe's Gospel trewely wolde preche,
> His parischens devoutly wolde he teche.
>   * * * *
> But Christe's love and His Apostles twelve
> He taughte, but first he folwede it himselve.

It is well to remember, too, that the story Chaucer makes his priest contribute to the *Canterbury Tales* is nothing but an excellent and complete tract, almost certainly a translation of a Latin theological treatise, upon the Sacrament of Penance.

As a sample, however, of what is popularly believed on this subject at the present day, I will take the opinion of by no means an extreme party writer, Bishop Hobhouse. "Preaching," he says, "was not a regular part of the Sunday observances as now. It was rare, but we must not conclude from the silence of our MSS. (*i.e.*, churchwardens' accounts) that it was never practised." In another place he states upon what he thinks sufficient evidence, "that there was a total absence of any system of clerical training, and that the cultivation of the conscience as the directing power of man's soul and the implanting of holy affections in the heart, seem to have been no part of the Church's system of guidance."

Further, in proof that this view as to the teaching of the English Church in the later Middle Ages is held even by Catholics, I need only quote the words of a well-known writer, to be found in the *Dublin Review* for July, 1891:

At the end of the fifteenth century (writes Mr. W. S. Lilly) the Church in England, as in the greatest part of Europe, was in a lamentable condition. There is a mass of evidence that multitudes of Christians lived in almost total ignorance of the doctrine, and in almost complete neglect of the duties of their faith. The *Pater noster* and *Ave Maria* formed the sum of the knowledge of their religion possessed by many, and not a few passed through the world without receiving any sacrament save that of Baptism.

It is, of course, impossible for us to pass any opinion on the "mass of evidence" to which Mr. Lilly appeals in proof of the soundness of his sweeping condemnation of the Church, not in England merely, but "in the greater part of Europe," since he has only given us the result, without furnishing us with the grounds of his judgment. For my own part, I think that such general judgments must be untrustworthy, and that it is necessary—so different were the circumstances of each—to take each country into consideration by itself. For Germany, the labours of the late Professor Janssen, even after the largest deductions have been made for a possible enthusiasm, or idealizing, have conclusively proved the existence of abundant religious teaching during the century which preceded the coming of Luther. As to England, about which we are at present concerned, we can only suppose that Mr. Lilly has been engaged in researches of which, as yet, the world knows nothing. For many years having been occupied in collecting information upon this very point, I may at once say, that so far from my studies tending to confirm Mr. Lilly's verdict as to the "almost total ignorance of the doctrines," and almost "complete neglect of the duties of the faith" in which Catholics were allowed to live and die, they have led me to the opposite conclusion—namely, that in pre-Reformation days the people were well instructed in their faith by priests, who faithfully discharged their plain duty in this regard.

Let me state the grounds of this opinion. For practical purposes we may divide the religious teaching given by the clergy into the two classes of *sermons* and *instructions*. The distinction is obvious: by the first are meant those set discourses to prove some definite theme or expound some definite passage of Holy Scripture, or deduce the lessons to be learnt from the life of some saint. In other words, putting aside the controversial aspect, which, of course, was rare in those days, a sermon in mediæval times was much what a sermon is to-day. There was this difference, however, that in pre-Reformation days the sermon was not so frequent as in these modern times. Now, whatever instruction is given to the people at large is conveyed to them almost entirely in the form of set sermons, which, however admirable in themselves, seldom convey to their hearers consecutive and systematic dogmatic and moral teaching. Mediæval methods of imparting religious knowledge were different. For the most part the priest fulfilled the duty of instructing his flock by plain, unadorned, and familiar instructions upon matters of faith and practice. These must have much more resembled our present catechetical instructions than our modern pulpit discourses. To the subject of set sermons I shall have occasion to return presently, but as vastly more important, at any rate, in the opinion of our Catholic forefathers, let us first consider the question of familiar instructions. For the sake of clearness we will confine our attention to the two centuries (the fourteenth and fifteenth) previous to the great religious revolution under Henry VIII.

Before the close of the thirteenth century—namely, in A.D. 1281—Archbishop Peckham issued the celebrated Constitutions of the Synod of Oxford which are called by his name. There we find the instruction of the people legislated for minutely:—

> We order (runs the Constitution) that every priest having the charge of a flock do, four times in each year (that is, once each quarter), on one or more solemn feast-days, either himself or by some one else, instruct the people in the vulgar language simply and without any fantastical admixture of subtle distinctions, in the articles of the Creed, the Ten Commandments, the Evangelical Precepts, the seven works of mercy, the seven deadly sins with their offshoots, and the Seven Sacraments.

The Synod then proceeded to set out in considerable detail each of the points upon which the people must be instructed. Now, it is obvious that if four times a year this law was complied with in the spirit in which it was given, the people were very thoroughly instructed indeed in their faith. But, was this law faithfully carried out by the clergy, and rigorously enforced by the bishops in the succeeding centuries? That is the real question, and I think that there is ample evidence that it was. In the first place, the Constitutions of Peckham are referred to constantly in the fourteenth and fifteenth centuries as the foundation of the existing practices in the English Church. Thus, to take a few specific instances in the middle of the fourteenth century, the decrees of a diocesan Synod order :—

> That all rectors, vicars, or chaplains holding ecclesiastical offices shall expound clearly and plainly to their people, on all Sundays and feast-days the Word of God and the Catholic faith of the Apostles ; and that they shall diligently instruct their subjects in the articles of faith, and teach them in their native language the Apostles' Creed, and urge them to expound and teach the same faith to their children.[1]

---

[1] Wilkins, iii. 11. Two curious instances of the care taken by the Bishops to see that Priests were able to instruct their people may be quoted. After the great plague of 1349, as is notorious, many were admitted to Holy Orders in order to fill the decimated ranks of the clergy, without sufficient learning and preparation. On June 24, 1385, the illustrious William of Wykeham, Bishop of Winchester, caused Sir Roger Dene, Rector of the Church of St. Michael, in Jewry Street, Winchester, to swear upon the Holy Gospels that he would learn within twelve months the articles of faith, the cases reserved to the Bishop, the Ten Commandments, the seven works of mercy, the seven mortal sins, the Sacraments of the Church, and the form of administering and conferring them, and also the form of baptizing, &c., as contained in the Constitutions of Archbishop Peckham. The same year—on July 2—the Bishop exacted from John Corbet, who had been instituted on June 2 previously to the Rectory of Bradley, in Hants, a similar obligation to learn the same before the Feast of St. Michael then next ensuing. In the former case Roger Dene had been Rector of Ryston, in Norfolk, and had only been instituted to his living at Winchester, by the Bishop of Norwich, three days before William of Wykeham required him to enter into the above obligation.

Again, in A.D. 1357, Archbishop Thoresby, of York, anxious for the better instruction of his people, commissioned a monk of St. Mary's, York, named Gotryke, to draw out in English an exposition of the Creed, the Commandments, the seven deadly sins, &c. This tract the Archbishop, as he says in his Preface, "through the counsel of his clergy, sent to all his priests":—

So that each and every one, who under him had the charge of souls, do openly, in English, upon Sundays teach and preach them, that they have cure of the law and the way to know God Almighty. And he commands and bids, in all that he may, that all who have keeping or cure under him, enjoin their parishioners and their subjects, that they hear and learn all these things, and oft either rehearse them till they know them, and so teach them to their children, if they any have, when they are old enough to learn them; and if parsons and vicars and all parish priests inquire diligently of their subjects at Lent time, when they come to shrift, whether they know these things, and if it be found that they know them not, that they enjoin them upon his behalf, and on pain of penance, to know them. And so there be none to excuse themselves through ignorance of them, our Father the Archbishop of his goodness has ordained and bidden that they be showed openly in English amongst the flock.

To take another example: the Acts of the Synod held by Simon Langham at Ely in A.D. 1364, order that every parish priest frequently preach and expound the Ten Commandments, &c., in English (*in idiomate communi*), and all priests are urged to devote themselves to the study of the Sacred Scripture, so as to be ready "to give an account of the hope and faith" that is in them. Further, they are to see that the children are taught their prayers; and even adults, when coming to confession, are to be examined as to their religious knowledge.[1]

Even when the rise of the Lollard heretics rendered it important that some check should be given to general and unauthorised preaching, this did not interfere with the ordinary work of instruction. The orders of Archbishop Arundel in A.D. 1408, forbidding all preaching without an episcopal licence, set forth in distinct terms that this prohibition did not apply " to the parish priests," &c., who by the Constitutions of Archbishop Peckham, were bound to instruct their people, in simple language, on all matters concerning their faith and observance. And further, in order to check the practice of treating people to such formal and set discourses, these simple and practical instructions were ordered to be adopted without delay in all parish churches.

To this testimony of the English Church as to the value attached to popular instruction, I may add the authority of the Provincial Council of York, held in A.D. 1466 by Archbishop Nevill. By its decrees, not only is the order as to the systematic quarterly and simple instructions reiterated, but the points of the teaching are again set out, in great detail, by the Synod.

There is, moreover, I believe, ample evidence to

---

[1] Wilkins, iii., 59.

convince any one who may desire to study the subject, that this duty of giving plain instructions to the people was not neglected up to the era of the Reformation itself. During the fifteenth century, manuals to assist the clergy in the performance of this obligation were multiplied in considerable numbers, which would not have been the case had the practice of frequently giving these familiar expositions fallen into abeyance. Of some of these manuals I shall speak presently, and here I would note specially that one of the earliest books ever issued from an English press by Caxton, probably at the same time (A.D. 1483) as the *Liber Festivalis* (or Book of Sermons for Sundays and Feast-days), was a set of four lengthy discourses published, as they expressly declare, to enable priests to fulfil the obligation imposed on them by the Constitutions of Peckham.[1] As these were intended to take at least four Sundays, and as the whole set of instructions had to be given four times each year, it follows that at least sixteen Sundays, or a quarter of the year, were devoted to this simple and straightforward teaching, to every soul in the parish, what every Christian was bound to believe and to do.[2]

---

[1] Probably there were many similar works issued by the first English printers. In Lansd. MS. 379, there is a *black letter* tract, printed by W. de Worde, to enable priests to comply with the command of the Synod.

[2] The work upon which Caxton's *Liber Festivalis* was founded is a volume written in the early part of the fourteenth century by John

Looking at the character of these instructions, we need not be surprised that priests should not often have thought it necessary to commit them to writing. They were given as a matter of course, as a necessary part of the round of their priestly duty, and there is naturally very little record of what must have been part of the routine of common clerical life. Let me take what is a parallel instance. Do we expect that some centuries hence there will be any evidence forthcoming to show that the clergy of the great city of London, in this year 1893, have been doing their duty in instructing the children of their schools in religious knowledge? Or, to put it another way: what explicit evidence is there likely to be, say, a couple of hundred years hence (even if meantime there be no such wholesale destruction of documents as took

---

Myrk. Of this see later. Here we may note that in several copies of the MSS. *Festivale* there may be found other matters useful for the priest in the work of instructing others. For example, "De magna sentencia pronuncianda, hoc modo;" the days on which no servile work might be done, according to Archbishop Arundel's *Constitutions*, notes on various Papal Constitutions, &c. In one MS. (Harl. MS. 2403), following upon the *Festivale*, is a short explanation of the Creed, *Pater noster*, &c. This latter instruction is introduced by the form, "Good men and women, ye shall know well yt each curate is bownden by the law of Holy Church to expound the *Pater noster* to his parischonys twyes in the yere." The substance of these instructions is used in many copies of the sermons of the period. In the copy (MS. Reg. 18 B. xxv.), the people are addressed as "Worschipful frendys," or "Worschipful and reverent frendys." The discourses for the time about Easter appear to have been prepared to be preached before the Court, as they commence with the words, "Worschypul sufferanc and frendys."

place in the sixteenth century), that, say, the Sacrament of Extreme Unction is regularly administered by our Catholic clergy to-day? For the same reason it would be asking more than we have any right to expect, to demand formal documentary evidence of the performance of this plain and well-recognised duty of religious instruction.

We have, however, I expect, sufficient material to satisfy most people. The Episcopal, or Chapter, Registers fortunately, in some few cases contain documents recording the results of the regular visitation of parishes. It is almost by chance, of course, that papers of this kind have been preserved. Most of them would have been destroyed as possessing little importance in the eyes of those who ransacked the archives at the time of the change of religion. The testimony of these visitation papers as to the performance of this duty of instruction on the part of the clergy is most valuable. Hardly less important is the proof they afford of the intelligent interest taken in the work by the layfolk of the parish, and of their capability of rationally and religiously appreciating the instructions given them by their clergy. The process of these visitations must be understood. First of all, certain of the parishioners were chosen and examined upon oath as to the state of the parish, and as to the way in which the pastor performed his duties. As samples of these sworn depositions we may take what are to be found in a

"Visitation of Capitular Manors and Estates of the Exeter Diocese," extracts from which have recently been printed by Prebendary Hingeston Randolph, in the Register of Bishop Stapeldon. The record of of the Visitations comprises the first fifteen years of the fourteenth century. At one place, Colaton, we find the *jurati* depose that their parson preaches in his own way, and on the Sundays expounds the Gospels as well as he can (*quatenus novit*)! He does not give them much instruction (*non multum eos informat*), they think, in "the articles of faith, the Ten Commandments, and the deadly sins." At another place, the priest, one Robert Blond, "preaches, but," as appears to the witnesses, "not sufficiently clearly;" but they add, as if conscious of some hypercriticism, that they had long been accustomed to pastors who instructed them most carefully in all that pertained to the salvation of their souls. But these are the least satisfactory cases. In most instances the priest is said to instruct his people "well" (*bene*) and "excellently" (*optime*), and the truth of the testimony appears more clearly in places where, in other things, the parish-folk do not consider their priest quite perfection; as for instance at Culmstock, where the vicar, Walter, is said to be too long over the Matins and Mass on feasts: or still more at St. Mary Church, where the people think that in looking after his worldly interests, their priest is somewhat too hard on them in matters of tithe.

The Register from which these details are taken is a mere accidental survival, but the point which it is of importance to remember is this: that during Catholic times in the course of every few years the clergy were thus personally reported upon, so to say, to the chief pastor or his delegates, and the oath of the witnesses is a proof how gravely this duty was regarded. And here I may note in passing, a fact little realised or even understood, viz., that one of the great differences between ecclesiastical life in the middle ages and in modern times lies in the fact that then people had no chance of going to sleep. There was a regular system of periodical visitations, and everything was brought to the test of inquiry of a most elaborate and searching kind, in which every corner was swept out.

In this special instance, before passing on, I would call attention to the manifest intelligence, in spiritual things, shown by these jurors—peasants and farmers—in out-of-the-way parishes of clod-hopping Devon, in the early years of the fourteenth century. I have a doubt whether, notwithstanding the Board Schools, any of our own country parish-folk could do better at the present day.

To assist parish priests in the preparation of these familiar discourses, various manuals were drawn up during the fourteenth and fifteenth centuries. It is possible now to refer to only one or two of the best known, but as a fact a large number of such works may be found in our national manuscript collections. I will first name the volume called *Pars Oculi Sacerdotis*, which was probably composed either by a certain William Pagula, or Walter Parker, about the middle of the fourteenth century. It was very popular and much sought after. It is named frequently in inventories and wills, and has thus sometimes been an evident puzzle to editors. No less than five complete copies, as well as several fragments, are among the MSS. in the British Museum. It well deserved its popularity among the pre-Reformation clergy, for it not only furnishes most useful matter for the usual parish instructions, but is really a very complete manual of teaching on almost every detail of clerical life. One portion of the tract is devoted to the subject of the parochial discourses, which the author declares have to be given by all priests once in each quarter. In delivering these the priest is urged to be as simple as possible in his language, and to suit himself in every way to his audience.[1]

In another treatise closely resembling this *Pars*

[1] Some further account of this important tract may be given with advantage. The tract begins by instructing the priest on the *praxis confessarii*: the kind of questions it is well to ask from various people —*e.g.*, religious, secular priests, merchants, soldiers, &c. Then comes a method of examination of conscience in detail, &c. The priest is advised to urge his penitents to say seven times daily the *Pater* and *Creed* to correspond to the seven canonical hours. Should any one be found not to know these he is to be enjoined to learn them, together with the *Ave Maria*, at once. The confessor is to inculcate upon those who come to him a devotion to the Guardian Angels, and teach them some little verses to say in order to beg the protection of these guardian

Oculi Sacerdotis—so closely, indeed, that it has sometimes been mistaken for a portion of it—is the better known *Pupilla Oculi* of John de Burgo, or Borough, rector of Collingham, in A.D. 1385. It was only to a certain extent original, for, as the author states in his Preface, he has called it *Pupilla Oculi*, " because it is to a large extent drawn from another work entitled *Oculus Sacerdotis*." This spirits. The verse given in the *Dextra Pars Oculi* may be Englished thus:

> O angel who my guardian art,
>   Thro' God's paternal love ;
> Defend and shield and rule the charge,
>   Assigned thee from above.
>
> From vice's stain preserve my soul,
>   O gentle angel bright ;
> In all my life be thou my stay,
>   To all my steps the light.

Then follow the various modes of absolving from excommunication, &c., and in this connection, copies of the reserved cases, with the *Magna Carta* and the *Carta de Foresta*, the keeping of which was enforced in A.D. 1254 by ecclesiastical censures.

The second part of the *Dextra Pars Oculi* deals minutely and carefully with the instructions which a priest should give his people, not only as to matters of belief, but as to decorum and behaviour in church, cemetery, &c. These materials for instructions are arranged under some thirty-one headings. Following on this are the explanations of the familiar instructions which priests were bound to give to their people four times a year, and sermons on various subjects, chiefly on temptations.

The third part of the volume, entitled the *Sinistra Pars Oculi*, is in fact a careful treatise on the Sacraments. The instructions upon the Blessed Eucharist are especially good, and in the course of them many matters of English practice are touched upon and explanation is given of the ceremonies of the Mass.

manual also was evidently much in demand by the clergy. Numerous manuscript copies of it are in existence, and it has been printed several times. One edition, that of A.D. 1510, was issued from the press by the printer Wolffgang, at the expense of an English merchant of London, named William Bretton, and was sold, as the title-page sets forth, at Pepwell's bookshop in St. Paul's Churchyard.[1] Both the *Pars Oculi* and the *Oculus Sacerdotis* bear a close resemblance to another tract called *Regimen Animarum*[2] which was apparently compiled as early as A.D. 1343.

Another sample of these priests' manuals, chiefly intended to furnish material for popular instruction, is a fourteenth-century tract called the *Speculum Christiani*. It was composed by one John Watton with the distinct purpose, as the Preface informs

---

[1] Its full title is *Pupilla oculi omnibus presbyteris precipue Anglicanis necessaria*. On the back of the title-page of the 1510 edition is a letter from Augustine Aggeus to W. Bretton. After saying that societies exist to propagate books, the author declares that Bretton has been induced to print the *Pupilla* by a desire that the rites and sacraments of the Church should be better known, and to secure "that nowhere in the English Church" these rites should be badly observed or understood. It is clear from the letter that W. Bretton had already had other works printed in the same way, and it is known that amongst those works were copies of Lyndwode's *Provinciale* (1505), *Psalterium et Hymni* (1506), *Horæ*, &c. (1506), *Speculum Spiritualium*, and Hampole, *De Emendatione Vitæ* (1510). (cf. *Ames*, ed. Herbert, iii. p. 16). Pepwell, the publisher, at *the sign of the Holy Trinity*, was the same who published many books printed abroad, and had dealings with Bishops Stokesley and Tunstall.

[2] The prologue to the *Regimen Animarum* (Harl. MS. 2272, fol. 2) says the work is compiled chiefly from the *Summa Summarum* Ray-

us, of aiding the clergy in giving the teaching commanded by the Constitutions of Archbishop Peckham. In many ways the *Speculum Christiani* is the most useful and important of this class of manuals. A considerable portion is given in English, each division, for example, being prefaced by simple rhymes in the vernacular, giving the chief points to be borne in mind. In fifteenth-century sermons I have frequently met with these rude rhymes, introduced into the text of a discourse, as if they were perfectly well known to the audience. At haphazard I take a couple of examples. The First Commandment is summed up thus:

> Thou shalt love thy God with heart entire,
> With all thy soul and all thy might,
> And other God in no manner
> Thou shalt not have by day nor night.

And the precept of keeping holy certain days is prefaced by the following:

mundi, Summa Confessorum, Veritates Theologie, Pars oculi Sacerdotis, &c. The work is divided into three parts: (1) *De Moribus et scientia presbyterorum et aliorum clericorum;* (2) *De exhortationibus et doctrinis bonis erga subditos suos faciendis;* (3) *De septem Sacramentis.*

In the second part the priest is urged to instruct his people constantly *in English*, and no one who will examine this portion can fail to be struck at the minute character of these instructions. It may be noted that at fol. 91b the priest is urged to teach his people to bow at the Sacred Name, and to add the name *Jesus* to the end of the *Ave Maria*, and to explain to them the Indulgences granted to such as do so by Popes John XXII. and Urban IV.

The third part begins, in this copy, at fol. 132, and treats of the sacraments most fully. In speaking of *Confirmation*, the necessity of *consecrated* oil is insisted upon. The volume closes with a description and explanation of the Canon of the Holy Mass.

> Thy holy days keep well also,
> From worldly works take thou thy rest;
> All thy household the same shall do,
> Both wife and child, servant and beast.

The number of copies of the *Speculum Christiani* to be found in the Museum collection of MSS. is some ten or twelve, and this may be taken as evidence of its popularity in the fourteenth and fifteenth centuries. It was translated into English by one John Byrd in the latter century, and was one of the earliest books ever put into type in England. An edition was printed in London by William of Machlin, at the expense of a London merchant, about A.D. 1480, and in the first decade of the sixteenth century it was reprinted, but without the English verses, at least three times.[1] I cannot pass from a brief notice of this excellent manual of instructions without pointing out that in it may be found some beautiful prayers to the Blessed Sacrament and our Lady, which were formerly used by our Catholic ancestors. The English verses beginning:

> Mary Mother, wel thou bee,
> Mary Mother, think on me.

---

[1] The Museum has four printed copies: (1) the supposed print of 1480; (2) a copy of 1500, printed at Paris; (3) another of 1502; and (4) one printed by Thomas Rees, A.D. 1513, in London. The later copies have no English verses; but that they were intended for English use seems clear from the fact that the prologue to the volume, in which the author says that it is intended to furnish priests with material for the instructions they are bound to give by the Constitutions of Peckham, is reprinted.

I should like to see reprinted, and, indeed, the entire manual deserves to be better known than it is amongst us to-day.[1]

Space obliges me to pass rapidly on to the second point for our consideration—that of preaching proper in the two centuries before the Reformation era. I would, however, ask you to believe that the question of popular instruction has only been touched upon. I could give many other examples of manuals such as I have here introduced to notice, and I have said nothing whatever of what may be called formal theological text-books, all of which were, of course, calculated to aid the clergy, in what the great Grosseteste calls, "as much a part of the *cura pastoralis* as the administration of the sacraments." I must, however, give one word of warning. When writers talk of people being taught

---

[1] Besides the volumes named in the text there are a considerable number of works of much the same kind. One such is the *Flos Florum*, a copy of which is among the Burney MSS. (No. 356) in the British Museum. It is divided into five-and-twenty books, the first being occupied with an explanation of the Lord's Prayer; the second with a tract on the virtues and vices; the third with an account of the priest's personal duties; the fifth with notes on the teaching which parish priests are bound to give to their people. Another book is called *Cilium Oculi Sacerdotis*, and is divided into two parts. The first treats about clerical duties, and especially of the duties of a confessor; the second part is a tract upon the Ten Commandments. Here, as in so many similar works, some interesting points of practice in Catholic England are touched upon. For example, we read that every rector of a parish should have a cleric to assist him at the public Mass, and to read the Epistle. This cleric may be vested in an alb, and besides Church duty should teach the children their creed, "*id est*, their faith," and their "letters," besides "teaching the singing." (Harl. MS. 4968.)

their *Pater*, something very different is meant from the mere repetition of the words. A large number of systematic instructions during the middle ages were based upon the explanation of the Our Father. Anyone who may care to pursue this subject cannot but be amazed at the ingenious way the petitions of the Lord's Prayer are made the pegs on which to hang a definite course of teaching on the whole of Christian doctrine.[1]

It is impossible to consider the subject of that systematic religious instruction which was constantly being repeated in mediæval times, without wondering whether it had its proper effect upon the minds of the people. The proof of the wisdom of our forefathers is, I think, sufficiently evidenced by the history of the change of religion throughout Europe in the sixteenth century. In other words (confining our attention to England), the way in which the Catholic faith had to be uprooted from the minds of the people is surely a proof that they had been well grounded in it. Now that the real facts are becoming known it is beginning to be suspected in several quarters that the change of

---

[1] Harl. MS. 1648, for example, is an instance of a book of instructions in Christian doctrine founded upon the petitions of the Lord's Prayer. It is arranged in tabular form, and is most ingeniously devised to convey a great amount of solid instruction. The key to the arrangement is on fol. 1 *b*, where it is said, "Per istas septem petitiones impetrantur septem dona Spiritus Sancti, que extrahunt a corde septem peccata mortalia et plantant in corde septem virtutes principales que nos perducunt ad septem beatitudines et ad earum merita."

religion was brought about, not by the spontaneous acceptance by the people of Protestantism in place of the Catholic faith, but by a process of systematic and deliberate religious starvation. And taking a comprehensive survey, the Reformation in Europe, as a whole, was by no means a popular movement; but, for the most part, the new faith was only, after many a struggle, imposed upon the nations by force and the will of the Prince.

But let us turn to the question of *sermons* in the later middle ages. The work of instruction may be said roughly to have been the special office of the secular clergy. In the same general way preaching may be regarded as coming within the special province of the Religious Orders. Of course, in such general statements the limit must be taken as understood; and as a fact, at the outset, it is necessary to guard ourselves against the impression that, because the friars gave a great impulse to popular preaching, it began with them; just as it is useful to guard against the notion that it was Wyclif who introduced the preaching of vernacular sermons. Indeed, unless the accounts of the preaching of the friars in the thirteenth century are mere myths, of this latter there can be no question whatever. The Dominicans and Franciscans were essentially popular preachers in the truest sense of the word. They went from village to village speaking to the people wherever they could, in public places as well as in the churches. They gathered their audiences together on the great roadways as readily as in consecrated spots. For the most part they had to do with the masses, and plain, unadorned speaking was their *forte*. As a rule, they made no attempt at set and polished discourses, refraining from elaborate argument or the discussion of abstract questions. They extemporised their teaching, suiting it to the needs of the moment, and pointing their moral with anecdotes, fables and examples. Hence their triumph. The people followed them in crowds, hung upon their words, were carried away by their earnest—albeit perhaps rough—eloquence, and made their conquest easy. But even the friars (a century and a half be it noted before Wyclif's "poor priests") by no means commenced, though they certainly gave an impetus to, the practice of vernacular preaching. From the earliest times the people were spoken to in the language they could understand. St. Bede, for example, describes the crowds of Saxons who flocked to their churches to hear the words of the Christian missionaries. What has misled so many writers, apparently, is the fact that the sermons which have been preserved to us from the middle ages are for the most part in Latin. This is true; but it is no less a fact that the preachers of those days used to compose discourses in Latin which they afterwards delivered in English, a practice which I fear might seem strange, or even intolerable, to the immense majority of the Anglican country clergymen, who in these more cultured days have received the best education the national Universities can afford.

In the same way as the work of instruction proper took a fixed form, so that of preaching was fashioned on a well-understood and well-recognised model. A short exordium, following upon the chosen text of Scripture, led almost invariably to a prayer for Divine guidance and assistance, which concluded with the *Pater* and *Ave*, and only then did the preacher address himself to the development of his subject. For the most part, until comparatively recent times, which have introduced somewhat strange themes into the sacred pulpit, the sermon was based almost entirely upon the Bible, and generally upon the Gospel, or other Scripture, proper for the day. This practice, whilst it imbued the minds of those who listened with a thorough knowledge of the sacred writings, gives the sermons as we read them now so great a similarity that we are apt to regard them as generally dull and uninteresting. With rare exceptions it is clear that, in England at least, brilliant, startling, and sensational sermonising was not regarded with favour, but, on the contrary, was looked on with suspicion, as savouring of the "treatise," or method of the schools, and founded on the practice of heretics.

Numerous tracts on the art of preaching, drawn up for the use on our English preachers during the fourteenth and fifteenth centuries, are still to be seen in our public libraries. I shall here only refer to one, written somewhere in the middle of the fourteenth century by the celebrated Dominican, Thomas Waleys, in order to teach the mode and form of pulpit oratory, in what he then describes as the "modern style." The whole tract is instructive, but I will here give only a brief epitome of the first chapter, which treats of "the preacher." He should, the master declares, undertake the duty, not from vanity or love of notoriety, but from pure love of God's truth; and prayer and study should go before his work. As to his gestures, he should endeavour not to stand like a statue, nor to throw himself about regardless of decorum. He is to refrain from shouting, and not to speak so low that his audience have to strain to catch his words. He is not to speak too rapidly, not to hesitate "like a boy who repeats lessons he does not quite understand." The theme should be spoken with great distinctness, so that all may understand the subject, and, if necessary, it should be repeated. Before his discourse the preacher should retire to some private place and thoroughly practise the sermon he is about to deliver, with the method of declamation, the gestures, and even the expressions of countenance suitable to its various parts. Finally, the author urges the advisability of having some candid and reliable friend to listen to the discourse, who will correct the faults of pronunciation, &c., when it is over. This is not such bad advice to preachers, given at a time when we are asked to believe that sermons were almost unknown.¹

Turning to the material aids to the intending preacher, we can describe them—even in the fourteenth and fifteenth centuries—as really vast. Confining our attention, of course, to England only, we may, in the first place, note some collections of sermons for Sundays and Feast-days very popular in the fifteenth century. The first course of such sermons I will mention is that drawn up by John Felton, the Vicar of St. Mary Magdalen and Fellow of Magdalen College, Oxford. His discourses won for him the name of *homiliarius*, or *concionator*, and his course of Sunday sermons—some fifty-eight in number, and of which there are many copies among the Museum manuscripts—were much used by subsequent preachers. In his Preface our author states, that on account of the poverty of those who are students in moral and dogmatic theology, and con-

---

[1] Friar Waleys, in other places in this tract—*De Arte Prediçandi*—gives much excellent advice from which we may cull one or two points. Speaking of the *subject* of a sermon, he says that it is the custom (*consuetudo apud modernos*) always to have some text upon which to found a discourse. This should be a real theme, taken from Holy Scripture, and always from the Lesson, Epistle, or Gospel of the day, except on great feasts, such as Easter. Generally it should be a sentence, but sometimes it is best to take the whole Epistle or Gospel and explain its meaning, for "this kind of preaching is easy and very often greatly profitable to ordinary people." The author warns the preacher that he is not to think sermons are merely arguments; a discourse should not only convince the mind, but lead it to good affections and implant in it devout thoughts. He urges priests never to finish a sermon without some mention of our Lady, Christ's Passion, or eternal happiness.

sequently by reason of the few books they are able to obtain to help them, he has been induced by the importunity of friends to draw up, for the use of any priest having the cure of souls, a course of sermons founded on the Gospels of the Sundays. "They are," he adds, "merely the crumbs I have collected as they have fallen from the tables of my masters, whose names I have given in the margin." A note in one of the copies among the Harleian MSS. says that the sermons were published in the year 1431.[1] They are, I fancy, for our modern taste too much divided and subdivided, and I have little doubt they would be to-day voted "dry." Various authorities are cited in the margin, as for example Waleys, the *Vitæ Patrum*, &c., and stories are frequently introduced to drive home a point, or fix the attention on a moral. Although the series is complete, I fancy

---

[1] In one copy of these *Sermones Dominicales* (Harl. MS. 861, fol. 2) is the following note: "In nomine Dni nri Ihu Xpi cui sit honor et gloria in secula seculorum. Amen. Hoc opus completum fuit a venerabili viro Domino, Johe Felton, vicario perpetuo ecclesiæ paroch. Beate Marie Magdalene, Oxon. Lincoln. diœc. in anno Dni: Mccccxxxi." Leland says of John Felton: "He was an eager student of philosophy and theology; (yet) the mark towards which he earnestly pressed with eye and mind was none other than that by his continual exhortations he might lead the dwellers on the Isis from the filth of their vices to the purity of virtue." Besides the *Sermones Dominicales*, in some copies (*e.g.*, Harl. MS. 5396, fols. 143—209) there is another collection of fifty sermons of a more miscellaneous nature. In his illustrative stories he uses Pliny, Seneca, &c., freely, and as a rule the sermon is shorter than the more formal discourse for the Sunday. Besides set sermons, Felton drew up for the use of preachers and other teachers an *Alphabetum Theologicum*, from the works of Bishop Grosseteste.

the discourses were really intended rather as a help to the priest in the preparation of his Sunday sermon than as a collection of sermons to be preached exactly as they are set down. The stories, for example, are often mere indications of what were then doubtless well-known anecdotes, but the memory of which has long since perished. Especially is this the case where English and local examples are referred to, as: "Note about the man in Bristol;" or, "About the woman in London, to whom our Lord showed His Heart." At the end of every copy of these Sunday discourses I have examined, there is a careful and copious subject-index; and many indications are given, by subsequent sermon-writers, of the influence of this collection upon the preaching of the age.

Another set of sermons, evidently much in use in the fifteenth century, and many copies of which are still in existence, is that known as the *Liber Festivalis* of John Myrk, a Canon Regular of Lilleshull. This author is perhaps best known by his tract entitled *Instructions for Parish Priests*, which was published some years ago by the Early English Text Society. He lived much about the same time as Felton, namely, about the middle of the fifteenth century, and his sermons were intended for use on the higher festivals of the Christian year. I should like to quote a few words of his Preface, putting it, however, into modern English.

God, maker of all things (he says), be at our beginning, and give us all His blessing, and bring us all to a good ending, Amen. By my own feeble lecture I feel how it fareth with others that are in the same degree (as I am), who having charge of souls are obliged to teach their parishioners on all the principal feasts of the year. But many have as excuse, the want of books and the difficulty of reading, and therefore to help such mean clerks, as I am myself, I have drawn this treatise.

The sermons themselves are short, and frequently afford interesting information as to Catholic practices in those days. There is always one anecdote, and often there are two or more, and whilst many of these may perhaps appear to us somewhat grotesque and absurd, a study of the whole series of sermons cannot but impress us with a belief that the priest who could use them must have been upon terms of most familiar intercourse with his people, and unless religious instruction had been constantly and regularly given, he never could have talked to them as he is made to do in these sermons.[1]

[1] A few extracts from some of these popular instructions on the feasts of the Church may be given. The following words, as the rubric directs, at the *Tenebræ*, or Office of Matins, on the last days of Holy Week, after the Hours were finished, and "before the discipline is given to the people," were to be addressed to the people; "good men and women, as you see, these three days, the service is said at eventide in darkness. Wherefore it is called among you *tenabulles*, but Holy Church calleth it *tenebras*, that is to say, 'darkness,' and why this service is performed in darkness the holy Fathers assign three reasons," &c. The people are then urged to be present at these services, and to obey the common practice of coming to them in silence and thinking upon Christ's Passion.

In the instruction on Maundy Thursday, after explaining that the

The *Liber Festivalis*, printed by Caxton in A.D. 1483, although by no means identical with John Myrk's, is practically founded upon it. It has sermons for nineteen Sundays and ferias, commencing with the first Sunday of Advent and ending with Corpus Christi day. These are followed by discourses for forty-three of the chief holidays and saints' days of the year, and one sermon, suited for the anniversary of the dedication of a parish church. Then come somewhat detailed explanations of the Lord's Prayer, Creed, and Commandments, &c. At the close of the fifteenth century the general popularity of the *Liber Festivalis* may be gauged by the fact that it was printed twice by Caxton, twice by Wynkyn de Worde, twice by Pynson, once by an English printer whose name is unknown, in A.D. 1486, and thrice abroad before the close of the century.

The foregoing are samples of the many collections of sermons—chiefly for the Sundays of the year—

Church calls it "Our Lord's Supper day," the author continues: "It is also in Englis tong schere thursday, for in owr olde fadur days men wolden yt day makon sheron hem honest, and dode here hedes and clyppon here berdes and so makon hem honest agen astur day ; for ye morowe yei woldon done here body non ese, but suffur penaunce, in mynde of Hym yt suffurd so harte for hem. On Saturday thai myghte nowte whyle, what for long service, what for othur occupacion that thai haddon for the weke comynge," &c. In the sermons there are many indications of Catholic practice, as for example, that procession was made to the font of the church for the seven days after its blessing on Holy Saturday. In the short instruction on the Assumption, the author introduces a hymn to our Blessed Lady, which he urges his audience to learn by heart and constantly repeat.

which were clearly used by the English preachers in discharge of their duty of teaching, in the later middle ages. But besides these collected sermons, which might be either used to draw material from, or preached just as they stood, there were many books intended for the purpose of helping priests in the preparation of their discourses. As an example of these aids to preachers, we may take the well-known *Summa Predicantium*, drawn up by the English Dominican, John Bromyard, about the beginning of the fifteenth century. There is a good copy in the King's Library at the British Museum, which formerly belonged to the Rochester monastic library. The book—a very large thick folio volume—is drawn up alphabetically, and information can thus be obtained with the greatest facility on most matters upon which a preacher is likely to need instruction. An examination of its contents will prove to any one who doubts, that it must have been a mine of wealth to a priest engaged in the work of preaching. Bromyard's work was printed abroad, twice in the fifteenth century and again in the middle of the sixteenth.[1]

---

[1] The theological *common-place books* which still exist in MS. prove that the clergy often took great pains to adapt their studies to the work of teaching. To take an example: Harl. MS. 2344, is a theological note-book certainly used, and possibly drawn up in the fifteenth century by one John Chapman, "Rector of Honey Lane," London. Chapman was a doctor in theology, and, from 1493 to 1505, appears to have sometimes occupied the pulpit at St. Paul's Cross, since he gives, on the first leaf of his note-book, a list of his sermons delivered in that celebrated London pulpit. The interest of the small volume lies in

Another work, similar to the *Summa Predicantium*, was drawn up by Alan of Lynn, a Carmelite, who wrote much in the fourteenth and fifteenth centuries. The mere list of his works fills the best part of a closely-printed page of Tanner, and a large portion of his labours was directed to lighten the work of preachers in the preparation of their sermons. Of course the writers of the period drew much, especially on all matters concerning natural history, from the work of Bartholomew the Englishman—sometimes called Glanville—a minorite friar who taught in France during the thirteenth century. His book, *De Proprietatibus Rerum*, alongside of that of Vincent of Beauvais, was the Encyclopædia of the middle ages, and all his facts were arranged with a moral and religious object. It was translated into English by Trevisa in A.D. 1398, and had been printed in fourteen or fifteen editions before the year 1500.[1]

the fact that it is a collection of notes on a great variety of theological matters. They are in a form which would probably be considered most useful for referring to. In the margin a number is set against each *distinction*, thus, | 71 |, and at the end is an alphabetical index—

e.g., *De Pilati et Herodis concordia mistice intellecta* | 71 |.

[1] The work of another Dominican, Robert Holcot, called *Pro Christi verbum Evangelizantibus*, deserves to be mentioned as much used in the fourteenth and fifteenth centuries. Wood states that Holcot was "first a lawyer, and afterwards a Friar Preacher." He studied at Oxford, and was the friend of Richard de Bury, Bishop of Durham. He was a great lecturer on Holy Scripture, and is said,

In sermons of the period about which we are engaged, I have met with many references to a work evidently very similar to Bromyard's *Summa*, called the *Alphabetum Predicantium*. The work also of another English Dominican, Nicholas Gorham—*Thema et distinctiones*—furnished not only the skeleton for a sermon, but material wherewith to clothe it, arranged alphabetically and with a good index of words. The influence of Gorham can be traced in the preachers whose works have come down to us (although, by the way, his name is not even mentioned in the great *Dictionary of National Biography*).[1] One northern priest, Robert Ripon, who was a monk of Durham,[2] for example, is constantly quoting him as his authority. The volume of sermons by this Durham monk may be noted in passing. It is not a complete course, but a somewhat miscellaneous collection. The Sundays of

with some probability, to have been the real author of the *Philobiblon*, now claimed for Richard de Bury. His work in aid of preachers was printed in Paris in 1510 and 1513. Besides this, a small work, which may be described as skeleton sermons for the *Themata Dominicalia*, was drawn up by him, and is known as the *Dicta Salutis*. Seven or eight copies of this work are among the British Museum MSS. Holcot died in the fatal year of the great plague, 1349.

[1] Gorham was certainly an Englishman (see Tanner). He was apparently first a fellow of Merton College, Oxford, and subsequently became a Dominican, and, going abroad, was confessor to Philip the Fair of France. He died in A.D. 1298. The Sunday sermons in Harl. MS. 755, fols. 1—148, were attributed by Wanley to Gorham, at least in part. His book of Dominical sermons was printed at Paris in 1509, under the title of the *Golden Foundation*.

[2] See p. 27 *ante*, note 2.

Lent, for example, and those of the spring quarter, have often as many as eight sermons for a single day, and there are some six or eight discourses preached at various Synods at Durham. In one of these the preacher strongly urges upon all who have the care of souls a diligent study of the Bible, for, he says, "Curates are bound to have a knowledge of Scripture, for preaching the Word of God to their people. Running through all the sermons *de Synodis*, moreover, is the same plain demand for learning and piety of life on the part of the priest, and the same insistence upon the obligations they were under to preach constantly to their people.

The study of Scripture urged by this northern preacher must certainly have been practised throughout the whole period of the fourteenth and fifteenth centuries. We have remarked before that the sermons were, as a rule, Scriptural expositions, illustrated chiefly from the Holy Writ, and it is impossible to read them without rising from the study with a profound belief in the detailed knowledge of the Bible possessed alike by priest and people. The clergy from early times had vast storehouses, both of Biblical and Patristic knowledge in the great *glossed* texts, which, together with the words of Scripture, presented the interpretations given by the chief Fathers of the Church. Before the close of the fourteenth century, moreover, the great value of an index for the purposes of study had been recognised in England, and many earnest workers had devoted their energies mainly to throwing open, by means of their *tabulæ*, or indexes, what had hitherto been unworked and closed mines of buried knowledge. The value of this all-important labour has not been sufficiently recognised in the past; but, amongst those conspicuous in this work, we may name Alan, the Carmelite, of Lynn, and later than him, Abbot Whethamsted, of St. Albans. A glance at the works of the former will show all that he did in this matter. Concordances and sub-indexes to the Bible, specially for the use of preachers, were multiplied in the early part of the fifteenth century; and the works of the Fathers, Chronicles, and even the sermons of such a comparatively recent preacher as Bishop Grosseteste, had copious and well-arranged indexes made to them.

Whilst upon this subject I cannot refrain from calling attention to the great catalogue of monastic and collegiate libraries of England, drawn up in the fourteenth century by a monk of Edmundsbury, " for the use and profit," as he says, " of students and preachers." For this reason it was called by him a *Promptuarium*. The list is arranged so that by the help of numbers attached to each monastery it might at once be seen where any given work could be found in the English fourteenth century libraries. Thus, for example, suppose a student or preacher wished to consult the sermons of St. Anselm, a glance at Boston of Bury's list would show him the numbers 89, 43, 19, 116, 166, and 65 placed against the title of this work. Turning next to the key list of monastic libraries he would at once be able to tell that complete copies were to be seen in the libraries of Bermondsey, Woburn, St. Paul's (London), Shrewsbury, Hexham and Ramsey. The use made of this catalogue for preaching purposes is evidenced by the way in which the Franciscans subsequently arranged the list of libraries for their own members, to correspond with the seven "Custodies," or divisions, into which the Franciscan Province of England was apportioned. But, although no account of the preaching in the two centuries before the change of religion would have been complete without some mention of this gigantic work of Boston of Bury, I have been able, of course, merely to refer to it. To do justice to it, the subject would require an article to itself.

Before passing away from the question of material aids to preachers in the later mediæval period, it is proper to advert briefly to the various collections of stories intended to adorn and lighten the dulness of ordinary discourses. Tales, examples, and even fables with moral applications were apparently introduced into the pulpit in very early times. From the days of St. Gregory the Great the practice of pointing a moral by the relation of an anecdote is clearly evidenced, but its ordinary use may be said to date from the rise of the Dominicans in the thirteenth century. Very shortly afterwards collections of "histories," suitable for the purpose, began to appear. In A.D. 1294, for example, a Dominican, Etienne de Besançon, composed his *Alphabetum exemplorum*, believing, as he says, in his Preface, that " an example is more efficacious than the most subtle preaching." From the first the authorities were urgent as to the need of caution in the use of these embellishments, but the practice once introduced soon became general. Even before the close of the thirteenth century Dante refers, with some regret, to the growing habit of making people laugh in sermons. But Chaucer's *pardoner* knew well the taste of lay people for pulpit stories when he says:

> For lewed (*i.e.*, unlearned) people loven tales olde.

The well-known *Gesta Romanorum*, probably of English origin, the *Vitæ Patrum* and the lives of the saints generally, furnished the mediæval preacher with ample material for his anecdotes, and many collections of appropriate stories, arranged under useful moral headings, were at hand to assist him. Local colouring is often met with, and several volumes of *historiettes* for English preachers, drawn up in the fourteenth century, are known. Quite recently one such work, by a hitherto unknown English Franciscan writer, Nicholas Bozon, has been published in France; and the evident common origin of stories found in sermons of the fifteenth century shows, as we should have expected, that there was no lack of material of this kind.

I have pointed out that for the most part parochial

sermons were founded upon Scripture—chiefly upon the Scripture proper for the Sunday upon which they were preached. There are, however, of course, many examples of set discourses at this period upon other, and, as some may think, more entertaining themes. The subject is so vast that I can give but few examples of such sermons. The first collection of English set discourses I recall to mind, not to speak of the great Grosseteste, is that of the sermons of the celebrated Richard FitzRalph, Archbishop of Armagh—a learned man, best known, perhaps, as the uncompromising opponent of the privileges claimed by the mendicant friars.[1] Al-

[1] FitzRalph was born at Dundalk, co. Louth. Some of his early life was spent in the household of that learned lover of books, Richard de Bury, Bishop of Durham. Amongst his companions here were Thomas Bradwardine, afterwards Archbishop, Walter Burley, and Robert Holcot, afterwards the celebrated Dominican preacher. When, as Archbishop of Armagh, FitzRalph was asked to preach at St. Paul's upon the great question of the friars' privileges, Richard Kilmington, also an old friend of his, was Dean. In his work, *Defensio Curatorum*, the Archbishop says that having come to London on business connected with his See, he found great disputes going on between the secular clergy and the Mendicant Orders; after much pressing he consented to preach on the subject at the Cross, *in vulgari*, some eight sermons. His propositions gave great offence to the Minorites, and he was summoned to Rome to answer their accusations. His chief contention appears to be that people ought to confess to their parish priest in their parish church at least once a year, just as they were bound to make their offerings in their own parish church twice or three times yearly. He complains that the friars use their faculties to entice children to join them, and that once they entered their ranks not even parents were allowed to see their sons except in the presence of professed friars. He adds that, for fear of the influence exerted by members of the Mendicant Orders, parents were beginning to hesitate about sending their children to Oxford.

though written in Latin, the discourses were, as they expressly state, preached in English. Many were delivered in the choir of Lichfield Cathedral during the time FitzRalph was Dean; others were preached in the cemetery of the hospital, in the Chapel of St. Nicholas, and elsewhere in the city and neighbourhood; whilst others again were delivered at St. Paul's Cross, London, and at various other places in England and Ireland. It may seem somewhat strange, perhaps, that the sermons of so well-known a man as FitzRalph have never been printed, but such is the case. I note that on more than one occasion FitzRalph, preaching about the year 1340, is said to have commenced his sermon by reading the whole Gospel in English—an interesting and significant fact. The most celebrated of these discourses were preached in A.D. 1356, at St. Paul's Cross, and in them he fiercely attacked the friars' privileges. They are certainly bold and vigorous enough in their language, and we cannot but be astonished at the way the Archbishop, speaking on behalf of the Bishops of England, could possibly have addressed himself to so burning a question in the public pulpit at St. Paul's. We judge, however, that he was not entirely free from interruption, for he tells us himself that in reply to an objection raised by a friend of the friars in one of these celebrated sermons, he replied: "If you will prove that our Lord ever really begged His bread, I will give you this Bible I hold in my hand."

St. Paul's Cross, be it remarked by the way, at that time and for many years before, "of which there is no memory," says Stowe, was the most celebrated pulpit in England. Some of the sermons preached there help us to realise a scene now long passed away, and to fix a spot upon which, in ages past, so many London audiences have gathered to listen to the voice of the most renowned preachers of the time. The very memory of the spot has almost faded away. It stood—a raised platform beneath a great timber cross—in the open air, and in the midst of the chief burial-ground of the metropolis. There, except in bad weather, when the covered space, called "the shrowds," was used, the great English sermons of the day were preached; and the site often suggested a moral to the speaker. "The audience of the dead bodies under your feet," one is reported to have said, "is as great and greater, as good and better, than you."

Learned and greatly interesting as are the sermons of Archbishop FitzRalph, they cannot, in my estimation, compare with those of another English preacher, whose name I need not give, who lived but a few years later, and who often occupied the pulpit at St. Paul's Cross, and must have deeply stirred the hearts of his audience by his exceptional eloquence. His sermons are, I fancy, but little known, but there are more than two hundred and fifty of them in existence. Though preached in English, they were written in free or even elegant Latin, and, if only by reason of the many historical and topical allusions to be found in them, they fully deserve a place among the monuments of our national literature. I only wish that time would permit me to quote a few samples, not only of this preacher's eloquence, but of the manly vigour with which he publicly attacked abuses, even in the highest places in the land.

The foregoing are imperfect, and, I admit most fully, but detached specimens of the information which lies ready at hand, but which, I fear, is little attended to either by the popular writer or the learned historian. In fact, the difficulty is quite to realise how best to bring the truth home to people in matters such as these. We have been so long accustomed to round assertions, evidently based upon fancy rather than on fact, that in treating a matter such as this, I myself feel as if I were exaggerating, and so hardly know how to deal with, or even justly to appreciate, the facts which crowd themselves upon the mind of any one who will take the trouble—the patient trouble—to inquire. Thus, in this supposed era of "no preaching," I find that, taking only those who have left evidence in the shape of collections of sermons, the names of at least two hundred English sermon-writers are known to us as having lived and written in the fourteenth and fifteenth centuries. Most of these, moreover, be it remarked, are Carmelites, the least numerous of the four Mendicant Orders. Are we to suppose that this phenomenon is due to the fact that the Carmelites had in Bale a capable bibliographer, or rather that, whilst the members of the Order of Mount Carmel preached, the other mendicants were all the time "dumb dogs"? On Mr. Lilly's hypothesis this latter is the more probable alternative. For my own part, I am inclined to think that the record of a vast mass of sermon literature of the two centuries previous to the Reformation has perished, simply because the Franciscans and Dominicans, not to mention the other great Orders, possessed no Bale to register their sermon-writers. Still less fortunate, of course, would be the secular clergy, who did not form a corporate body with corporate interests. Hence I would conclude that the list of preachers and sermon-writers during the fourteenth and fifteenth centuries (given in, say, Pitts or Tanner) only contains a proportion—in fact, I may say a small portion—of those who actually lived in that period. Yet even this list contains a very respectable number of names.

It must be long before even a fair sketch of the history of preaching and instruction in England during the later middle ages can be drawn. Even in the British Museum alone it is necessary to examine and weigh the contents of some hundreds of manuscript volumes. It is a case of which we may truly say *labor est ante nos*. But already one or two points of importance stand out clearly from a background of much that is yet vague. First and foremost, it is certainly untrue that religious instruction, in the highest sense of the word, was neglected in pre-Reformation England. Next to this is the prominence given to familiar instruction, as distinct from preaching, and the importance which in Catholic days was attached to the constant —the perpetual reiteration of the same lessons of faith and practice. It may be said that this must have produced a certain sense of sameness, and that education has altered matters in our own times. In point of fact, however, no amount of education really affects these truths, still less does it advance them. The only question is, how best the truths of religion are impressed upon the mind. I must own to a belief that at the present day our Catholic people have not that clear understanding nor that firm grasp of the great simple truths of their religion which they ought to have. Nor need we be astonished if this be the case; for is there much exaggeration in the statement that after leaving school Catholics now seldom receive regular and systematic instruction upon the elements of faith and practice during the rest of their lives? Here we are, living in the midst of Protestants, and I would ask if, when the whole nation was Catholic and had been so for generations, when the very atmosphere which Englishmen breathed was impregnated with Catholicity, it was considered necessary never to cease repeating instructions of what, for lack of a better expression, I may call "the Penny Catechism type," it can be safe in these days of vagueness and latitudinarianism to rely—I may say exclusively—for the teaching of our people on the formality of set sermons?

Of course I must not be understood as wishing unduly to obtrude these considerations; but in investigating the history of religion among the English people many doubts such as these force themselves on the attention of the inquirer, and many a practical question is raised in his mind of which at the outset he had no suspicion.

VII.

A ROYAL CHRISTMAS IN THE FIFTEENTH CENTURY.

BEING AN ACCOUNT OF HOW KING HENRY VI. SPENT THE CHRISTMAS-TIDE OF A.D. 1433-4 WITH THE MONKS OF EDMUNDSBURY.[1]

I.—INTRODUCTION.

THE Christmas of 1433 Henry VI. spent at Edmundsbury. Although events were taking place which already threatened the overthrow of English rule in France, as yet the heritage left to his infant son by Henry V. was intact, and the English people greeted their young sovereign with every confidence as the monarch of the two great realms of England and of France. A child of but

[1] This narrative was compiled for the *Tablet*, Christmas, 1892, in conjunction with Mr. Edmund Bishop. There exists a contemporary account of the king's visit printed in Dugdale's *Monasticon*, but this has been worked into a mosaic of minute details gathered from the various registers and liturgical remains of the abbey of Edmundsbury, of which a large collection has been accumulating in our hands for many years past.

12 years, he had, at the time of which we speak, been recently crowned in Paris, whither he had proceeded amidst every sign, fallacious though it might have been, of popular rejoicing; "attended by the chief of the English nobility and 3,000 horse, he left Pontoise and was met by the clergy, the Parliament, the magistrates, and the citizens of the capital. Triumphal arches had been erected, mysteries were performed, and devices were exhibited to honour and entertain the young king." The ceremony of coronation "was performed by an English prelate, the Cardinal of Winchester, and the high offices of state were filled by Englishmen, or by natives of inferior rank." Herein lay the weakness which time was to disclose; but as yet the Maid of Orleans had not appeared on the scene, and there was no indication that the fugitive Charles VII. would ever enter into the full possession of the kingdom which had been ruled by his fathers. On Henry's return to England, therefore, the people of this country could welcome their twice crowned Sovereign with unrestrained exultation and joy—feelings heightened by the ingenuous and noble character of the child, and by the bright hopes of the future to which the thought that he was the son of a hero gave birth.

II.—THE PREPARATION FOR THE VISIT TO BURY.

On All Saints' Day, in 1433, presiding at the meeting of Parliament at Westminster, the king publicly announced that, in accordance with the custom of his royal house, he, by the advice of his Council, intended to spend the season from Christmas to St. George's day at the abbey of Bury St. Edmunds. The unwonted news reached abbot Curteys whilst he was staying at his manor of Elmswell, some six miles distant from the abbey. At first he seemed hardly able to understand this novel proposal. At St. Albans, on the high road to the north, the monks had been accustomed for two or three centuries to frequent visits of king and court, but, said the abbot, when the message was brought him, nowhere in the chronicles can we find that the king of England, at least for such a time, ever fixed his stay with us, by the expression of his royal will.

The burden, be it understood, was no light one. A king, a court, and all the numerous attendants, from the lords and knights to the lowest valet—to house and board all these in a fitting manner would put the resources of even such a house as Edmundsbury to the test. However, the abbot quickly determined to do his best to maintain the honour of St. Edmund's church and monastery, and a few days later found him returned to Bury in order himself to superintend the needful preparations. His house, or "palace," as the record calls it, was in an indifferent state of repair, and eighty workmen were at once engaged, not merely to set it all in order, but to decorate and beautify it, as so loyal a subject as abbot Curteys would best wish to do.

Before proceeding further, it is well to understand something of the position of the abbot and convent of Bury in the county. Like St. Cuthbert in the north, St. Edmund in the east held the most extensive franchises. Quasi-regal is the way the local writers speak of them, and as the charter of the Confessor granting the liberty of the eight hundreds and a half to St. Edmund's monastery, says: They are bestowed as fully as his mother Emma held them, and as they were after in the king's own hands.

But whilst the abbot held such temporal rule (albeit with certain restrictions) over the famous eight hundreds and a half, nothing could be done in taxing the borough without the will of the convent, for the town belongs chiefly to St. Edmund and his altar, and all the profits pertain of right to the convent, unless they be voluntarily granted to the abbot, or perhaps to some one else. Accordingly the horn, which is called the *Mote Horn*, and the keys of the town are every year on St. Michael's day delivered in the chapter house to the sacrist by the town bailiffs: and the sacrist delivers them to the prior, who in the same way through the sacrist returns them to the town authorities. And this observance is annual, so that it may be known that the town altogether belongs to the convent, and that during the vacancy of the abbacy the king does not take it into his hands.

Still, although such care was taken to guard

vested rights, no less watch was kept that the abbot's dignity should, in no sense, suffer. With such ample jurisdiction it will be readily understood that abbot Curteys found no difficulty in securing among his own dependents a sufficient suite to wait upon a king. He appointed, says the record, one hundred officers of every rank to attend on Henry during his stay. Even the most minute points were not overlooked in his desire to do honour to his royal master. He summoned the aldermen and the chief townspeople of Bury to discuss with him how they might best receive their prince, and in what dress. Everyone will easily understand that this last was no light matter, for even in small country towns in the fifteenth century, no less than in the present day, there were evidently many ticklish matters of precedence to settle, and, what is even more difficult to agree upon, the exterior marks which manifest these differences. After much discussion, therefore, says the account, and a great variety of opinions expressed, it was agreed, under the moderating counsels of the abbot, that the aldermen and burgesses should be content with the fine material known as scarlet, and their inferiors with red cloth gowns with hoods of blood-colour.

III.—The Reception.

At length all was ready for the day of the king's arrival. The convent among themselves had already for three days past sounded the note of the coming feast of Christmas by the antiphon *Orietur sicut sol*. For at St. Edmundsbury, at least, it was the custom to watch for the coming festival from the third day before Christmas, and the 23rd of December stood in their calendar as the vigil of the vigil of our Lord's Birthday, from the first vespers of which day, out of reverence for the coming feast, the whole divine services were performed with special solemnity.

Christmas Eve was the day fixed for the royal arrival. At daybreak the town was all astir, and the aldermen and burgesses and other townfolk, five hundred in number, in their scarlet robes and red cloth gowns with blood-colour hoods, set out on horseback, in open ranks, stretching a mile along the road, to meet the king at the Newmarket Heath and bring him into Bury. Henry was accompanied by a stately train, and with this brilliant addition to his retinue, he rode on to the monastic enclosure.

The bell tower over the great gateway was then in ruins, and so, to avoid all possible danger, Henry and his gay cavalcade entered the precincts by a safer if a lesser entrance. But this can in no way have detracted from the splendour of his reception. The burgesses, who, on the part of Bury, had taken so prominent a part in the proceedings, had only come to introduce the king to the reception prepared for him.

It is no difficult task for the imagination to

picture the vast court of Bury abbey, crowded with the inhabitants of the town and the villages of the franchise of St. Edmund, eager to catch a first glimpse of their sovereign. Meantime, the hosts themselves had done their part to arrange a ceremonial of reception worthy of a king. As rumour heralded his near approach, the great western doors of the abbey church—works of beaten bronze, cunningly chiselled by the skilful hands of Master Hugh, and inspired possibly by what abbot Anselm, the nephew of the sainted archbishop, had himself seen at Monte Cassino—were thrown open. Forth issued the community, some sixty or seventy in number, all vested in precious copes, headed by cross and candles, and preceding their abbot in full pontificals, with whom walked an honoured guest, bishop Alnwick of Norwich, whom on this occasion they associated with themselves in the part of host. The ranks of the vested monks opened on either side, and through them the bishop and abbot advanced to meet their boy king. Then the Earl of Warwick, quickly alighting from his horse, ran forward, and, receiving the king in his arms, assisted him to dismount. Henry now advanced towards the procession, and kneeling on the silken cloth spread out on the ground, was sprinkled with holy water by the abbot, who also presented the crucifix for adoration, which was reverently kissed by the king.

The procession here turned to re-enter the stately

church, and was followed by the whole crowd. The building was large enough to accommodate even such a multitude as was then assembled. The western front from end to end stretched for nearly 250 feet; and within, an unbroken length of over 500 feet met the eye. The massive Norman architecture was relieved by the painted vaulting—that of the choir by the monk "Dom John Wodecroft, the king's painter," in the days of abbot John I. de Norwold (1279-1301), that of the nave to match—executed in the taste of the fourteenth century at the expense of the sacrist, John Lavenham (*circa* A.D. 1370), who during his term of office had spent something like £50,000 of our money on beautifying the church. The new lantern tower above the choir was his work, as well as the clerestory windows round the sanctuary; and the painted glass in the southern side of the minster had been the gift of king Edward III. to St. Edmund.

As the procession passed up the stately nave, the organ burst forth in jubilant strains of music, and the vaulting of the vast basilica rang with the anthem of the martyred King, chanted in harmony by the whole body of monks as they led their sovereign to the altar. And these were the words they sang :

> Ave Rex gentis Anglorum,
> Miles Regis Angelorum,
> O Edmunde flos martyrum,
> Velut rosa, velut lilium ;
> Funde preces ad Dominum
> Pro salute fidelium.

Which may be turned into English thus:

> Monarch of our English race,
>   Soldier of the Angels' King,
> Edmund, Flower of Martyr's grace,
>   Rose and lily round thee spring:
> Let thy prayers ascend on high
> For thy clients' sanctity.

The procession finished, and Henry having prayed before the Blessed Sacrament, he passed out of the sight of his people by one of the side doors in the altar screen, which had been adorned with paintings by the care of abbot Edmund Brundish, into the feretory beyond, to pay his devotions at the shrine of the Saint. This priceless work of art rested on a base of gothic stonework, and was itself covered with plates of solid gold enriched with every kind of jewel. The monks loved to recall how king John had every year of his reign bestowed ten marks on the work of beautifying the shrine, and how among the stones which sparkled on it a great and precious sapphire and a ruby of great price had been his special gifts. On the right side, too, was the golden cross set with many jewels surmounting a flaming carbuncle, the rich gifts of Henry Lacy, the last Earl of Lincoln of that name, whilst a second golden cross weighing 66 shillings, from the same generous benefactor, formed the apex of the shrine.

On the east side, at the head of the saint, two small columns supported a smaller shrine containing the relics of Leofstan, the second abbot, and others; whilst on the western side, at the feet of the saint, was placed the altar of the Holy Cross. Above the whole stretched a canopy, which prior Lavenham had adorned with painted pictures, and at the four corners were the great waxen torches, which burned day and night, and were paid for by the rent of a Norfolk manor left for the purpose by king Richard I.

Having ended his devotions, king Henry turned to the abbot and thanked him for the reception given him, and then, accompanied by the members of his suite, he passed into the abbot's palace, where all expressed their pleasure at the preparations which had been made for them.

IV.—The Vestry of the Abbey.

The reader, it is hoped, will be patient of an account, even in some detail, of the religious services of this Christmas season as they were actually observed at Bury St. Edmunds at the time of this royal visit. The destruction of records, especially of such as deal with ritual, has been immense, but in the fragments which survive more has really been preserved than is commonly understood, and here advantage will be taken of such Edmundsbury records as we possess.

But first, before the immediate preparation for the service begins, and whilst the king is dining in the hall, let us take a survey of the vestry of this great abbey and peep into the presses and strong chests for vestments, jewels, and objects of gold and silver. Unfortunately, we have no inventory of the goods of Bury such as exists for St. Albans, but a little anecdote of one of the guardians of this church, Walter de Diss, which has come down to us, is sufficient to show that the care of the valuables in this vestry was no light charge to an anxious-minded monk. Walter was appointed sacrist by the well-known abbot Samson; but after four days' experience in the office, he came and asked to be relieved of it, saying that since his appointment he had never closed his eyes, and could neither rest nor sleep.

Doubtless, like St. Albans, Bury possessed large " sets " of vestments, including ten, thirty, or even sixty copes; for one example at least will meet us in our survey. The fragmentary notices which remain, afford, at all events, some idea of that of which all exact record is now lost. Here, for example, is the cope woven with gold, and the precious chasuble given by abbot Samson himself; here the chasuble adorned with gold and precious stones, and a cope of the like set given to the house by abbot Hugh II., afterwards bishop of Ely. Then in this press are kept the precious copes and silken hangings and other most noble ornaments provided by abbot Richard I. (A.D. 1229-1234); in this other the set of fifty copes and other things thereto belonging (that is, doubtless, albs, apparels, &c.) which prior John Gosford had done so much to acquire. Then, to mention one or two more instances, there were the vestments obtained at a cost of over £200 by John Lavenham; the vestment *bloden cum botterflies de satyn* given by Dom Edmund Bokenham, chaplain to king Edward III.; the embroidered cope of prior William de Rokeland: the precious cope bought for over £40 by prior Edmund de Brundish; the sumptuous embroidered cope given by Henry Lacy, Earl of Lincoln.

Of the plate, the most precious was doubtless the great chalice of gold, weighing nearly fourteen marks, the gift of Eleanor, queen of Henry II. This had a history, for it had been given up by the convent as its contribution towards the ransom of king Richard. Queen Eleanor, the King's mother, however, had herself paid its value, and subsequently returned it to the monastery on condition, as she says in her charter, that it is never alienated, and is preserved as a perpetual memorial of her son, king Richard.

Then, to proceed on our inspection, here we have the chalice of fine gold weighing five marks, procured by the sacrist Hugh; here the cross of gold given by the abbot Samson; here the third golden cross, which had been among the presents of Henry Lacy, which was set with precious stones, and contained a relic of the Holy Cross. The same generous benefactor had presented the convent with a cup more prized still. It was a bowl of silver gilt, of the most wonderful workmanship, which he asserted had belonged to St. Edmund himself, and which on great feast days his chaplain, wearing a surplice, had been wont to offer to the most dignified guests keeping holiday with him. The last acquisition would doubtless be regarded with particular pleasure, and it would probably be specially pointed out to the visitor among the precious things in the treasure chests of Bury.

As abbot Curteys was himself the donor, and as he was about to use his gift in the pontifical functions of the feast, we may delay a moment over a more detailed description of a work of art—a pastoral staff—which must have done honour to the English workman who had made it. For it had been made by one John Horwell, goldsmith of London. It was ordered by abbot Curteys in January, 1430, and it was to be ready for the feast of All Saints in that year. In the crook itself are figured two scenes—on the one side the Assumption of our Blessed Lady, on the other the Annunciation; below the springing of the curve is a richly ornamented niche enshrining the figure of St. Edmund, whilst below this again and forming the summit of the staff are twelve such canopies each containing a figure of one of the Apostles. The weight of this precious pastoral staff is 12lbs. 9½ozs, and the abbot, we are told, paid £40 to the London goldsmith for it.

This mere glance at the vestry of a single

monastery may afford some idea of the devastation which took place some century later. Of the treasures gathered together at St. Edmundsbury nothing whatever remains; the destruction was complete. No wonder the eighth Henry's Royal Commissioners could write of Bury: "we found a riche shryne which was very comberous to deface," and that, although they had "taken in the said monastery in gold and silver 5,000 marks and above, over and besides a rich cross with emeralds, as also divers and sundry stones of great value, they had yet left the house well furnished;" and no wonder too, that Camden, in lamenting over the ruin of the house, could write: "Greater loss than this, so far as the works of man go, England never suffered."

V.—The Beginning of the Feast.

At Bury, as at Glastonbury, at Evesham, Coventry, and elsewhere, the parish churches, although standing in the very enclosure of the abbey, were noble structures. And though they could not vie in splendour with the great monastic church hard by, we have in extant records the best warrant for believing that the divine service was performed in them with a dignity and a fulness which were inspired by their great neighbour.

To-day, however, at Bury, there can hardly be a doubt that the two parochial churches in the minster precincts were fairly deserted. All who possibly could must have thronged into the great church for the first vespers of the Christmas feast. In great houses like these, everything connected with the place had its history, which was affectionately remembered by the inhabitants, even the very bells. It was borne in mind how prior John Gosford had provided the peal for the choir, and how one big bell added to it was called the Newport, after prior Newport, who had procured it; also how the sacrist, John Lavenham, at a cost equal to £3,000 of our money, had bought the biggest bell, and Reginald of Denham had obtained the four bells for the clock chime with one of wonderful size.

Even the ringing, like everything else in an orderly house, was subject to rule, and the inhabitants of Bury knew perfectly well from the character of the peals the quality of the feast. Christmas Day was rung in by four successive changes; first came the tones of the two Londons—the greater and the Holy-water bell; the second and the third peals were sounded on the bells in the cemetery, and amongst them Gabriel, the bell rung in thunderstorms, and its companion, Galiena. The beginning of the third peal was the signal for the cantors and all the rest of the vested ministers to enter the choir for vespers, whereupon the younger monks began ringing the bells in the great lantern tower, and then all the bells of the monastery took up the music, and above them all was heard the well-known tongue of *Haut et cler;* and thus, all sounding together, there rang out what the townspeople knew as *le glas*, which was the signal for the beginning of the office.

With the first peal the monks prepared for vespers. Coming from the dormitory they repaired to the lavatory and washed their hands. Then those who were not to be vested in copes put on albs which lay ready set out for them in the choir, whilst the abbot, prior, and others prepared for the functions in the vestry. The abbot, and to-day, of course, the Bishop of Norwich, would be in full pontificals. Meantime the torches and candles were being lighted throughout the church. Besides the four great wax candles mentioned as ever kept burning at the four corners of the shrine of St. Edmund, twenty-four, each of a pound weight, were lighted on the walls surrounding the feretory, and seventeen more of the same weight were placed in the seventeen windows round the presbytery. In the choir, the great candle, five large torches standing before the high altar, each weighing four pounds, and seven of the same size in the great gilded seven-branch candlestick, were lighted. These last were reflected in the plates of gold which adorned this great candelabrum, and, together with one torch before the high altar, were kept burning until the close of the second vespers of the feast. Then twelve more great torches were ablaze in the choir and rood, and a second dozen in the lantern tower, whilst twenty-six in either transept, one before each of twenty-four altars of the church, one great candle set under each arch of the nave, and twelve more huge waxen torches, each of eight pounds, before the altar of the Blessed Virgin in the chapel—a church itself in size—on the north side of the choir, completed the illumination of the vast church.

This evening it must have been a goodly procession that passed into the choir to the vespers, for besides the prelates, the coped cantors and the attendant ministers, the king himself took part in the sacred pageant. After the psalms and their antiphons, the responsory *O Juda* was sung in triple harmony. As soon as the anthem before the *Magnificat* had been begun, the prior, who had been waiting either in the vestry or before the altar of St. Sabas, entered the choir, and, with the abbot, sub-prior, sacrist, the abbot's chaplains, and the vestiar, preceded by two acolytes and two thurifers, went to the incensing. The abbot putting the incense into both thuribles, took one, the prior taking the other, and then both together censed the Blessed Sacrament hanging over the altar in the cup of pure gold which king Henry III. had given for the purpose, and then the altar. This over, they passed through the doors of the altar screen, the abbot by the south door preceded by the two acolytes, the prior by the north, each accompanied by his side of the procession, the sub-prior always carrying the abbot's thurible; and so went to incense the shrine of St. Edmund and the other relics, and lastly the altar of SS. Botulph, Thomas and Jurmin, situated at the extreme end of the church. This done, the whole procession returned to the choir, censing on the way the shrine of abbot Baldwin and the little altar of the choir in front of it. Arrived at their places, the king, the bishop, the abbot, cantors, and finally the convent are censed. Then once more the prior and his procession proceed to cense the altar of the Holy Cross at the foot of St. Edmund's shrine, and lastly the altar in the Lady chapel.

For so lengthy a ceremonial it was necessary that the *Magnificat*, should be sung with solemnity, and its antiphon was repeated as well before as after the *Gloria Patri*. The vespers finished by the solemn *Benedicamus* called *Flos Filius*, sung in triple harmony by many monks standing in the middle of the choir. Then the brilliant procession passed out of the church and through the throng. The multitudes dispersed to their homes to talk over the doings of an eventful day and prepare for the further festivities of the morrow.

VI.—THE MATINS AND MASSES OF THE FEAST.

Between nine and ten o'clock the bells rang out once more for matins and the midnight Mass. The manner of life in the fifteenth century was more hardy than ours, and, what is more, religion was interwoven with all the thoughts and habits of the English people. There is little doubt, therefore, that the building was once more filled with an expectant multitude. The proportions of the spacious church would have been magnified to the imagination by the solemn shadows of the Christmas night. The altar and feretory was a perfect blaze of light, which only threw the nave into deeper darkness. For it is evident that in the disposition of the lights there was a settled purpose. Whilst the vast nave was left in comparative shade, the great crossing was brilliantly lit up, and from the lantern a strong light was cast down upon the Rood with the attendant figures of Our Lady and St. John, an incomparable production of the same master Hugh, who had made the great brazen doors of the church. The intermediate choir was again but moderately lighted up, contrasting with the brilliant illuminations of the altar and the place of the shrine beyond.

The long matins were yet more magnificent in their ceremonial than had been the vespers. The closing responsory of each succeeding nocturn was sung by an increasing number of coped cantors standing around the great antiphonal of prior Brundish, whilst the *O magnum mysterium*, though sung by only two, had a thrilling effect. For these two were the picked voices of the community, chosen because their clear and resonant tones would make the vaulting ring, and would penetrate to every corner of the vast basilica.

The close of each nocturn was marked by the same elaborate ceremonial of censing as at vespers, and by the time the *Te Deum* was reached the whole church was filled with fragrant incense. During the singing of the hymn of praise the abbot and his numerous ministers went to vest for Mass, and at the close of matins the Holy Sacrifice began with the *Introibo*, the *Confiteor*, and so on, as usual.

The Introit was sung by the precentor, the succentor, and four companions in copes, and, according to the practice at St. Edmundsbury, into the *Kyrie* was inserted the *O Rex clemens*, one of the two *farsuræ* allowed by the old use of the house. The *Gloria in excelsis*, as was then the custom on all principal feasts, was sung by the whole convent in a body; and glorious indeed was the chant of such a number of trained voices, re-echoed by the vaulting of that mighty roof.

The Prophecy was sung by two with well-according voices, and the Mass was followed by lauds, and only after this the community retired, if not to sleep, at least to rest, awaiting the sound of the big bell of the great tower, which it is the duty of the sacrist's servants to ring on this morning at the first streak of dawn. At this sound all went once more into the church to the Aurora Mass.

The third Mass was preceded by procession, for which, while tierce was being sung, preparations were made. First walked the servers, carrying the

Holy water and two thuribles; next, two cross-bearers in copes with two torch-bearers on either side; then the shrine with the *Camisia* of St. Edmund, borne by two secular chaplains in albs and copes; then three sub-deacons followed, of whom the middle one—the epistolar of the Mass—reverently bore the great Gospel Book, the sumptuous gift of abbot Samson, and the other two other "texts" of lesser price. Then walked three deacons carrying relics, the middle one—the gospeller—having the reliquary with *Ave* on the top. Last, in this first part of the great procession, walked a priest, a grave and ancient senior, carrying the arm of St. Edmund, and after him, two and two, in open ranks, followed the whole convent, whilst in their midst walked the precentor and the succentor ruling the chant, the former with the seniors, the latter with the juniors. On this day the procession was closed, after the two prelates in full pontificals, by the king clad in regal dress, followed by his court, and doubtless by some, if not all, of the scarlet-clothed burgesses of the town of Bury.

In this wise they passed along the cloister, by the marble effigy of Anselm, the first mitred abbot of the house, whose memory after three centuries was still fresh, and so by three sides of the cloister to the crypt, the entrance of which was from the eastern alley. This crypt, over a hundred feet long by almost as many broad, supported on twenty-four columns, and dedicated like that at

Canterbury to the Blessed Virgin, extended under that part of the eastern limb of the church occupied by the shrine of St. Edmund. The procession entered it singing the responsory *Descendit;* the relics were placed on the altar, the ministers ranging themselves within the presbytery. When all had entered and had taken their places, the prior and sub-prior censed the altar and the dignitaries, and the thurifers the community. After a prose sung by six voices, and the prayer of the Station, the procession returned through the cloister to the church, and there, singing the *Sancta et Immaculata* they entered the nave. A supreme moment this for the Bury people. Our imagination can well picture the eagerness with which they crowded round to look at the splendid pageant and to get a glimpse of their youthful monarch; and the delay, necessitated by a second *statio* before the great cross in the rood loft, gave them time to satisfy their curiosity.

Here the abbot intoned the anthem *Hodie Christus,* singing which the procession passed into the choir, where, to-day, as on all greater feasts, the relics were venerated by the convent. Then followed the Mass, one part only of which need delay us here. To heighten the jubilant character of the sequence before the gospel, as was the practice on all principal feasts, it was prefaced by a peal from the great tower; and so soon as the Mass was over the joy bells rang out again, whilst the king left the church.

VII.—The Christmastide.

After the religious celebration of the day, Henry returned to the palace and there held high festival such as Bury had never seen before. On Christmas Day, as on two or three other of the greater festivals of the year, it was the practice of the house to invite all the dependents of the monastery of every grade to dinner. This crowd of guests was distributed in accordance with their rank or character. Thus, all those who were connected directly with the service or the custody of the church itself and all that pertained to the church, dined with the community in the great refectory. The chief officers, the abbot's gentlemen and yeomen, with other persons of credit and position, would dine with the abbot in his hall; while, again, the chief officials of the obedientiaries of the monastery, forty-eight in number, were accommodated in the guest-hall; and so on with others of lesser degree down to the turnbroach and the disher. In this way, all connected with the abbey were ever reminded that they formed, with the monks themselves, one great family—the family of St. Edmund —bound together by ties of interest and affection.

But to-day there must naturally be some displacement when the king took the place of abbot and a kingly court had to be provided for. But Bury abbey was big enough, and its hospitality ample enough for all—the new guests and the old friends also. The stores of plate which had accumulated were sufficient to supply the table even of a king, although abbot Curteys had already sold much as superfluous. Abbot Thomas, for example, had alone given to the house 18 large silver dishes, 18 salts, 25 silver cups—of which 8 were gilt—4 water pots, 3 bowls, and other pieces of plate, weighing in all over 105 pounds.

Moreover, the establishment as a whole, in the number of persons who were engaged on some duty or other, was on such a scale as in these days it is difficult to realise. Every part of the complicated service was accurately mapped out, and for every piece of work there was a special servant or officer, whose duty and responsibility was clearly defined. Moreover, the housekeeping of a great abbey was continuous from year's end to year's end, and the house was always open and the family on the spot. Nothing strikes one more, in looking through the records of a complicated administration like this, than the way in which all needs were foreseen. Nothing is too small to escape attention, or too minute to be left to the chance of accident, and nothing was left to be counted as anybody's business; thus, on the one hand all knew for what they had to answer; on the other if there were defaults the failure could be visited on the defaulter personally.

Unfortunately, in this case we have not, as in so many others, the actual menu of the dinner, but on the evidence of similar records it may be safely asserted that each man was expected to do justice to the ample hospitality in a way alarming to us with our modern appetites. Fortunately, the hours were early, and all had time to prepare themselves for further functions, for in those days in matters of religious observance everyone was called upon to do his duty manfully.

During the first portion of the king's stay, that is, up to the Epiphany, he seems to have devoted himself mainly to the solemn services of the season, and to have surrendered himself to the life of the place in which he was stopping. Westminster was after all but a suburb of the capital, and life there was full of the interests and distractions of a town; but at Edmundsbury there was no life but that of the Abbey and the country. The stay must accordingly have been in this sense a novelty to the young Sovereign. We will not weary our readers with more details of the church services, although they were marked in those days by an ever-studied variety; one or two points, however, may be permitted as of interest in the present day.

Thus, after the second vespers of Christmas the commemoration of St. Stephen was made with a degree of solemnity which is no longer observed. One of the deacons among the community, whose voice was most suitable, immediately after the *Benedicamus* of the vespers, assumed the precentor's cope, and with all the other deacons of the house vested in copes sang the antiphon of St. Stephen, which was again followed by the whole *Magnificat* when the high altar, the relics and the altar in the choir were a second time censed by the prior and sub-prior. To the deacon-precentor was entrusted the ordering of all the office for St. Stephen's feast, and he had the satisfaction of inscribing the name of abbot, prior, sub-prior, and all the seniors of the house on the *tabula* to take the part he assigned to them in the services. Further, as an additional mark of honour, to the deacons were assigned the most precious copes and albs that the vestry could provide, and the deacon-precentor placed his companions in the highest places of the choir according to his discretion, and his assignment was law.

The same ceremonial in all its fulness was observed after the vespers of St. Stephen and St. John the Evangelist; but on St. John's day the whole office was taken by the elders among the priests. It is not too much to suppose that in the observances of the feast of Holy Innocents the little king would take a special interest. After St. John's vespers were over, for the commemoration of the Innocents, a boy assumed the succentor's cope, and with his youthful companions, also vested, began the antiphon, which was followed by *Magnificat*.

The boy precentor and his companions ruled the feast to-day, as the deacons had done on St. Stephen's. They were not, however, left without guidance, for the precentor always accompanied them, although leaving to them the precedence; and there was this further difference, which tells a tale of the lessons taught in Bury school. To the precentor-deacon it fell to intone, in place of the abbot, the antiphon at *Benedictus* and *Magnificat*, but for the boy on Holy Innocents' it was prescribed that he should offer these antiphons to the abbot, who, if it so pleased him, should sign to the youth his permission to intone. Advantage was taken of this day to introduce into the music the pleasing alteration of the treble of the boys, singing either alone or together, with the full chorus of the deeper voices of the monks.

In this season too occurred the notable anniversaries of abbot Baldwin and abbot Samson. The character of these is sufficiently indicated by the well known verse current among the juniors in the Edmundsbury vestry—verses which the critic may possibly think halting and somewhat too familiar when applied to a person so remarkable in his day as abbot Baldwin:—

Bald cum thure cappas et Samson postulat abbas,

Which in English is

Bald and Samson both require
Copes, with incense set afire.

The Epiphany was marked by many compliments and, what is more solid, valuable presents made by the abbot and convent to king and courtiers. For the latter purpose the community had taxed itself to the extent of £100, promising the abbot a proportion of such further expense as he should find it necessary to incur; and so, with twelfth night rejoicing was closed the celebration of this memorable Christmas-tide at Bury.

VIII.—Royal Recreation.

"Changing and loving change is ever human nature," so moralizes the monastic annalist. In plain words, the king had evidently had enough of church services, and the monks were not such as not fully to understand the feeling; and were quite ready to provide even on the spot a pleasant change.

Of course they would not have been happy until they had taken him to every nook and corner of their house and told him the story attached in their fond recollections to every building and adornment. It would not be difficult even at the present day to take a similar survey and to repeat much that the king must have heard; but we will spare the reader what perhaps the king himself found a little tedious. The interest displayed by these guides in their home affairs, however, had this advantage, that before long Henry knew the place well, and by the time Christmas was over he was quite at home at Edmundsbury.

After the Epiphany celebrations he at once dispensed with the more ceremonious observances of the abbot's palace, and moved into the prior's house.

This, although a less splendid dwelling, had the advantage of a most pleasant site. One part of it, the work of prior John Gosford, was thrown across the running stream which passed through the monastic enclosure. In front stretched that which was the pride of the house—the vineyard, which had been bought by abbot Samson for the recreation of the community, and on the beautifying of which successive generations had bestowed all their care. Fresh and sweet-smelling was the air which was wafted over it, says the chronicler of the house. Dom Thomas Rudham, a contemporary of prior John Gosford, had taken advantage of the running water of the river to fashion in this pleasant vineyard two lakes. And here the king, as a step to further sport, could have the rather tame fun of watching the larderer and his men employ their "dragnet" and "trameyll," their "flewes" and "bowenettes" to provide fish from the stews for the consumption of the convent, and seeing them choose the eels from the great perforated iron barrels where they were kept, just below the outshoot at Teynene.

The great and sumptuous wall of Dom Thomas did not prevent a view of the far-stretching woods beyond, whilst the gates of the vineyard gave the hunting parties direct access to them. So, very soon the king and his court were all engrossed in the healthy pastime of the chase, and great and noteworthy in the annals of Edmundsbury was the havoc made among the wolves and foxes by the royal party.

As a relief from these exciting pleasures, Henry would very probably have had many a talk with the now aged Dom John Lydgate, at the time prior of Hatfield Broadoak, but whose heart was ever at Bury. Lydgate was the poet of his day, and now without a rival in England. His journeyings through France and Italy, his acquaintance with the literature of the latter country especially, his love for youth, to whose education the best years of his life had been dedicated, the store of tales he had gathered alike in travel and in reading, his extraordinary mastery over his native tongue, all would combine to draw towards the aged monk the fresh and open mind of Henry.

After a fortnight's stay in the prior's house, the king moved to the abbot's establishment at Elmswell, six miles off. This manor-place is situated in an exceedingly pleasant part of Suffolk on high ground. The air is fine and wholesome, the prospect beautiful and extensive. The house at this time was in excellent repair, the neighbourhood thickly wooded, and abundant water near. Here was a change of sport, and the king and his companions varied their amusements between sedate attempts to catch the fish in the streams and the more lively recreation of hawking. All this, says the contemporary writer, they found most delightful. And meanwhile the abbot had care to provide

Henry and his courtiers, from the wide-spreading domains of the abbey, with swans and pheasants and partridges and other game, and with pike and toothed eels and every sort of fish in abundance.

On the vigil of the Purification, Henry returned to the palace at Bury to keep the festival. That over, he went back to Elmswell until Ash Wednesday ushered in the solemn season of Lent, when he came again to Bury to pass the holy time in the prior's house; whilst the great feast of Easter, with its rejoicing, no less secular than religious, was kept like Christmas at the palace.

On Easter Tuesday two of the court accompanying the king, the Earl of Warwick and his countess, were received into the fraternity of the house of St. Edmund. For those who do not understand the ancient and present Benedictine system of admission to such fraternity, it may be well to give a few words of explanation. Such admissions to fraternity, which date from almost the earliest days, differ from the Third Orders, which had their rise in the thirteenth century, mainly in this, that the bond of union was not to the order, but to the particular house to which the individual admitted henceforth stood in a distinct and personal relation. On the one hand he received a share in the prayers and good works of the monastery, and on the other he made its interests his own. In a word he became to a certain extent one with the actual members of the monastic family in which he was admitted to fraternity.

The example of the Earl of Warwick was soon followed by others of the king's followers, and as the time of Henry's departure drew near it came to the minds of many that they could not leave Edmundsbury and the friends there made without the special tie implied by enrolment in the family of St. Edmund. Humphrey, duke of Gloucester, the king's uncle, who was already a *confrater* of the St. Alban's monks, made his petition and others with him. This was granted, and they all received the fraternity of St. Edmundsbury. But Henry himself would not be left behind, and determined to sue for the like privilege. First he prostrated himself before the shrine of the Saint, and then, followed by the Duke of Gloucester and the other nobles, he went into the chapter house and sent to inform the abbot of his desire. Abbot Curteys and the whole convent at once came to chapter and granted the pious petition of the young king; he was admitted with all the solemnity usual on such occasions, and he and all the new *confratres* received the kiss of peace.

Then the Duke of Gloucester, kneeling, begged the king to thank the abbot for all his kindness, and Henry, taking the prelate by the hand gleefully and gladly thanked him again and again, and bidding farewell to all the community there assembled, he affectionately commended himself and all his to God, St. Edmund, and to the fervent prayers of the abbot and his brethren.

17

Once more the king and all his train passed out of the abbey precincts amidst, we cannot doubt, the acclamations of the crowd assembled. Once more to do honour to him the five hundred good and true men of Bury would have donned their scarlet robes and their red cloth gowns with blood-coloured hoods and conducted him the first stage on his way to London to take up again the business of a life, which as the years passed on was to be one of growing anxiety and trouble, until in bitterness of soul, once more at Bury, he should exclaim:

> For in the shade of death I shall find joy;
> In life, but double death now Gloster's dead.

The visit of Henry VI. to St. Edmundsbury for the Christmas-tide of 1433-4, which we have attempted to describe, seems more like a journey to dreamland, so changed is all the world. Of Edmundsbury itself and all its glories scarcely one stone remains upon another. But of this visit one special memorial is left. It is a book often shown as one of the treasures of the national library at the Museum, and is the copy of the poet Lydgate's life of St. Edmund, which was not only written as a memento of this royal visit, but is the identical volume presented by the author to king Henry. The illustrations from this precious manuscript have become familiar to others besides the antiquary. How many are there, we wonder, of those who have examined this volume, and turned over its pages, who have ever realised the circumstances in which it had its origin? But it remains a witness of the life that indeed is past and gone, but which was once as real and as absorbing as our own.

VIII.

THE CANTERBURY CLAUSTRAL SCHOOL IN THE FIFTEENTH CENTURY.[1]

MEDIÆVAL education is a subject about which much has been written, but about which, it must be confessed, we remain very much in the dark. Those who have not made the attempt would hardly believe how difficult it is to obtain any reliable information as to pre-Reformation schools in England. Still more impossible is it to find the book which gives any account of what may be called scholastic " manners and customs," whether in cathedral, monastic or grammar schools. There are many works, it is true, which deal professedly with this matter of ancient education; but, for the most part, they quickly land the unwary reader in some abstruse and interminable discussion concerning the *trivium* and *quadrivium*. To some, I know, it may appear a matter of considerable importance to determine whether grammar, rhetoric and logic formed

[1] Reprinted from the *Downside Review*, vol. x., p. 31, *seqq*.

the basis of the education bestowed upon our English youth some centuries ago, or whether this apparently somewhat eccentric elementary course was supplemented by the more enlightened and equally curious higher course of the *quadrivium*, consisting of arithmetic, music, geometry, and astronomy. To me—I confess it with a feeling that I may be lowering myself in the estimation of my learned readers—the whole subject, when thus confined to this narrow horizon, has the most depressing effect. It results in no mental picture whatsoever of the educational methods pursued by our national forefathers. What I should like to know, and what I never can find any writer to tell me, is something about the conditions under which our mediæval ancestors learnt and their masters taught; and it is in the hope that others besides myself are more interested in trying to realise the actual working of the old school, in picturing the student at his task and the pedagogue in the act of teaching, than in exploring this *trivium* and *quadrivium* desert, that I here put on paper some thoughts suggested by the examination of a monastic lesson book of the fifteenth century.

Before, however, entering on this, I would ask my readers to understand the material conditions under which this book was really used. The monastic school-room was the cloister of the monastery, or rather one portion of it. "On coming out from the morning chapter," says the custumary of

St. Mary's, York, "let the brethren sit in the cloister. . . In one part, where the Abbot is, or he who takes his place, those come whose business it is to speak to him." The others were to attend to their tasks and reading, whilst the officials and seniors were discussing with their abbot the necessary business of the house. In the western walk of the cloister, the junior brethren, who had finished their studies, had spiritual conference with at least one of the superiors. Directly opposite, in the eastern part of the quadrangle, the novices and the junior monks who were still students, or, as the Rule says, were "*adhuc in custodia*," sat at their books and were taught the observances of regular life—"the disciples asking their masters about things they did not know; the masters instructing their pupils, and above all teaching them to master the rule of St. Benedict."

At Westminster, the abbot, "as his dignity demands," says the customary of Westminster, sat at the top of the eastern part of the cloister. The prior took the first place on the north, next to the door of the church, and the rest of the monks sat according to their seniority after him. The western walk was sacred to the novices, whose master took the first place, with the youngest nearest to him. Their method of sitting was peculiar: they were placed one behind the other, so that the face of one looked on the back of his neighbour. And this was always the case, except when there was general conversation in the cloister. The only fixed seats were those of the abbot, prior and master of novices; the rest were placed according to the disposition of the prior, sub-prior, or novice master, to whom the care and due order of the cloister were specially committed. There, in the morning after the chapter, and at other intervals during the day, the novices attended to their tasks and one by one took their books to their master, who either heard their reading himself or sent them to some other senior for help or instruction. Such was the practice at St. Peter's abbey.

We who see the cold, deserted and damp-stained cloisters of Westminster at the present time may well feel a difficulty in bringing to mind a picture of the busy scene which was enacted there, day after day, for centuries. The four cloisters, there as in every other abbey in Catholic England, formed the work-room of the inmates. There the chief business of the house was transacted, and the estates by which it was supported were managed by the superior and his officials. There the older monks laboured at the tasks appointed to them, or discussed questions relating to ecclesiastical learning and regular observance; and there the younger members toiled under the eye of their master and his assistants at their daily lessons. Cold and uncomfortable enough must that cloister life have been there in the dull days of our northern winter before hot-water pipes and suchlike luxuries of modern life were invented, in spite of the skin-lined almuces, and notwithstanding the thick carpet of hay, which the sacrist had thrice a year to find for the cloisters and the church of Westminster, from the farm at Kilburn. How the hand could have held the pen and written so neatly and so regularly, or have used the pencil and brush so cleverly; or how the somewhat thick wits of our ancestors could continue to work at their daily lesson through the long winter months, quite passes our comprehension. But this we know, that somehow or other they did manage to do so; and although the rush of modern life was little dreamt of in the cloisters of mediæval England, still daily progress was made in spite of all those drawbacks, which would simply paralyse the efforts of the modern monk, and the pampered nineteenth century school-boy. In some places, it is true, as in northern Durham, screen-work divisions appear to have been devised to somewhat shelter the student and the scribe from the sharper draughts which wandered round the vaulted cloisters. For does not the ever-delightful "Rites of Durham" say that in the "cloister there were carrels fynely wainscotted and verie close, all but the forepart, which had carved worke to give light in at their carrel doores, and on every carrel was a deske to lye their bookes on, and the carrel was no greater than from one stanchell (central bar) of the window to another." And for the use of the younger monks and novices the same writer tells us that "over against the said treasury door was a fair state of wainscott where the novices were taught, and the master of the novices had a pretty seat of wainscott adjoining to the south side of the treasury door over against the state where the novices sate, and there he taught the novices both forenoon and afternoon. No strangers or other persons were suffered to molest or trouble the said novices or monks in their carrels while they were at their books within the cloister. For to that purpose there was a porter appointed to keep the cloister door." But at southern Westminster (according to Abbot Ware's Constitutions), and we may suspect in most of our monastic houses, there were only very few of these sheltered carrels, designed for those who had special and constant business to transact within the cloister.[1]

So much for the schoolhouse where lessons of all sorts were learnt—a very important matter to bear in mind when estimating the results obtained. One

[1] The earlier and purer form of the Westminster Customs, written out with adaptations for St. Augustine's, Canterbury, contained in Cotton MS. Faustina, c. xii., thus speaks of these carrels: "De karulis in claustro habendis hanc considerationem habere debent quibus committitur claustri tutela, ut videlicet celerarius seu alii fratres qui raro in claustro resident suas karulas in claustro non habeant; sed neque aliqui fratres nisi in scribendo vel illuminando, aut tantum notando communitati aut etiam sibimet ipsis proficere sciant." (MS. Cott. Faust, c. xii., f. 96.) What is called abbot Ware's Consuetudinary of Westminster (also a Cotton MS., Otho c. xi.) is a *rifaccimento* of this earlier compilation—a compilation, be it said, by no means representative of English monasticism; its origin can be not obscurely discerned.

mediæval aid to learning should not be overlooked. Although we in this more enlightened age have learnt to scout the notion that wits are stimulated by whippings, the rod was ever held in mediæval philosophy to be the readiest and surest method of imparting wisdom. The ideal pedagogue is always represented with birch and cane ready to help his stumbling scholar over a difficulty with a well-timed castigation. By master—and, be it added, by his pupil too—the discipline of the rod appears to have been accepted as the inevitable, if somewhat painful, accompaniment of scholastic exercises. In all places of learning, from the grammar school to the monastic cloister, every scholar, from the plough-boy to the tonsured monk, accepted the inevitable, administered either *coram publico*, as an encouragement to the others, or in the somewhat more sacred seclusion of the daily chapter. So true is this that the very term *bacularius* (now the proud title of a finished student at the University) is said to be derived from the dignity of deputy-beater, or wielder of the stick, conferred only on those who had passed through their course, and who were thus considered sufficiently advanced to stimulate the younger generation, under the eye of the master, with healthful stripes.[1]

[1] We should hardly perhaps be inclined to count the sound whipping of boys among the works of piety. It was however sometimes so accounted in the mediæval days. Thus, in a book relating the miracles of St. Erconwald, there may be found the story of a boy from St. Paul's school flying for protection to the Saint's shrine in the London

One other matter of great importance must be named in this connection. We, who have known the paths of learning since they have been made plain and smooth by every variety of printed manual and carefully-planned table, can hardly realise the time when these things were not. In the days when schemes for the easy learning of cases and of genders were undreamt of, and before Thomas Kerchever Arnold had set Balbus to build his wall through every mood and tense, so that in following his actions the youth of England might acquire the rudiments of the Latin tongue, the royal road was broken with many pitfalls for the unwary. Books were few and precious, and the student's grammar and dictionary, instead of being acquired by the expenditure of a few parental shillings, had to be laboriously transcribed from the dictation of a master. Such a thing as a whole treatise of grammar, even as the common property of a school, seems to have been rare enough. Thus in the fourteenth century it is recorded as a matter of note that at the grammar school supported by the funds of the almoner of St. Albans, an old tome was discovered in a box. It turned out to be a copy of Priscian's *De arte grammatica*, and with great ceremony and under the

cathedral. The anecdote begins thus: "Fuit itaque in Doctoris Gentium familia Londoniæ (St. Paul's school) didascalus quidam nomine Elwinus, moribus bonis insignis et artibus, qui *inter cetera pietatis opera* puerorum disciplinis vigilantissimam impendere curam solitus fuit." (Hearne, *Leland's Collectanea*, i., 21.)

safeguard of stringent precautions (the schoolmaster being bound to find security for its safe custody), it was handed over to him for the boys to examine when they liked. How precious these books, even such as were in the hands of students, were esteemed in those days may be learnt from the treatise on books composed by Richard of Bury, bishop of Durham, in the fourteenth century. The seventeenth chapter of the *Philobiblon* is so very much to the point that I quote freely from it.

It is entitled, "Of handling books in a cleanly manner and keeping them in order." "We hold," he says, "that it is expedient to exhort students upon various negligencies which can be avoided, but which are wonderfully injurious to books.

"In the first place, then, let there be a mature decorum in opening and closing of volumes, that they may neither be unclasped with precipitous haste, nor thrown aside after inspection without being duly closed, for it is necessary that a book should be much more carefully preserved than a shoe. But school folks are in general perversely educated, and if not restrained by the rule of their superiors, are puffed up with infinite absurdities; they act with petulance, swell with presumption, judge of everything with certainty, and are unexperienced in anything.

"You will perhaps see a stiff necked youth lounging sluggishly in his study, while the frost pinches him in the winter time. For such a one I would substitute a cobbler's apron in the place of his book. He has a nail like a giant's, with which he points out the place of any pleasant subject. He distributes innumerable straws in various places, with the ends in sight, that he may recall by the mark what his memory cannot retain. These straws, which the stomach of the book never digests, and which nobody takes out, at first distend the book from its accustomed closure, and being carelessly left to oblivion, at last become putrid. He is not ashamed to eat fruit and cheese over an open book, and to transfer his empty cup from side to side upon it; and because he has not his alms-bag at hand he leaves the rest of the fragments in his books. . . What is worse, he next reclines with his elbows on the book, and by a short study invites a long nap; and by way of repairing the wrinkles he twists back the margins of the leaves, to the no small detriment of the volume. He goes out in the rain and returns; and now flowers make their appearance upon our soil. Then the scholar we are describing, the neglecter rather than the inspector of books, stuffs his volume with firstling violets, roses, and quadrifoils. He will next apply his wet hands to turning over the volumes, then beat the white parchment all over with his dusty gloves, or hunt over the pages, line by line, with his fore finger covered with dusty leather.

"But impudent boys are to be specially restrained from meddling with books, who, when they are learning to draw the forms of letters, if the copies of the most beautiful books are allowed them, begin to become incongruous annotators, and wherever they perceive the broadest margin about the text they furnish it with a hideous alphabet, or their unchastened pen immediately presumes to draw any other frivolous thing whatever that occurs to their imagination. There the latinist, there the sophist, there every sort of unlearned scribe tries the goodness of his pen.

"Our Saviour, by His own example, precludes all unseemly negligence in the treatment of the books, as we read in Luke iv., for when He had read over the Scriptural prophecy written about Himself in a book delivered to Him, He did not return it to the minister till He had first closed it with His most holy hands; by which act students are most clearly taught that they ought not in the smallest degree whatever be negligent about the custody of books."

So much about the general conditions of school life in the middle ages. I now ask leave to introduce to the reader a monastic schoolboy dwelling in the cloisters at Christ Church, Canterbury, in the latter half of the fifteenth century. His name is William Ingramm, as in defiance of good Richard of Bury's advice, he has scribbled it on many a page of his lesson book. I may be permitted to remark that it is a fortunate thing that there were some boys who would "try their pens" and "draw their monstrous alphabets" on the margin of their books, for all the bishop could say. It is by these boyish tricks that we have learnt much of what we know about these old world students. And so far as this class of book goes, it is the student, not his manuscript, that we prefer to know about.

My acquaintance with my Benedictine ancestor at Canterbury is entirely due to the delightful way he has of illustrating his course of studies. By this I mean "*illustration*" in its literary rather than its pictorial sense. Of pictures, if they may be dignified by such a name, there are but two. One represents an animal with two legs and a very curly tail, which, according to some interpreters of mediæval drawings, should be taken as an accurate likeness of a Canterbury dog of that period; the other I have little hesitation in pronouncing to be a rude drawing, in both senses, of the monastic teacher.

Below these rough sketches are five lines telling how the book belonged to Dom William Ingram, monk of Christ Church, Canterbury, as "Reginald Goldstone, monk of the said Church of Canterbury and his senior testifies." Of the former, William Ingram, I am sorry to say that all I know, except what this book tells us, is that his name is inscribed in another Canterbury book—a most wonderful psalter—as its possessor, and that the name of "*Willmus Ingram, frater noster,*" is entered in the Canterbury obit book (Arund. MS. 68, f. 38), on the

Ides of August, and in a hand which, judged by other entries, was written about the beginning of the sixteenth century. This and the fact that he is not described as being either in priest's or deacon's orders would lead us to suppose that his name was added to the great roll of the majority when he was but a young man. "Those whom the gods love die young," we are told, and William Ingram informs us several times in his lesson book that: "Ego sum puer bonus quem Deus amat." Reginald Goldstone was probably a relation of a prior of that name who ruled over the Canterbury priory at that time, and the same who in 1480 signs himself in a letter to the prior as "your chaplayn" (*Litt. Cant.* III., pp. 304-6).

The lesson-book I am now to describe is a stout quarto of about 220 folios of paper. The first portion consists of what we should call a dictionary, or what was then known as a *nominale*. There is nothing remarkable about this, except that it is different from any printed in Wright's volume of mediæval vocabularies. Following on this, and filling about 30 folios, is the elementary grammar. The ground-work, of course, of all school learning was the knowledge of the Latin language, and the first tasks set to beginners were easy lessons in grammar, the learning of words and their declensions and the practice of turning sentences of English into Latin for the purpose of Latin conversations. Fundamentally all these first grammars were the same and generally known as the *Donat*, from Donatus a celebrated grammarian, who lived in Rome in A.D. 354, and was the preceptor of St. Jerome. A traditional peculiarity of this grammar is the collection of all the words of one signification together: thus we have

Hoc Mare	is.
Hoc Equor	is.
Hic Pelagus	gi.
Hoc Salum	i.
Hoc Amphitritus	is.
Hic Pons	tis.

} A Sea.

This portion of the book is closed with one of those pious rhyming prayers that so clearly reveal the influence of religious thought and practice over even the ordinary actions and labours of life: a fact which is patent in every book, or we might almost say in every document, of those ages. The lines run :—

"Presens huic operi sit gratia neumatis almi

Mando lecto   ⟩ri⟨ Xpum roget ore fide   ⟩li
Ut det scriptor /   \ post mortem gaudia ce /

Deo gratias,"

which in English is :—

"May the grace of the loving Spirit of God be present to the work.

"I beg the reader with faithful prayer to ask of Christ that He would grant the writer after death the joys of heaven. To God be thankfulness."

One might illustrate this beautiful practice of jotting down little ejaculatory prayers in copy books of this sort to almost any extent. Thus in the Museum we find a lesson book of about the same date as this Canterbury one, which belonged to a certain "John Jones." On the top of many leaves is the prayer, "Jesus mercy, Ladi helpe." In the same book, before a series of questions and answers on the verb *sum*, we find, "Oh Ladi, helpe me in ye beginning." This prayer for a blessing at the commencement of a work is very common.

At the risk of wearying my readers I cannot refrain from quoting one petition of the kind somewhat more lengthy, printed by Caxton. The book in which this is found is a translation of Bartholomeus, *de Proprietatibus rerum*, and on the back of the title are the following verses :—

"In nomine Patris et Filii et Spiritus Sancti. Amen. Adsit principio Sancta Maria meo."

> " Cross was made all of red
> In the beginning of my boke
> That is called God me sped
> In the first lesson that I toke.
> Then I lerned *a* and *b*,
> And other letters by her names;
> But alwaye God spede me
> Thought me nedefull in all games.
> If I played in felde other medes,
> Stylle other wythe noys;
> I prayed helpe in all my dedes
> Of him that deyed upon the croys.

> Now divers playes in his name
> I shall lette passe forth and fare,
> And aventure to play oo long game.
> Also I shall spare
> Wodes, medes and feldes,
> Places that I have played inne,
> And in his name that all things weldes
> This game I shall begynne.
> And pray help, counseyle, and rede
> To me, that he wolde sende,
> And this game rule and lede
> And bring it to a good ende."

Even the lessons very often are conceived in the same spirit. Thus, John Jones is asked to translate and parse such sentences as this: "Ego sum creatura Dei creatoris mei." And even the boyish relaxations of our friend John are indications of the same.

He writes, for example, in one place:—

> " Qui scripsit scripta sua dextra sit benedicta
> Qui scripsit *scrape away* non possum scribere *all daye*
> Qui scripsit certe Johannes vocatur aperte
> Qui legit emendat scriptorem non reprehendat."

To return, however, to our young Canterbury monk. The elementary Latin grammar is followed by some apparently miscellaneous notes on religious subjects. The seven gifts of the Holy Spirit are explained, and Scriptural authorities are quoted for the due observance of the Sabbath day. One piece of information on a liturgical point may be recorded, not as possessing much authority, but as a curiosity.

Our student answers the question, "Why is the *pax* not given in Mass for the dead?" by stating that this is because we are in doubt whether the departed are in the peace of eternity or not.

Our scholastic, after devoting two leaves of his copy book to these notes, resumes his studies of the Latin language, and turns his attention to a series of words, the meaning of which, together with the gender of each, is expressed in some rhyming sentences. The following examples are taken at random :—

> "Hec tibea for a leg
> Hoc ovum for a nege
> Hec Margareta for Meg."

or :—

> "Canto-Cantas for to sing
> Pulso-Pulsas for to ryng
> Hic rex for a king."

or again :—

> "Hic urcius for a pote
> Hec alapa for a knoch
> Hec cachinatio for a mok."

After treating of adverbs and prepositions, and giving, in the catechetical form, some short explanations of Holy Scripture, followed directly by rules for the use of the verb *sum*, our student devotes some 30 folios to his Latin exercises. These mostly consist of simple sentences or of proverbs and such like old saws in English, followed by the translation of them into Latin. Some of the proverbs we recognise as old friends in still older dresses;

others strike me as being new, or, I should rather say, very old wise sayings, so old that they have not survived to our days. As instances of the sentences, we may take: " John, ye lerning of grammar long lyeing in bed little shall profit "—" My father for to be beatyn woe is me beholding his bloody body "—" Pilgryms are gone to Canturbery to worship ye Shrine of Seynt Thomas "—" I and thou Robert shall gather grapes in the yerd "— " A sodear fighting at Pomfret was rewarded in France for his doghty dedys."

The proverbs are of more interest, but I merely note the following :—" He that wyl not when he may, he shall not when he would "—" When the gam is beat it is tyme to rest "—" Ther is no man so shrewd as a beggar made a lord "—" Better is a bird in hand than four out "—" It is evil to tech an old doge curtesi "—" It is a hard batel where no man skapis "—" The blynde eateth many a flye "— " A piper laketh much that laketh his over lip "— " When the foot warmeth ye sho harmeth "— " It is better late than nevyre "—" The brent hound dreadeth the fyre."

We come now to an interesting part of this very instructive study book. It is a set of lines, some 150 in number, designed to teach the young monk the manners and behaviour fitting in one who wears the habit of St. Benedict. It is evidently of the same character as the lines known as *Stans puer ad mensam*, or those attributed to Lydgate, the monk of Bury, known in their English dress as "the Book of Curtesie," both of which are printed in the "Babees Book" of the Early English Text Society. It would be expecting too much from anyone to ask him to read this tract on mediæval manners, or even an English translation which I had attempted; but a few indications of the teaching given may perhaps be permitted. The young monk is to kneel when answering the abbot, not to take a seat unasked, not to loll against the wall, nor fidget with things within reach of his fingers. He is not to scratch himself—probably a more difficult matter of self-restraint than it may appear, in the days of woollen clothing and hay carpets—nor must he cross his legs like a tailor. He is to give place to his seniors, remembering that honour paid to others is honour given to God. He is not to interrupt conversation nor to laugh or shout aloud, ever remembering that a man without manners is rightly called a clown. Criticism and mockery of others are to be avoided as a habit wrong in itself and leading to a foolish manner of looking down on all but self. Thanks are to be given for every act of kindness or word of praise.

After these general rules for good manners the tract goes on to speak specially of the daily life. The youthful monk is bidden to wash his hands before his meals, to keep his knife sharp and clean, and say his grace. If talking is permitted in the hostel, he must speak in Latin, not in English, must avoid idle tales, and when the Bible or other book is being read he must attend. He is not to seize upon the vegetables; not to use his own spoon in the common dish; not to lean upon the table; not to cut or dirty the table cloth; not to pick his teeth in public, as it is not gentlemanly to let his jaws be seen. Further, he is not to use his knife to carry the gravy to his mouth, but to help others, as only the ill-mannered and clowns take everything for themselves. He is to wipe his knife before he cuts the common cheese, and not to taste first whether it be good enough for him. Finally, his meal ended, he is to clean his knife and cover it with his napkin. Special care is enjoined of all the lights, in view of fire, and he is admonished of the necessity for seeing them properly extinguished. The tract then goes on to direct that in school time English is never to be spoken, and that the student do diligently write in his book what has been taught him. If anyone come to call him whilst lessons are going on, he is never to leave without his master's permission, no matter who it is that bids him come, and while being taught he is to be quiet, and not to fidget or sniff so as to disturb the class.

About sixty folios of our young monk's book are now devoted to the grammatical treatise of "Ebrard the Grecian," whose syntax was so very generally used in the middle ages, and who apparently was an inhabitant of Bethune, in Artois, about the close of the twelfth century. Finally, the last portion is occupied with William Ingram's copy book proper, and is a revelation of the methods by which caligraphy was taught to young aspirants to a place in the monastic scriptorium. There are pages devoted to the letters small and capital, to a series of proper names, days of the week, and to the titles of the months. The copies proper are verses or sentences, generally consisting of four lines, beginning with the various letters of the alphabet, which have been written out in the hand of the master. The initial letter is generally quite a study in the art of flourishing.[1] Below this come the various attempts of the student to imitate the master's copy. Here and there one may see marks set underneath a word which has been badly written, and then the special word is practised in the margin. For example, in the first copy the word *chaos* had to be written. In the first attempt this is badly done; it is underscored and we find it practised five or six times in the margin. In those days, as in ours, the copies chosen were apparently of a decidedly bombastic

---

[1] This art was much esteemed in the middle ages. A curious and interesting example of this may be here given. In 1489, a monk of Westminster, named Edward Botiller, obtained permission of his abbot, John Estney, to be transferred from Westminster to the Cluniac Priory of Wenlock. On 9th April the abbot gives him his "dismission under scale," and a letter of recommendation to Wenlock. In the course of his letter he says: "The same Edward hath competent lerning and understandyng, and can syng both playn song and prikked song, and also a faire writer, a florisher and maker of Capital letters." (Hearne, *Adam de Domerham*, I., lvii.)

and priggish character. Somehow I suppose this
"Honesty-is-the-best-policy" kind of copy has been
found by generations of writing masters to be the
best. I will take one example of a copy set to
William Ingram:—

> "Est melior probitas quam nullo sanguine claret
> Quam sit nobilitas que probitate caret.
> Nobilitas morum plus ornat quam genitorum;
> Non eget exterius qui moribus intus habundat."

One could easily imagine a nineteenth century
writing master setting his pupils its English counterpart:—

> Uprightness of life with ignoble blood is to be esteemed
> before nobility without honour.
> A nobility of morals is a greater glory than a nobility of
> forefathers.
> He whose life is right does not need the external glory of
> noble blood.

The jottings on the margin of this portion of the
instructive study book may be noted in passing.
William Ingram, of course, tries his name in many
places, both in his native tongue and in the Latin
version. On one page we can recognise that his
native tongue has been exercised over a blot or two
in the approved boy fashion. A curious note finds
a place on folio 210^d :—

"Memorandum that William Ingram oeth the
Mastir for ij pennes knyvys and papir,"
and at another folio, like a bad workman, our

youthful monk complains of his tools, in the following rhyme :—

"Est mala scriptura quia penna non fuit dura"
(The writing is bad for a soft pen I had);

over against which complaint a wag has written:

"Penna non valet dixit ille qui scribere nescit"
('Tis surely the pen, say all ill-writing men).

I may perhaps be allowed here to make a slight digression, in order to give a sample of a draft-letter written by a young monk of Canterbury about 1530, almost on the very eve of the dissolution. It is taken from a bundle of such drafts in the library of Christ Church, Canterbury, and is one of three transcripts I owe to the kindness of Dr. Sheppard. The mother of the young writer had apparently just died, and he drafts the following to his father:—
"(God rest) her sowl and send her sowle good religion, and I send you knowlegg of the great benefyte that my mother hathe by the relygion of this place. Sche ys nowe suster of our chapter and her name schall (be read out) and her sowle to be prayed for yerely as long as ower church doothe stand (and her) name schall be sent to every relygyous place monastic, as to monks and nonnes and her name shall be read and sche shall be prayed for."

"An other cawse of my wrytyng it ys of the joyfull tydyngs of my brother's marryage; the which ys a thynge that dothe please me ryght (well).

He hathe an honest young woman of her and I trust they wyll do well. (I pray Almygty God to send them joye of it.)

"An other cawse of my wrytyng ys to bring to youre knowledge of syngyng of my first masse yf it do please Almyghty God. . . . I beseech you to be good father unto me at that season and help me. It will be a grete koste unto me for I must pay for bread for dry——that doth belong to yt. And yf yt do please God that I may live it shall be a great gladness and a great comfortte to you, to me and to everyone of my brethren. Then I, which am but a wretche and a synner and unworthye, shall have autoryte and full power with my vyle hondys to handle the verray (flesh) of Jesu Crist, also yt ys soche an hye offyce that yt must be done with moche reverence, grate perfection and with great cleanness. Therefore yt behoves me to do some kost upon raiment, also that I maye do that same hye offyce with reverence and cleanness in honesty as (far) as I can do y^t yt may be to (the honour of God) and to the salvacyon of my soul. And God knoweth y^t I have (great need to do) as I thynke that I shall do and therefore I beseech you to help me at that tyme so that you do not hurte yourself. For if yt (was) to your hurte suerly you myghte saye that I were an unkind son, the which you shall never fynde in me as longe as I do live.

"Also I desyre you to have me commendyd to my ij brethren and to my new suster and to all other.

So no more to you at thys tyme; but I wish you hartely (farewell, begging) you also of your dayly blessyng, and so I betake you to God who (watches over us all)."

In conclusion, I would note that obviously books such as the one I have tried to describe must have been rare, and would probably have been handed on from one generation of schoolboys to another. It is often possible to trace the descent by the names of the various owners found inscribed in the pages. Of course when William Ingram was drawing up his study book the art of printing was already well established, and we cannot expect to find many possessors subsequent to the first owner. There is, however, one name written at folio 208, and it makes us ask ourselves, "Could he have been a boy at Canterbury in his early days?" It would be interesting to know, for the name is none other than that of "Reynoldus Poulus."[1]

---

[1] It seems by no means unlikely that Cardinal Pole received his early education at the claustral school of Canterbury. His love for the Benedictine order is well known, and it was to the monastery of Polirone, near Mantua, then so gloriously restored by his friend Cortesi, that he retired to spend the happiest years of his life. The following letter, dated May 28, 1557, shows not merely the intimacy in which he had for many years lived with the Cassinese Congregation, but, what is more to the present purpose, his intention to have restored the Benedictines to Canterbury had he lived:—

Cardinal Pole to the Abbot of St. Paul's at Rome.

Very Reverend in Christ as a brother,—I received from my Henry (Penning) your Reverend Paternity's letter, and thereby learnt the diligence used by you in sending to the fathers-visitor resident in Spain the licence to come hither, as in truth I should have been very glad to see them for the purpose which induced me to ask for them. Your Paternity will perhaps have heard that the affairs of St. Peter's Monastery (Westminster Abbey) go on well, and thus, by God's grace, they still continue proceeding from good to better, and I am not indeed without hope that one of the two monasteries at my church at Canterbury may soon be restored. I am certain that I do not, and never shall, lack the constant aid of the devout orisons of your Paternity and of the whole congregation, to whose members I greatly recommend myself, and pray our Lord God ever to assist and comfort you all in His holy service, and to free you of the troubles you of necessity endure on account of these wars, by speedily granting Christendom that peace and quiet of which there is so much need in every quarter. I salute with all affection our father Dom Sylvester.

Croydon, 28th May, 1557.

—"Calendar of State Papers Venetian, vol. vi., No. 904."

IX.

THE NOTE BOOKS OF WILLIAM WORCESTER,

A FIFTEENTH CENTURY ANTIQUARY.[1]

PROBABLY to many people the idea of a "note-book" will suggest something too utterly dry and unentertaining. Visions of miscellaneous notes and statistics concerning places, peoples, and things —a very Sahara of dry-as-dust lore—rise up in the mind on the very mention of the word. I quite believe that a volume of disjointed jottings *de omnibus rebus et quibusdam aliis* is hardly the most cheerful form of reading, or calculated to rouse unbounded enthusiasm in those who have not served an apprenticeship in the art and craft of literary "cinder-sifting." For myself, I will confess to a partiality for note-books in general, and for old, time-worn, paper-stained note-books in particular. It gives me pleasure to turn over the pages of even a modern note-book—that is, of course, the note-

---

[1] Reprinted from the *Downside Review*, vol. xiii., p. 235 *seqq.*

book of one who knows what to note, and how to note it. It is possible to learn a great deal from marking different methods of work and seeing what has been of interest to others. But above all there is much pleasurable excitement to be got out of an old note-book. There is something of the nature of a "lucky bag" about it. You may thrust your hand in and bring to light very little worth the trouble, but it may come out with some item of precious information which will repay with interest the time spent in turning over its pages. If you get nothing else for your pains you will at least have got some insight into the period covered by the note-book, and into the manners and customs of the people living when the original owner made his jottings. To get this, however, out of the book requires patience and a good portion of perseverance. No scribble must be accounted too insignificant to be read, no scrap of paper too small to be regarded. It is wonderful how much a miserable little scratchy scribble may tell one; and how great a tendency precious letters and memoranda have to hide themselves away in the leaves of note-books, and sulk away there until someone has proved himself to possess patience enough to seek them.

In this brief paper on two fifteenth century note-books I hope to illustrate some of these remarks, and to prove that something of interest may be extracted from what at first sight would appear to be a rather unpromising source. Let me first of all introduce the person who, now four hundred and thirty years ago, made what are certainly rather unconnected jottings in these volumes. The name of William Worcester, or William Botoner, as he calls himself indiscriminately, is not unknown, although perhaps it deserves a wider fame than it has yet attained to. All who are acquainted with the Paston Letters will need no introduction to one who occupies so prominent a place in those delightful volumes. They will remember that Worcester, or Botoner—which you like—was the faithful friend and secretary of Sir John Fastolf. He was one of the executors of the will of this knight-Crœsus on his death in 1459, and expected, not without good reason, to have inherited some of his patron's great wealth. That he did not was not his fault, and the reason for his disappointed hopes appears in those old Paston letters clearly enough. But that, as the saying goes, is another story, which, although full of interest, has not much to do with the matter in hand.

To those who are not read in the Paston family archives William Worcester perhaps requires a few lines of formal introduction. According to Bale he was born about the year 1415, and the little that we know about his family he tells us himself. The place of his birth was Bristol, where in the early years of the fifteenth century his father had rented the house of one John Sutton, "Super-le-back," in the parish of St. James. His mother's name was

Elizabeth Botoner, and she was the daughter of Thomas and Matilda, who at the close of the fourteenth century were apparently traders in Bristol. Another Botoner, Adam,[1] the brother of Thomas, and consequently great-uncle to William Worcester, was settled at Coventry; upon his death of the plague in 1386, his only child Agnes was sent on to her relations in Bristol, and subsequently married there a man named John Randolf, whose family were related to the Tychmershes, or Tidmarshes, of Pershore, near Worcester.[2]

In 1402 Matilda Botoner, William's grandmother, died at Bristol, where William Worcester, the father, was then living. He was already married to Elizabeth old Mrs. Botoner's daughter, since she leaves her son Thomas and her son-in-law William executors of her will. From this note of time and the fact that our William was seemingly the eldest son, having as far as appears only one sister, Joan, it is not unlikely that his birth may be put rather earlier in the fifteenth century than the date usually assigned to it. Of his early education we know nothing; but Wood tells us that he spent some years at Oxford at the expense of Sir John Fastolf, and applied himself much to books; especially to

[1] This Adam and his brother William, together with their two sisters, Anne and Mary, defrayed the entire cost of the beautiful tower and spire as well as the nave and chancel of St. Michael's, Coventry, as we see it to-day.

[2] A descendant of this same family and born in the same place, is now the senior member of the monastery of St Gregory's, Downside.

astronomy, in which science he was helped by a doctor of the University, one friar John Hobby. That he really was an exceptionally good student and knew the real value of learning, the note books that have survived to our times bear ample testimony.

William Worcester did not take to the church at the end of his Oxford career, as in those days so many of the learned University men did; but as a layman went to Caistor and became the secretary and general *factotum* of Sir John Fastolf, his patron. With him he remained till the old knight died in 1459, during which time he seems to have married into a family of Norfolk. Fastolf's death was the greatest misfortune to the faithful client. It looks as if he regarded that event as an epoch in the world's story, since in one part of the diary of his journeyings, when he found himself again in Norfolk, he begins in the most odd way to note events according to time reckoned from the "*obitus Johannis Fastolf.*" For example, some event at St. Benet's Hulme is described as taking place seventeen years after his patron's death, and the foundation of the various churches of Yarmouth so many years before. Thus the church of the friars minor we learn was dedicated in the year A.D. 1200, or 259 years before Fastolf passed away at the age of seventy-nine.

His benefactor's death released Worcester from the ties which kept him in Norfolk, and the year 1460 finds him already commencing his wanderings through England, which only came to an end apparently at the very close of his life in the last decade of the fifteenth century. The two literary works by which he is chiefly known are the *Annales* or short chronicle, from the year 1324, printed by Hearne from a MS. in the College of Arms, and the *Itinerarium*, published by James Nasmith from a Corpus Christi College MS., at Cambridge, in 1778. Of the first of these works nothing need be said here; the second deserves a somewhat extended notice.

The itinerary of Worcester is in many respects the most important book of its kind that exists, so far as England goes. It is, of course, not absolutely the first account of any travels in the country; but it is certainly the first to furnish any detailed descriptions of places and buildings. The fame of another and later traveller, Leland, and the account the latter gives of his journeyings in the well-known *Itinerary*, has somewhat eclipsed the work and fame of the earlier antiquarian rambler. Yet, in some respects at least, Worcester's *Itinerary* is more valuable than that of Leland, in spite of the very exceptional advantages possessed by the latter in travelling over the country in the capacity of Henry the Eighth's "own antiquary." In the eagerness of his search after the treasures of the monastic libraries Leland frequently forgets to note details of the monastic churches and conventual buildings, for which we should now be only too grateful. The fact is that he had no eye for mere architectural beauty, and can in no sense be regarded as an architectural student. He was before all things a bookworm, and other things are subordinated to his love of antiquity as it appealed to him from the dusty shelves of the old libraries of monastery and cathedral. This was his first care, the rest came as it might; and, although, after ten years' roaming over England and Wales, he could write that there remained "almost no cape, nor bay, nor haven, creek or pier, river or confluence of rivers, breeches, washes, lakes, meres, fenny waters, mountains, valleys, moors, heaths, forests, chases, woods, cities, burghs, castles, principal manor places, monasteries and colleges, but I have seen them," still the natural features of the country through which he passed were evidently considered chiefly in relation to the store-houses of ancient manuscripts he had already explored or expected to discover. I believe that it is true to say, that in regard to architectural detail he never once makes use of a technical term in the whole of his *Itinerary*, whilst we may look in vain for any evident appreciation of the glorious churches and majestic buildings he certainly inspected. To take an example: Leland visited Glastonbury before its overthrow, and must have been conducted, probably by abbot Whiting himself, over the vast church adorned with its countless treasures, for he speaks of the crucifix before the choir. But, though he "observed six goodly windows in the top of each side of the east part of the church," and notes that abbot Bere "made a vault to the steeple, which he supported by two arches like St. Andrew's cross, else it had fallen," he yet makes no attempt to describe as a whole what must have been one of the most majestic minsters of Christendom.

William Worcester, on the other hand, half a century before, with eyes hardly less keen for literary treasures than Leland's, did not neglect to note dimensions and mark peculiarities of construction. Although not to the exclusion of other things, he was devoted to architecture, and may be said to have been the first to furnish us with a glossary of terms of the Gothic style. He was evidently in many respects an ideal traveller. Note-book in hand he went forth on his tours, always ready to pick up information from chance acquaintances upon any subject of interest. The pages of his Itinerary reveal him almost in the character of a modern interviewer, eager to put down whatever the person he has captured can tell him about places or people. To take some examples: He meets a Dominican friar, one John Burges, at Exeter, and finds that he knows a good deal about the saints of the district. Out comes the note-book, and down go the details: "*Ex informatione Fratris Johannis Burges.*" At Tavistock the information of Thomas Peperell, a notary public, extends not only to the relics to be found in the district, but apropos of Mount St. Michael's, Cornwall, to the various apparitions of the archangel he has read of. These notes are relieved by descriptions of the Cornish water-courses, about which Mr. Thomas Peperell seems inclined to brag somewhat much. Worcester, however, on this latter point is further instructed by a relation living at Fowey who also seems to know all about the Cornish saints. Other information he gets from a priest at St. Mary's Ottery "loquendo et potando"; from a ferryman, and from the keeper of a prison at Bristol, and from a workman to a "plump-maker" in the same place, from whom he had inquired about a tree growing in the streets. A Scotchman tells him all about Scotland and the Isle of Skye, so called—at least so he says—because its mountains are so high. A merchant from the Isle of Man speaks about that island, and also about Ireland, of which latter country Worcester learns more from a native he falls in with riding from Walsingham. A wayside hermit is found to have lived—at least according to his own account—for eleven years in Denmark, and so can tell our traveller a great deal about that land which he eagerly jots down in his note-book. At times—or, at any rate, once—there is perhaps a spice of sarcasm in his remarks. Coming from Norfolk, and having been a retainer of so important a man as Sir John Fastolf, he doubtless knew the Bishop of Norwich, Walter le Hart,[1] well. On one of his

---

[1] Walter le Hart was Bishop of Norwich from 1446 to 1472.

journeyings to St. Michael's Mount he rested with a relation at Fowey, and there discovered, in conversation, that this good bishop was a native of the place. Down goes a note: "Memorandum. Walter, the Bishop of Norwich, was born in this place, and he is the son of a miller, and Saint Wileon was martyred quite close to the house where the bishop was born."

Nor does Worcester neglect such sources of information about saints and others as the calendars and martyrologies of the religious houses and churches afforded him. For instance, besides giving the measurement of the church and monastic buildings at Tintern, he notes the chief obits entered in "an ancient calendar" there; at Newenham abbey, near Axminster, he takes extracts from the Martyrology, and in the church of the canons at Bodmin he finds various entries, "written in a good hand," in the general calendar prefixed to the chief antiphonarium. At St. Michael's Mount, in Cornwall, where, by the way, he had, as he says, devoutly heard mass, he discovers and copies the legendary life of St. Nectan, the eldest son of a family of four and twenty children of Brokan and Gladewysa, "all, both sons and daughters, saints, martyrs and confessors in Devon and Cornwall."

Passing through London in 1478, our antiquary finds, in the hands of a scribe whom he calls a "text wryter," an old book, which he forthwith borrows to copy some extracts from the calendar.

Another time he speaks of making excerpts from a "French book of the Chronicles of Brittain," which afterwards he gave to a lawyer of Bodmin, named Benedict, together with another paper book, written in French, called "Aristotle to Alexander." Another time he copies largely from Giraldus Cambrensis, and later on he puts into his note-book a list of all the works of Bishop Grosseteste. At Oxford, in the Merton College library, he chances upon what he calls "the most ancient book in the University," which proves to be a copy of Gildas, and from which copious extracts are made; and at the Dominican Friary at Thetford he jots down some information as to English saints which he discovers in a volume of their lives, written in a small hand in the English tongue; and, to take a last instance, he extracts from the fraternity lists of St. Benet's Hulme, in Norfolk, the names which appear to him to be of most general interest.

Of course, among the notes of a traveller like William Worcester, with such a keen eye to literary antiquities, as well as such a correct sense of important details, there are many things of more than ordinary interest. I pass over his Bristol memoranda, including the account of Cannyng—the celebrated Cannyng—and what he had done for the port of Bristol, with names of the ships he built there, as well as the very detailed notes on the great church of St. Mary, Redcliff, manifesting as they do a mastery, strange in those days, of architectural technicalities. To those interested in Somersetshire, the description of the wonders of "Wookey Hole," with its fantastic images of men, and its roof of hanging stalactites, which Worcester was shown by the light of burning "shevys of reede segge," will repay an examination; as also his account of the stream which runs out of the cavern. In this, he tells us, all the people of Wells and the neighbourhood were wont to fish at their sweet wills, and to catch "troute, colys called Miller's-thumbs, loches, flokes, pickerel, pyemis, prides like lampreys, craveys, and dewdow," whatever all these may be; and, wonderful to relate, he continues, no matter how much fish was taken out one year, the next it was always plentifully stocked. Travellers proverbially tell strange tales, or, as they might prefer to have this fact stated, gather them on their way, and Worcester has his marvel to relate about the stream flowing out of Wookey Hole, by which —at least, according to the story of the countryside—Providence plainly vindicated to the public the common right to fish. Bishop Beckington thought to stop the general fishing, and reserved whatever was taken in the stream for his own table. Forthwith—so runs the tale—the fish departed from their usual watery haunts, even the most likely pool remained deserted, and the poor greedy bishop got no "prides like lampreys," nor any favourite fry of miller's-thumbs, for the episcopal table. Two years passed in this way, and at last the bishop gave way and proclaimed the public right of fishing again, when, *ecce!* the fish at once swarmed into their stream, only too ready to make sport and furnish savoury suppers for the people of Wells and the neighbourhood. Snake stories were not invented in the days of William Worcester; but this fish story may perhaps be considered by modern sceptics as somewhat of a similar nature.

I will take but one more example of the interesting items of information to be found in this book, before passing on to Worcester's second note book, less known even than his *Itinerary*. Our traveller is speaking of the Charterhouse at Shene, and in the church there he describes what appear to be cards of various prayers and devotions which we are accustomed to see in our modern churches and chapels. I had better give the entire note on the subject. "Memorandum," it runs, "that on both walls of the nave of the church there hang some four-and-thirty *tabulæ* with various devotions and practices proper for exciting devotions for the souls of all Christians, both high and low. These tables are written in a good text hand, in bastard letters (whatever they may mean), and I have never come across," continues our antiquary, "any church of any monastery with so many or indeed even the twentieth part of the number of these *tabulæ*."

So far these chance notes have been taken from William Worcester's record of his journeys in the edition of his *Itinerarium* printed a hundred and twenty years back. I hope I have quoted sufficient to prove that these jottings contain much that is of considerable interest, and that the book deserves to be better known. In fact, William Worcester is so far forgotten that his name is not even mentioned in the last edition of the *Encyclopædia Britannica*, in which others of far less national importance find a place. It is about time that a new edition of the Itinerary should be given to the public, or, at least, included in the publications of some one of our many antiquarian societies. It is, perhaps, a more important work, from an historical point of view, than we might at first be inclined to suspect. I could mention a case in which a lawsuit about a right of way was finally determined in favour of the public through evidence furnished by Worcester's pages, and in the light of his description of a pilgrim track to a holy well and long-forgotten shrine in the neighbourhood of Bristol.

The second note book of our fifteenth century antiquary is to be found among the Cotton manuscripts in the British Museum. So far as I am aware the volume in question—Julius F. VII—has hitherto remained unnoticed, and consequently its material has been altogether unused, although Nasmith, in his preface to the print of Worcester's *Itinerary*, speaks of the book. I should hardly, perhaps, like to claim that it possesses the same general interest as the printed notes of Worcester's journeyings; but I believe that it throws considerable light upon his serious studies of classical literature, as to which no evidence—or what practically amounts to none—is forthcoming in the pages of the *Itinerary*; and, indirectly, as I hope to show, it illustrates that highly-important and much-debated subject, the renaissance of letters in England.

The volume in question is a long, narrow and stout book, with paper leaves, covered all over with writings of various sizes and degrees of excellence. It is a mere note book in every sense of the word; the papers which compose it form a heterogeneous collection of scraps, by no means all of a size, but the bulk of them inclining to the long and narrow shape, which gives its form to the volume. Amongst its leaves, as may be gathered from a direction, "To William Worcester, dwelling in Norwich," still visible, are blank sheets of old letters, used to jot down notes of matters interesting or important to remember; and, looking at the book as it exists now, one can well believe that as an old bundle of handy paper, it has done much travelling in Worcester's saddle-bags four centuries and more ago.

So much for the volume itself: its chief interest does not lie in its outward appearance, or, indeed, in the fact that it is a mere relic of an eager and well-equipped English antiquary. Although at first sight there would appear to be little order and method in the miscellaneous collection of jottings, on examination it seems that both as to matter there is a well-marked unity of subjects touched on, and as to time a definite chronological arrangement of materials. Without being in any sense an *Itinerary*, or record of travels as such, it affords evidence of Worcester's journeyings in various parts of England, and his occupations at a time which immediately followed the death of his patron, Sir John Fastolf, and almost immediately preceded the years occupied by the journeys described formally in the pages of the *Itinerarium*. Fastolf, as we have seen, died in 1459, and towards the close of that year, namely, on November 5th. Within a few months, Worcester was thrown on his own resources, and the period covered by this note-book is roughly the ten years from 1461; the published *Itinerary* would appear to relate to a time subsequent to 1470.

Whilst the notes of travels are chiefly, as we have said, descriptions of buildings and places, relieved by local colouring of legends of the saints, this manuscript note-book is entirely—or at least in the main—filled with literary jottings on both sides of its 208 folios. Perhaps the best way will be to take a rapid and general survey of its contents before pointing out wherein it would appear to be chiefly of interest and importance. The first pages of the volume manifest an intimate knowledge of the works of Virgil and Ovid. The heading of the chief chapters, or divisions, of the Georgics and the Æneid are followed by a table, extending over fourteen pages, giving the substance of the Metamorphoses of Ovid. This, it is true, is taken not from the original, but from a translation into French by "Ipien le Goways de Seyntmore, vers Troys, de l'ordre de Freres Minoures," as Worcester tells us, adding that it was a big volume of 422 folios written in double columns. His notes are made exceptionally interesting by his sketches of the illuminations which adorned the volume, and which he has here drawn in outline in a very remarkably good style, with here and there some notes indicating the colours of the original.

After this come catalogues of writers collected from the works of St. Isidore, Gennadius, Ivo of Chartres, and other ancient authorities, to which Worcester adds the names of illustrious Englishmen, collected by a "Master William Clyff." He extracts various notes upon Terence from a grammar by Querinus, called "*The flower garden*," gives a list of the works of Cicero, which he writes upon the back of a letter sent to him whilst at Norwich, and jots down a number of proverbs from an old book lent him by one John Hall, a Doctor in Theology.

Many of the notes show our patient antiquary at work in the libraries of Cambridge. From one he takes down the names of the chief English cities in Welsh; from another—Peterhouse—he copies out of a "very old psalter" the Hebrew alphabet and the proper pronunciation of the same; from Caius

College library he borrows a book to make various excerpts, literary and philosophical. In the same University city he critically examines a martyrology he was shown in the choir of the Austin Friars' church. From the evidence of its calendar he concludes that it probably belonged originally to Peterborough, and certainly to some Lincolnshire religious community. Then at other times and places he copies epitaphs and inscriptions, such as that of the poet Gower and that of St. Ethelbert, as it appeared on his tomb in the crypt of St. Augustine's, Canterbury. In 1471 the Bishop of Winchester at Esher lent him a copy of St. Thomas' works, and he enters on his notes—" The definition of the soul according to Thomas of Aquin, the Doctor of Paris, in the second book of the 'De Veritatibus Theologie.'" About the same time he writes on " The seven kinds or colours of music," as he found them described in a book of great antiquity borrowed from a Master William Bale. I will take one more item only from the mass of these notes before passing on to speak of the chief point of interest. At folio 169 begins a tract of Worcester's own composition, or to speak more strictly, compilation; he calls it " Of the various orders of Christian religions, both as to name and habit, drawn up by William Wyrcester, a native of Bristol, in the diocese of Worcester, from divers chroniclers in the City of London, with the approval of Dom Nicholaus Average, Prior of St. Leonard's, near the City of Norwich, in the County of Norfolk, about the year 1465."

I have already pointed out the interest manifested by Worcester in the classics. His knowledge of them is clearly proved by these notes. It must be borne in mind that the times were then ill-suited for such studies in England. The active period of his life fell in very turbulent days indeed, and his researches and travels had to be undertaken during the civil commotions and the wars in the struggle between "The Roses." The very period covered by this manuscript note book commenced with the rise of King Edward IV., and terminated with the death of Warwick in the battle of Barnet. London, Norwich, Bristol, and Coventry were distinctly Yorkist in their feelings, and as these were above all others the cities of William Worcester, he was, in all probability, a Yorkist at heart. We are not, however, concerned with his political opinions, and only note the strife between the Houses of York and Lancaster for the purpose of pointing out the external difficulties under which he continued to prosecute his studies and conduct his researches. But perhaps then, in England, as a writer has lately remarked about Paris during the Prussian siege and under the Commune, in the midst of war and constant danger the ordinary avocations of daily life could still be carried on by the student and scholar as if profound peace reigned in the land.

Of Cicero's works we have more than one notice in the papers of this note book. I have already referred to a list of his works which Worcester had given. In another place we have evidence that he himself had translated the *De Senectute* into English, for he notes that he presented the book in 1473 to the Bishop of Winchester, William Waynfleet, and adds, " sed nullum regardum recepi de Episcopo " —" I got nothing in return from the Bishop." Poor fellow! it was rather hard upon him after all his trouble with Cicero's Latin, but perhaps the Bishop thought *De Senectute* hardly appropriate to himself.

Perhaps the most interesting thing in the whole of the note book is an original letter regarding the books of Livy. It is written by a monk of Christ Church, Canterbury, Dom William Sellyng—a man famous, it is true, but not so famous as he deserves to be. I cannot resist translating the whole of this letter.

" The bearer of these presents," he writes, " is well known to a venerable man who is my dearest friend. He is very desirous to see the *Decades* of Titus Livius, which he has learnt from me is in your possession; and since we are united by a special bond of affection I could not refuse to write to you at his request. I consequently ask you, in your kindness to me, and your special courtesy to all, to allow him to look at your copy of Livy's *Decades*, and hope that it may be of profit to you should he wish to purchase the said work.

      Vale feliciter.

Canterbury, 15th August.   Thine,

          W. SELLYNG.

   Monk of Christ Church, Canterbury.

To the Venerable Umfrido Gentyll of Luca, at London, in the parish of St. Bartholomew named '*The Little*,' my special friend."

Is it possible that the missing books of Livy were actually existing in this England of ours in the second half of the fifteenth century?

The mention of the name of William Sellyng in connection with that of Worcester, and especially in regard to classical literature, raises a most interesting question. It has become the fashion with a certain school of writers to take for granted that, in England at least, the renaissance of letters sprang from secular humanist scholars altogether outside, if not distinctly at variance with, and antagonistic to, the religious orders, and even to the spirit of religion itself. The accounts of the revival of Greek studies may be taken as an example of this tendency. Professor Montagu Burrows, in an otherwise excellent memoir of Grocyn, published by the Oxford Historical Society, takes for granted that wherever this celebrated man acquired the rudiments of the Greek tongue, it must have been from teachers hostile to the monastic orders. "It is scarcely necessary to remark," he says, "that wherever

Grocyn was educated for college life, the mere circumstance of his obtaining a place on Wykeham's foundation determined his career as distinct from that of a member of the religious orders of the day; or to remind the reader that it was from amongst the colleges founded by those statesmen and bishops whose statutes excluded the religious orders, that the precursors of the Reformation came forth, as Wyclif and his friends, still earlier precursors, came forth before" (p. 336).

Can any good come out of Nazareth? we feel inclined to ask on reading this passage. And, indeed, Professor Burrows is so overpowered by his thesis that although he is obliged by his subject to refer to Sellyng he speaks of him merely as "the learned man who had been his (*i.e.*, Linacre's) tutor at Canterbury, Henry VII.'s ambassador." Certainly no one would gather from this that Sellyng was a *monk* of Canterbury, who subsequently was prior of his house, and that it is to this learned Benedictine of Christ Church, Canterbury, that England owes the first beginnings of the revival of Greek in the country. Dates are important things when it becomes a question of who has, or has not, the right to be considered the first in such a matter as this. Grocyn was admitted as a Winchester scholar in 1463, and was at Oxford in 1467. In 1488 he left England to study Greek in Italy; but he apparently had already some acquaintance with the language. Erasmus (Ep. ccclxiii.) says of him, "Did not Grocyn himself learn the rudiments of the Greek tongue in England? Afterwards when he visited Italy, he attended the lectures of the chief scholars of the day, but in the meantime it was an advantage to him to have learnt the rudiments from whoever were his teachers."

Now I fancy that there is some evidence to show that the revival of Greek studies came from Canterbury—from the monastery and monks of Canterbury—and that in William Sellyng, the friend of William Worcester, we have the man who was the pioneer of the movement in this extreme western world. He was born probably somewhere about 1430, and becoming a professed monk in 1448, proceeded in due course to Oxford. He has been described as "greedy for work," and the mass of papers in his handwriting which survives even to our day is the best monument to his industry and evidence of his capacity. In 1464 he obtained permission from Prior Chillenden and the chapter of his house at Canterbury to go abroad for three years to study in any university, and he proceeded with another monk to Italy, where, after having visited Venice, he settled down at Bologna, and there obtained his degree as doctor.

Thus whilst Grocyn was but beginning his career as a boy at Winchester, William Sellyng, a man of thirty-four, a trained Oxford scholar, with the highest aspirations to profit by every opportunity, was drinking at the fountain head in the cup of the new learning. The story of the revival of Greek studies reads almost like a romance. So far as the part taken by Sellyng in this renaissance is concerned, the account given in the *Encyclopædia* will be sufficient for my purpose. "Gradually," says the writer, "the contagion of the learned frenzy which created a hundred academies and literary societies in the Italian cities spread itself across the Alps. England was but very little, if at all, behind France, as without lingering over the names of Gray, Phrea, and Vitelli, by each of whom something was done towards promoting Greek study at Oxford, we will begin with Linacre's master, William Sellyng. An Oxonian and a monk of Christ Church, Canterbury, Sellyng conceived a fervent desire to partake of the intellectual banquet provided in the schools of Florence, where the great Lorenzo was then ruling the republic. About the year of Sir Thomas More's birth, 1480, he went to Italy, and attended the lectures of that prodigy of learning and talent, Angelo Politiano." Here I may remark that the writer is, of course, wrong in his dates. Sellyng went to study in Italy sixteen years before 1480, namely, in 1464. After his three years' study he seemingly returned to Canterbury, for we find him setting out for Rome on business of his monastery on October 3, 1469; this time in the company of another monk, Reynold Goldstone, also an Oxford student, who had been previously warden of Canterbury College.

In Italy Sellyng learnt to read and speak Greek, and collected Greek manuscripts, which he brought back to England; but these were unluckily burnt seventy years later, as we shall see. As Sellyng became prior of his house in 1472, the letter I have given above, written as an introduction to William Worcester, must be placed before that date, and looking at the few indications of time which are afforded us in the note book, it seems probable that Worcester visited Canterbury and obtained his letter from Sellyng between the time of his return from Italy, somewhere in 1468, and his second journey thither at the end of 1469. In view of the evident interest in classical literature taken by Worcester, it seems hardly far-fetched to suggest that his chief if not only object in visiting Canterbury was to confer with one more fitted than anyone else in England to give him every information on these matters.

There is evidence that upon his return Sellyng was occupied in establishing a school of Greek at Canterbury, and his long priorship would have enabled him to watch over his special creation. At this Canterbury school Thomas Linacre, a Derbyshire boy, was fortunate enough to have Sellyng as his master, and when in 1486 the latter was sent over to Italy as ambassador by King Henry VII., he took his former pupil Linacre with him and left him at Bologna to pursue his studies of Greek under Politiano. Here two years later he was joined by a somewhat older man who is mentioned as a *sodalis*, and who was apparently attracted to this literary paradise by the enthusiasm of Linacre. This was Grocyn, of whom we have before spoken, and who, some time between 1491 and 1500, was the first to lecture publicly at Oxford on the Greek language. In this he was followed by Linacre, from whom Sir Thomas More learnt between 1496 and 1498.

It is, of course, impossible here to pursue the subject of the revival of Greek studies beyond this mention of a few salient points. Up to the middle of the fourteenth century the knowledge of the classical Greek authors was confined to Calabria, a small corner of Southern Italy, and Petrarch and Boccacio were the first to understand and be influenced by the educating power of the classics of ancient Greece. Whilst the first made but little progress himself in the tongue, the second not only obtained a stipend for a Greek professor in the schools of Florence in 1360, but from his explanations prepared a literal translation of Homer's Iliad and Odyssey. It was not, however, till forty years later that, at the beginning of the 15th century, "a new and perpetual flame," as Gibbon calls it, was enkindled in Italy. The gradual decay of the Imperial rule on the shores of the Bosphorus, and the ever-encroaching power of the Turks, forced the emperors to look to the Christian nations of the West for aid in their necessities. Three emperors in succession made a pilgrimage from Constantinople to the courts of the Western world to petition for assistance against the infidel, and although small success attended their efforts to save the imperial city, it is in these journeys in Europe that the historian sees the instrument destined to bring about the renaissance of letters. "The travels of the three emperors," writes Gibbon, "were unavailing for their temporal, or perhaps their spiritual, salvation, but they were productive of a beneficial consequence, the revival of the Greek learning in Italy, from whence it was propagated to the last nations of the West and North."

May we not perhaps add that what is true of Italy is perhaps true also of other nations. Manuel, the second pilgrim emperor, the son and successor of Palæologus, was not contented to rest his hopes of assistance on Italian influence merely. He crossed the Alps, and after a lengthened stay in Paris determined to cross over to England. In December, 1400, he landed at Dover, and was entertained, together with his imperial retinue of Greeks, in the monastery at Canterbury. Is it by chance that here at Canterbury, and among the monks of Canterbury, some half century later, we find the first glimmering of the dawning light of a revival of Grecian studies? Striking events, such as the presence of the Emperor of Constantinople and his suite in the monastery, would long be remembered and discussed at Canterbury, and it is perhaps hardly too much to fancy that the tradition of this imperial visit may have fired the eager mind of the young monk, William Sellyng, with a desire to learn the language, and dive deep into the literature of the East.

To return to our note book, from which the mention of William Sellyng's letter has taken us somewhat far away: The fact of Worcester's connection with the monk of Canterbury, and the evidence afforded by his notes that he was greatly interested in classical literature, confirms the belief that among the monks at Canterbury we must look for the first beginnings of the new learning in England. As to Greek in particular, one item among the notes of William Worcester casts some light upon Sellyng's connection with the revival of a study of that language. It is a very slight indication, but in this matter all indications are only of the very slightest kind. I should date the entry about the time of the letter from Sellyng: that is, somewhere about the year 1468 or 1469. The notes are, as Worcester says, "about certain terminations in Greek grammar explained (*declaratis*) by Doctor Sellyng, of Christ Church, Canterbury." Thus once more we are brought back by the evidence of Worcester's note book to Canterbury and to the monk Sellyng teaching Greek grammar. With this we may take leave of the note books of our fifteenth century antiquary.

But it will be well to add a few more words on

the interesting subject of the revival of learning in England. It has been mentioned that Sellyng brought back Greek manuscripts from Italy; and not Greek manuscripts merely, for Leland tells us that he also returned with a copy of Cicero's *De Republica*, afterwards a long-lost work which was, at length, discovered in a palimpsest of the Ambrosiana, by Cardinal Mai, and edited by Niebuhr. From the suggestion, coming from a collector like Sellyng, that Worcester might be willing to purchase of Gentyll his copy of Livy, makes it appear not improbable that a manuscript was also to be found at Canterbury.

There was a moment in the reign of Henry VIII. when it appeared not impossible that English scholars might, north of the Alps, lead the van in the restoration of the new learning. The attention of Germany had been drawn off by Luther into quite other paths. As we see from indications among the great churchmen Warham and Fisher and Stokesley and Colet, there were Englishmen fully alive to the opportunities of the movement. King Henry, too, was within an ace of gathering into our libraries those treasures of Greek manuscript which Francis I. secured and placed at Fontainebleau. But already the great measure of the "divorce" clouded over every hope in that direction. The chief concern of scholars according to Henry's own heart was to discover passages of the Greek Fathers which would help to support the royal arguments in favour of the divorce from Catherine.

The new spirit which gained the upper hand is fitly expressed in Layton's description of the fire at Canterbury, which consumed the treasures so carefully brought together by Prior Sellyng, including the precious Cicero, *De Republica*. Although it has often been in print it deserves repetition here in a new connection. "This Saturday, at night, I came to Canterbury, to Christ Church," he writes. "At one of the clock after midnight, one of my servants called me up suddenly, or else I had been burnt in my bed. The great dining chamber called the king's lodging, where we supped, &c., was suddenly fired by some fire-brand or snuff of some candle, that first set the rushes on fire. My servants lying nigh the said lodging were almost choked in their beds, and so called me. And anon, after I found a back door out, called up the house and sent into the town for help, and before ladders and water could be got that great lodging was past recovery, and so was the chamber where I lay . . . . As soon as I had set men to squench and to labour, I went into the church and there tarried continually, and set four monks with bandogs to keep the shrine, and put the sexton in the re-vestry, there to keep the jewels, and walked continually in the church above, and set monks in every quarter of the church with candles, and sent for the Abbot of Saint Augustine's to be there with me in readiness to have taken down the shrine, and to have sent all the jewels into St. Augustine's."[1]

Fortunately, Leland has preserved some other details of the destruction wrought at this fire, in which perished Prior Sellyng's manuscripts. From the time the great "divorce" question began to engross men's minds, however, the hopes of learning in England were over, and Sir Thomas Pope, in refounding Durham College, under the name of Trinity, emphasises the need of special attention to the study of Greek, which, he says, has greatly fallen since his young days.[2] In fact, from the time of the change of religion in this country all energies were devoted to polemics until the day when Casaubon came hither and found his disappointment, and until Laud, profiting by the destruction wrought by Gustavus Adolphus, in the "Thirty-years War," opened out a new prospect for English scholarship.

The whole question of the revival of Greek

---

[1] *Calendar of Papers, Henry VIII.*, ix., No. 669.

[2] He submitted the statutes of his proposed college to Cardinal Pole for revision, and received some valuable suggestions about the studies. In a letter to the first President of the College he says: "My Lord Cardinal's grace has had the overseeing of my statutes. He much lykes well that I have therein ordered the Latin tonge to be redde to my schollars. But he advyses me to order the Greeke to be more taught there than I have provyded. This purpose I well lyke; but I fear the tymes will not bear it now. I remember when I was a yong schollar at Eton, the Greeke tongue was growing apace; the studie of which is now alate much decaid." (A. Chalmers, *History of the Colleges, &c., of Oxford*, ii., p. 351.)

studies in England, though much laboured at, seems to have been greatly obscured. A recent and careful writer, speaking about More's education at Oxford, states that we are " unfortunately unable to ascertain at what college he was educated."[1] The writer seems not to know the testimony of Cresacre More, namely, that on going to Oxford the future Chancellor went to Canterbury College. This is just what we should have expected; for what is more likely than that Cardinal Morton should have sent his *protégé* to the house which was specially under his patronage, and which was directly under the rule of Prior Sellyng? In no circumstance could the young aspirant after learning be brought into closer contact with the new humanism than at Christ Church, Canterbury, and Canterbury College, Oxford.

The monasteries have been labelled as corrupt, and, as a necessary consequence, the monks as ignorant and indifferent to learning.[2] It is time to look facts in the face, and it seems a pity that writers who have dealt with the question of the revival of letters should so frequently content them-

[1] J. H. Lupton, *The Utopia of Sir Thomas More*, p. xix.

[2] I may here, perhaps, recall the fact that Erasmus submitted his translation of the sacred Scriptures from the Greek, to Abbot Bere, of Glastonbury, whose opinion he acknowledged as most weighty in these matters. (Ep. lib. xviii., 46; Warner, *Glastonbury*, p. 213). From Leonard Cox's *The Art or Craft of Rhetoric*, which was printed at Reading, it may be gathered that Cox had been a *protégé* of Abbot Cook, who had bestowed much care in advancing the interest of promising youths, and that Greek was taught as well as Latin in " your grammar scholl,

selves with deductions from pre-conceived notions, rather than labour at the sorting out of the evidence which exists, to see what story it tells. The mere clue to be gleaned from William of Worcester's note book shows how much there is to be done in this direction.

founded by your antecessours in your towne of Redynge." It may be worth while to mention that in the years 1499 and 1500 a Greek, one John Serbopoulos, of Constantinople, was copying Greek MSS. in Reading. Two of these thick folios written on vellum now form MSS. 23 and 24 in the library of Corpus Christi College, Oxford. They were among Grocyn's books, and came to the College through the instrumentality of John Claymond, who was known and patronised by Abbot Bere, of Glastonbury, and himself a collector of Greek manuscripts.

X.

HAMPSHIRE RECUSANTS IN THE TIME OF QUEEN ELIZABETH.[1]

WHEN Elizabeth succeeded to the crown in 1558, many problems of practical import at once presented themselves for solution. Not the least in importance was the great religious question, which, during the previous five-and-twenty years, had exercised the mind of the nation by the frequent and violent changes of policy of successive sovereigns and their advisers. The queen herself, now in her twenty-fifth year, was in reality the creature of strife, and had been cradled amid the turmoil of the religious dissensions in England, which had their beginning, if not their origin, in the circumstances attending her birth. In her earliest recollection, practically, although not of course theoretically, England had ceased to be one in matters of religion, and the experiences of the quarter of a century during which she had lived before she was herself

[1] A paper read at the Petersfield Literary and Debating Societ

called upon to grasp the reins of power must have taught her how deep and bitter were the feelings engendered by theological dissensions. Her own personal religious opinions are somewhat difficult to fathom; but probably the popular historian of the English people, Mr. J. R. Green, is not far wrong in saying of her: "No woman ever lived who was so totally destitute of the sentiment of religion."[1] Theology was to her apparently but a branch of statecraft, and differences of creed were to be regarded, at least by the ruler, "in a purely political light."

It is, of course, not my purpose in any way to discuss the Elizabethan policy from a religious point of view. For the purposes of this paper I am quite prepared to assume that in her attempt to coerce the nation into following her lead, she had ample justification in the circumstances of the time, and ample precedents in the example of her immediate predecessors. Circumstances, which are too well known to need mention here, determined her to make choice of the Protestant, or Reforming party, upon which to build up the system which Mr. Gladstone has well called "the Elizabethan Settlement of Religion." And to do Elizabeth justice, it could hardly have entered her mind to suppose that the English people, or any considerable section of them, would finally question the royal right to settle

---

[1] *Short History*, p. 369.

the legal basis of the national creed. The Tudor principle *cujus regio ejus religio*, which may be Englished, " he who rules a nation determines its creed," had practically been acquiesced in, or at least acted upon, in the various religious changes England had seen in the quarter of a century which had intervened between Henry the Eighth's rejection of Roman Supremacy and the accession of Elizabeth. We who live in these days of religious liberty, and of a recognised diversity of religious opinion, can with difficulty appreciate the attitude of mind in which men in the middle of the sixteenth century must have regarded the possibility of national divisions and differences in matters of religion. Such a state of things must have appeared to them a peril to the ship of State not to be admitted on any principle of government, and strenuously to be resisted by the strong arm of the law.

The notion of being able " to agree to differ " in matters which touched the conscience, and yet of being united in other matters of national, foreign and domestic policy, had yet to be born of experience in the course of the coming centuries. Whatever we may think about the measures subsequently adopted by Elizabeth to coerce the consciences of her subjects, or at least to secure the external observance of those who remained attached to the older forms of religion, we should in fairness recognise this side of the burning question, and understand that the fundamental idea of unity in religion was still the dominant belief of the nation when Elizabeth came to the throne. The Queen's personal motives, her individual preferences, are of no present concern to us. I have already given Mr. Green's opinion (and I need not say he is not biassed in favour of the Catholic side) that with her it was a matter not of religion but of State; and that is as deep as we need here go into the question.

I am of course aware that there was an attempt made by the Queen's all-powerful minister, Lord Burleigh, to claim for the recusant laws the higher sanction of duty—a duty which made it incumbent on those who held the reins of power to extirpate the erroneous doctrine of the Sacrifice of the Mass from the hearts of the people. "It is not to be doubted," he writes, " but the usage of the present Popish Mass, wherein the use of the Sacrament is turned into a sacrifice for sins, and intercession is made to saints with other things derogatory to the first institution of Christ, is to be rooted out of the church as a great evil."[1]

As far as my present purpose, however, is concerned, any one who pleases may consider that in all Queen Elizabeth did to secure uniformity of religion she was actuated by high and holy motives; nay, more, that the measures she adopted to secure her settlement of the religious difficulties, although

---

[1] State Papers Dom. Eliz. (undated) 1590. No. 445 D. The paper was copied before the documents were arranged in volumes, and it is now impossible to say where it has been placed.

perchance to our more humane and tender hearts somewhat harsh and excessive, were justified by the circumstances of the time. I have no wish to disturb any conviction of this nature; for all I propose to do is to examine historically into the operation of the religious laws passed in the reign of Elizabeth, and to illustrate their action in regard to Hampshire in general, and to the neighbourhood of Petersfield in particular.

I do not think such an examination as I propose to make in any way unnecessary. To many people the very notion of coercion by the State, in matters of religion, is at the present day highly repugnant. What is unpleasant or distasteful is naturally ignored and passed over, if not designedly hidden away, till we are in danger of forgetting its very existence. I gather from several recent books that this is the case in regard to this portion of our national history; and more than once lately have I been gravely informed by people, who might have been supposed to know better, that Queen Mary Tudor was the only English sovereign who disgraced the annals of English history by interference between man and his conscience. Now, while I to a certain degree sympathise with the old lady of the story, who steadily refused to read any history of the past, on the high moral principle "that bygones should be bygones," I do not think it possible to form any right estimate of the latter half of the sixteenth century and even of the seventeenth and eighteenth centuries, without submitting the religious laws in force during that period to some examination. Let me take one example of what I mean. Most people have probably seen, or at any rate heard of, a work on *Social England*, which is being published by the well known firm of Messrs. Cassell. It purports to be an attempt to do for the general history of England what the introductory chapter of Macaulay's *History* did for the Stuart period. Such a book could only have been produced by the collaboration of many writers, and on the whole the result is excellent. There are, however, to my mind serious defects in the third volume, which deals with what is known as the Reformation period. I do not desire to be too sweeping in my condemnation, for I was myself a contributor to a small portion of the volume, but the book serves to illustrate the danger of leaving out unpleasant portions of our history. When I knew that I should have the pleasure of reading this paper I thought I would have a look to see what new lights the writer on the Elizabethan religious history in this volume had to give me about "*Recusants.*" Knowing that the author was a Fellow of one of the Oxford colleges and I believe also an examiner in the Modern History schools, I expected to get some information, and perhaps even to be able to ask you to accept his account of the religious legislation and its effects during this period as likely possibly to be more satisfactory to you than any I might give. I am sorry to say that at the outset my hopes were disappointed. The index of the volume does not so much as contain the word *recusant* or anything of a kindred nature, and the word penal law is equally conspicuous by its absence. I do not profess to have read every word of the book itself; but I have certainly read sufficient to be able to say with confidence that the subject of " recusancy " is not merely inadequately treated, but is barely touched upon at all in the otherwise full account of Elizabeth's reign. How a fair idea of the social condition of England at this time can possibly be obtained without a proper treatment of this subject I do not profess to be able to understand, and I hope before I have finished my paper you may be induced to agree with me.

Before passing to speak of matters of special local interest in connection with the subject of the recusant laws, it is necessary that I should recall briefly a few facts as to the general history of our country immediately subsequent to the accession of Elizabeth, and place before you some account of the laws as to religion by which, as I have said, the Queen sought to vindicate the right, claimed by the later Tudor monarchs, to give the form of religion to the country over which they ruled. It is necessary to describe these laws at some considerable length, since, as I have just pointed out, there is a real danger of their very existence being ignored.

I am not going to ask you to take my account

of this history, or of the measures to secure a uniformity in religion, known as the penal laws; the first we may conveniently take from Green's *History of the English People;* the second from Hallam's standard work, *The Constitutional History of England.* Neither author can be accused of having any bias towards the Catholic side; and for this reason, and because their works are easily within the reach of all, I have selected them. My part will be confined chiefly to an endeavour to illustrate the incidence of the laws against Recusants by reference to persons and places in this neighbourhood of Petersfield.

I may perhaps premise one word as to the meaning of the word *Recusant*. It does not mean, as is so often supposed, and not infrequently stated, one who had refused the oath of allegiance to the sovereign; or even the oath of supremacy. A *recusant* was simply one who refused to be present at the public services in the parish churches. This is the only meaning which the word has in the official documents of the period. Let us now, under the guidance of Mr. J. R. Green, take a glimpse at the general history of the times when Elizabeth came to the throne.

"The first interest in Elizabeth's mind," writes this historian, "was the interest of public order, and she never could understand how it could fail to be first in everyone's mind. Her ingenuity set itself to construct a system in which ecclesiastical unity should not jar against the rights of conscience; a compromise which merely required outer 'conformity' to the established worship, while, as she was never weary of repeating, it 'left opinion free.' . . . The first work of her Parliament was to undo the work of Mary, to repeal the Statutes of Heresy, to dissolve the refounded monasteries, and to restore the Royal Supremacy. . . . Further she had no personal wish to go. A third of the Council and two-thirds of the people were as opposed to any radical changes in religion as the Queen. Among the gentry the older and wealthier were on the conservative side, and only the younger and meaner on the other. But it was soon necessary to go further. If the Protestants were the less numerous, they were the abler and the more vigorous party, and the exiles who returned from Geneva brought with them a fierce hatred of Catholicism."

"The whole machinery of public religion had been thrown out of gear by the rapid and radical changes of the past two reigns. In some dioceses a third of the parishes were without clergymen. The churches themselves were falling into ruin. The majority of the parish priests were still Catholic at heart; in the north, indeed, they made little disguise of their reactionary tendencies.[1] On the

---

[1] There is a very general idea that, with the exception of a very small number, the entire body of the English clergy took the required oath of supremacy on the accession of Queen Elizabeth. This idea is

other hand, the Protestant minority among the clergy were already disgusting the people by their violence and greed. Chapters had begun to plunder their own estates by leases and fines, and by felling timber. The marriages of the clergy

based upon an entire misconception of the facts. Mr. R Simpson (*Life of Edmund Campion*, p. 196-7, new ed.) has put these most clearly. Before the end of 1559 all the Bishops had been deprived of their Sees. On May 23, 1559, a royal commission, partly lay, partly clerical, was appointed to tender the oath to the clergy generally. They were directed to proceed with caution, but in October it was found that they had been too zealous, and several laymen were appointed to supersede the clerical members. But even then the inquisition had such serious effects, that in December the Queen had to write to the commissioners to suspend their proceedings. The general result of the proceedings was, that of the multitude of clergymen who refused to subscribe only a few were at once deprived, some had three years given for consideration, and others seem to have been connived at. The province of York was visited in August and September, 1559, with the following result: out of 90 clergymen summoned, 21 came and took the required oath, 36 came and refused to swear, 17 were absent without proctors, 16 were absent with proctors. In the province of Canterbury, the dean and canons of Winchester Cathedral, the warden and fellows of the College, and the master of St. Cross, all refused the oath. The visitors for the whole province returned 49 recusants and 786 conformists, significantly omitting the absentees. Out of 8,911 parishes and 9,400 beneficed clergymen, only 806 took the oath, whilst all the bishops and 85 others expressly refused to subscribe, and the rest absented themselves. The assertion of Camden that only 189 clergymen were deprived in this visitation proves nothing, even if it were true. At the end of *State Papers, Domestic Elizabeth*, vol. x., is an abstract of the number of rectors, vicars and curates who refused to attend when summoned in the four dioceses of York, Chester, Durham, and Carlisle. The total is 314. There is no abstract of the number who attended but refused to take the oath, but the book proves that in this province 370 clergymen refused to swear, or would have refused had they been pressed. Probably the real number, had we the means of knowing, would be found to be double that figure.

were a perpetual scandal—a scandal which was increased when the gorgeous vestments of the old worship were cut up into gowns and bodices for the priests' wives. The new services became scenes of utter disorder, where the clergy wore what dress they pleased, and the communicant stood or sat as he liked; while the old altars were broken down and the communion table was often a bare board upon trestles. The people, naturally enough, were found to be 'utterly devoid of religion,' and came to church 'as to a May game'" (p. 371). "The Marian bishops, with a single exception, discerned the Protestant drift of the Queen's changes, and bore imprisonment and deprivation rather than accept them" (p. 370). Under Archbishop Parker "The vacant sees were filled for the most part with learned and able men; the plunder of the Church by the nobles was checked, and England was settling quietly down again in religious peace, when a prohibition from Rome forbade the presence of Catholics at the new worship. The order was widely obeyed, and the obedience was accepted by Elizabeth as a direct act of defiance. Heavy 'fines for recusancy,' levied on all who absented themselves from church, became a constant source of supply to the Royal Exchequer."

So much for Green's account of the general history. I pass on now to give, from Hallam's *Constitutional History of England*, some account of the laws by which Elizabeth and her advisers hoped to secure general adherence to her "settlement of religion" in England. The Parliament which met about two months after Elizabeth's succession re-established the Anglican Liturgy, and restored the royal supremacy, as we have seen. "These two statutes, commonly denominated the Acts of Supremacy and Uniformity," writes the historian, "form the basis of that restrictive code of laws, deemed by some one of the fundamental bulwarks, by others the reproach of our constitution, which pressed so heavily for more than two centuries upon the adherents to the Romish Church. By the former all beneficed ecclesiastics, and all laymen holding office under the crown, were obliged to take the oath of supremacy, renouncing the spiritual as well as temporal jurisdiction of every foreign prince or prelate, on pain of forfeiting their office or benefice; and it was rendered highly penal, and for the third offence treasonable, to maintain such supremacy by writing or advised speaking. The latter statute trenched more on the natural rights of conscience; prohibiting, under pain of forfeiting goods and chattels for the first offence, of a year's imprisonment for the second, and of imprisonment during life for the third, the use by a minister, whether beneficed or not, of any but the established Liturgy; and imposed a fine of one shilling on all who should absent themselves from church on Sundays and holidays."

"This Act," continues Hallam, "operated as an

absolute interdiction of the Catholic rites, however privately celebrated. It has frequently been asserted that the Government connived at the domestic exercise of that religion during these first years of Elizabeth's reign. This may possibly have been the case with respect to some persons of very high rank, whom it was inexpedient to irritate. But we find instances of severity towards Catholics, even in that early period; and it is evident that their solemn rites were only performed by stealth, and at much hazard. Thus Sir Edward Waldegrave and his lady were sent to the Tower in 1561, for hearing Mass and having a priest in their house. Many others about the same time were punished for a like offence. Two bishops, one of whom, I regret to say, was Grindal, write to the Council in 1562, concerning a priest apprehended in a lady's house, that neither he nor the servants would be sworn to answer to articles, saying they would not accuse themselves; and after a wise remark on this, that 'papistry is like to end in anabaptistry,' proceed to hint that 'some think that if this priest might be put to some kind of torment and so driven to confess what he knoweth, he might gain the Queen's Majesty a good mass of money by the masses that he hath said; but we refer to your lordships' wisdom.' This commencement of persecution induced many Catholics to fly beyond the sea, and gave rise to those re-unions of disaffected exiles, which never ceased to endanger the throne of Elizabeth.

"It cannot, as far as appears, be truly alleged that any greater provocation had as yet been given by the Catholics than that of pertinaciously continuing to believe and worship as their fathers had done before. I request [adds Hallam] those who may hesitate about this, to pay some attention to the order of time before they form their opinions."

I here interrupt Hallam's account of the penal laws to briefly corroborate what he tells us as to the early dates at which the celebration of Catholic rites was prevented by the strong measure of imprisonment. The Sir Edward Waldegrave he mentions as having been sent to the Tower in 1561 had been previously confined in the same prison during the reign of Edward VI. for refusing to force the Protestant service upon Queen Mary. The notice given of this imprisonment in the valuable contemporary diary of a resident in London, known as *Machyn's Diary* (p. 256), is "The xxii. day of Aprell was had to the Towre ser Edward Walgraff and my lade his wyff, as good almes-foke as be in thes day, and odur caried thethur." The cause of this imprisonment is given in many State papers, and also by Machyn when, on September 1 of the same year, 1561, he records the death of "the good and gentle knight whyle in the Towre, the whyche he was put for herrying of masse and kepyng a prest in ys howse that dyd say masse." In this and the following year, 1562, according to an official paper now preserved among the Harleian MSS. at the British Museum,[1] there were some sixteen or seventeen ladies and gentlemen prisoners in the Fleet prison for " matters of religion," and in almost every case it is stated that the offence was " for hearing mass." In the Marshalsea there was a gentleman and a priest, in the King's Bench a gentleman and two priests,[2] whilst in the Tower, besides Sir Edward and Lady Waldegrave, there was a goodly company, including Sir Thomas and Lady Wharton, and their priest, William Joly. " Their faults be well in remembrance " is noted against them as bracketed together with the Waldegraves and others; and we are not left in any doubt what those faults were, as they all appear in another paper, dated June 3, 1561, and endorsed " prisoners for mass." This last paper, annotated in the writing of Cecil himself, contains some forty names of persons—gentry and priests, who were indicted at the general assizes at Brentwood, in Essex, for offences against the religious laws.[3] But all this, as Mr. Rudyard Kipling is so fond of saying, " is another story," and I return to the guidance of Mr. Hallam.

" I have not found," he writes, " that Pius IV., more moderate than most other Pontiffs of the sixteenth century, took any measures hostile to the temporal government of this realm; but the de-

---
[1] Harl. MS., 360 f. 34.
[2] State Papers, Dom. Eliz., vol. xvi., No. 65, No. 35; vol. xvii., No. 13.
[3] Ibid., vol. xvii., No. 18.

prived ecclesiastics were not unfairly anxious to keep alive the faith of their former hearers; and to prevent them from sliding into conformity through indifference and disuse of their ancient rites (p. 115), questions of conscience were circulated, with answers all tending to show the unlawfulness of conformity. There was nothing more in this than the Catholic clergy were bound in consistency with their principle to do, though it seemed very atrocious to bigots. . . . Partly through political circumstances, but far more from the hard usage they experienced for professing their religion, there seems to have been an increased restlessness among the Catholics about 1562, which was met with new rigour by the Parliament of that year."

"The Act entitled 'for the assurance of the Queen's royal power over all estates and subjects within her dominions' enacts with an iniquitous and sanguinary retrospect, that all persons who had ever taken holy orders, or any degree in the universities, or had been admitted to the practice of the laws, or held any office in their execution, should be bound to take the oath of supremacy, when tendered to them by a bishop, or by commissioners appointed under the great seal. The penalty for the first refusal of this oath was that of a præmunire, but any person who, after the space of three months from the first tender, should again refuse it when in like manner tendered, incurred the pains of high treason. The oath of supremacy was imposed by statute on every member of the House of Commons, but could not be tendered to a peer, the Queen declaring her full confidence in those hereditary councillors. Several peers of great weight and dignity were still Catholics " (p. 116).

"I am never very willing," continues our authority " to admit as an apology for unjust or cruel enactments, that they are not designed to be generally executed; a pretext often insidious, always insecure, and tending to mask the approaches of arbitrary government. But it is certain that Elizabeth did not wish this act to be enforced in its full severity." (p. 117.)

In reply to the application of the Emperor Ferdinand that Catholics might be reasonably allowed the use of one church in each city, the Queen declared that she could "not grant churches to those who disagree from her religion, being against the laws of her Parliament, and highly dangerous to the state of her kingdom, as it would sow various opinions in the nation to distract the minds of honest men, and would cherish parties and factions that might disturb the present tranquillity of the commonwealth" (p. 120).

" Camden and many others have asserted that by systematic connivance the Roman Catholics enjoyed a pretty free use of their religion for the first fourteen years of Elizabeth's reign. We find abundance of persons harassed for recusancy, that is, for not attending the Protestant Church, and driven to insincere promises of conformity. Others were dragged before ecclesiastical commissioners for harbouring priests, or for sending money to those who had fled beyond sea. Students of the inns of court, where popery had a strong hold at this time, were examined in the star-chamber as to their religion, and on not giving satisfactory answers were committed to the Fleet. The Catholic party were not always scrupulous about the usual artifices of an oppressed people, meeting force by fraud and concealing their heart-felt wishes under the mask of ready submission, or even of zealous attachment. A great majority both of clergy and laity yielded to the times; and of these temporising conformists it cannot be doubted that many lost by degrees all thought of returning to the ancient fold. But others, while they complied with exterior ceremonies, retained in their private devotions their accustomed mode of worship. It is an admitted fact that the Catholics generally attended the Church, till it came to be reckoned a distinctive sign of their having renounced their own religion. They persuaded themselves (and the English priests, uninstructed and accustomed to a temporising conduct, did not discourage the notion) that the private observance of their own rites would excuse a formal obedience to the civil power" (p. 120). "There is nothing . . . which serves to countenance the very unfair misrepresentations lately (*i.e.*, 1845) given, as if the Roman Catholics generally had acquiesced in the

Anglican worship, believing it to be substantially the same as their own. They frequented our churches, because the law compelled them by penalties so to do, not out of a notion that very little change had been made by the Reformation. It is true of course that many became real Protestants, by habitual attendance on our rites and by disuse of their own. But these were not the recusants of a later period" (p. 121, note).

"The Romish scheme of worship, though it attaches more importance to ceremonial rites, has one remarkable difference from the Protestant, that is far less social; and consequently the prevention of its open exercise has far less tendency to weaken men's religious associations so long as their individual intercourse with a priest, its essential requisite, can be preserved. Priests therefore travelled the country in various disguises, to keep alive a flame which the practice of outward conformity was calculated to extinguish. There was not a county throughout England, says a Catholic historian, where several of Mary's clergy did not reside, commonly called the old priests. They served as chaplains in private families. By stealth, at the dead of night, in private chambers, in the secret lurking-places of an ill-peopled country, with all the mystery that subdues the imagination, with all the mutual trust that invigorates constancy, these proscribed ecclesiastics celebrated their solemn rites, more impressive in such concealment than if surrounded by all their former splendour. . . .

"It is my thorough conviction that the persecution, for it can obtain no better name, carried on against the English Catholics, however it might serve to delude the Government by producing an apparent conformity, could not but excite a spirit of disloyalty in many adherents to that faith" (p. 122).

As a consequence of the northern insurrection of 1570, and the celebrated Bull of Pope Pius V., new and more stringent laws were passed against the Catholics by the Parliament in 1571 (13 Eliz. c. 2). This enacted "that all persons publishing any bull from Rome, or absolving and reconciling any one to the Romish Church, or being so reconciled, should incur the penalties of high treason; and such as brought into the realm any crosses, pictures, or superstitious things consecrated by the Pope or under his authority, should be liable to præmunire. Those who should conceal or connive at the offenders were to be held guilty of misprision of treason. This statute exposed the Catholic priesthood, and in a great measure the laity, to the continual risk of martyrdom; for so many had fallen away from their faith through a pliant spirit of conformity with the times, that the regular discipline would exact their absolution and reconciliation before they could be reinstated in the Church's communion" (p. 138). . . "We cannot wonder to read that these new statutes increased the dissatisfaction of the Roman Catholics, who perceived a systematic determination to extirpate their religion. . . Many retired to foreign countries, and, receiving for their maintenance pensions from the Court of Spain, became unhappy instruments of its ambitious enterprises. Those who remained at home could hardly think their oppression much mitigated by the precarious indulgences which Elizabeth's caprice, or rather the fluctuation of different parties in her councils, sometimes extended to them" (p. 140).

"This indulgence, however, shown by Elizabeth, the topic of reproach in those times, and sometimes of boast in our own, never extended to any positive toleration, nor even to any general connivance at the Romish worship in its most private exercise. She published a declaration in 1570, that she did not intend to sift men's consciences, provided they observed her laws by coming to church, which, as she well knew, the strict Catholics deemed inconsistent with their integrity. Nor did the Government always abstain from an inquisition into men's private thoughts. The inns of court were more than once purified of popery by examining their members on articles of faith. Gentlemen of good families in the country were harassed in the same manner" (p. 140).

"It will not surprise those who have observed the effect of all persecution for matters of opinion upon the human mind, that during this period the Romish party continued such in numbers and in zeal as to give the most lively alarm to Elizabeth's administration. One cause of this was, beyond doubt, the connivance of justices of the peace, a great many of whom were secretly attached to the same interest, though it was not easy to exclude them from the commission, on account of their wealth and respectability. The facility with which Catholic rites can be performed in secret, as before observed, was a still more important circumstance."

In this way another ten years of Elizabeth's reign passed away. The Parliament which met in 1581 was "discontented with the severities used against the Puritans, but ready to go beyond any measures that the court might propose to subdue and extirpate popery. Here an Act was passed, which, after repeating the former provision that had made it high treason to reconcile any of her Majesty's subjects, or to be reconciled, to the Church of Rome, imposes a penalty of £20 a month on all persons absenting themselves from church, unless they shall hear the English service at home. Such as could not pay the same within three months after judgment, were to be imprisoned until they should conform. The Queen, by a subsequent Act, had the power of seizing two-thirds of the party's land and all his goods for default of payment. These grievous penalties on recusancy, as the wilful absence of Catholics from church came now to be denominated, were doubtless founded on the extreme difficulty of proving an actual celebration of their own rites. But they established a persecution which fell not at all short in principle of that for which the inquisition had become so odious. Nor were the statutes merely designed for terror's sake—to keep a check over the disaffected, as some would pretend. They were executed in the most sweeping and indiscriminating manner, unless perhaps a few families of high rank might enjoy a connivance" (p. 145).

"The public executions, numerous as they were, scarcely form the most odious part of this persecution. The common law of England has always abhorred the accursed mysteries of a prison-house, and neither admits of torture to extort confession, nor of any penal infliction not warranted by a judicial sentence. But this law, though still sacred in the courts of justice, was set aside by the Privy Council under the Tudor line. The rack seldom stood idle in the Tower, for all the latter part of Elizabeth's reign" (p. 148). "Such excessive severities, under the pretext of treason, but sustained by very little evidence of any other offence than the exercise of the Catholic ministry, excited indignation throughout a great part of Europe" (*Ibid.*).

"In 1584 a law was enacted, enjoining all Jesuits, seminary priests and other priests, whether ordained within or without the kingdom, to depart from it within forty days, on pain of being adjudged traitors. The penalty of fine and imprisonment at the Queen's pleasure was inflicted on such as, knowing any priest to be within the realm, should not discover it to a magistrate. This seemed to fill up the measure of persecution, and to render the longer preservation of this obnoxious religion absolutely impracticable" (p. 153).

After testifying to the loyalty with which Catholics in every part of England united with their fellow-countrymen in preparing to resist the Spanish Armada (p. 62), the historian Hallam continues: "It would have been a sign of gratitude if the laws depriving them of the free exercise of their religion had been, if not repealed, yet suffered to sleep, after these proofs of loyalty. But the execution of priests and of other Catholics became, on the contrary, more frequent, and the fines for recusancy were exacted as rigorously as before. A statute was enacted, restraining Popish recusants—a distinctive name now first imposed by law—to particular places of residence, and subjecting them to other vexatious provisions. All persons were forbidden by proclamation to harbour any of whose conformity they were not assured" (p. 163).

With this I will finish my quotations from the pages of Hallam's *History*, only remarking, as an apology for their length, that there are many other passages which deserve to be cited, which I hope you may be induced to read for yourselves. I now pass on to illustrate the incidence of the recusancy laws in Hampshire, and especially in this neighbourhood of Petersfield.

The most important sources of information upon

this subject (and sources which have hitherto been little regarded), are the *Recusant Rolls* in the Public Record Office. Unfortunately these systematic accounts of fines levied upon those who refused to attend the service in their parish churches, and of the rents received from property belonging to such recusants which, as the the record says, " by reason of recusancy " was held altogether or in part by the crown, are very far from being complete; that is to say, they do not begin until late in Elizabeth's reign, although from that time the series runs without a break for sixty-three years. There is, of course, a record of the fines paid under the recusant laws in the years previous to the thirty-third of Elizabeth, A.D. 1590; but this is to be found on the general receipt rolls of the Exchequer, known as Pipe Rolls. It would take a very long time to thoroughly examine these rolls, and pick out from the mass of payments of every kind the special sums received by the royal officials in the way of recusant fines. The special recusant rolls are sufficiently difficult to deal with, and we must be content to confine our attention chiefly to this source of information. For the benefit of those who have no acquaintance with the original records of our country, I may perhaps say one word in description of the recusant rolls. When rolled up these records look more like a good size drain-pipe than anything else; they are about two feet in height and eighteen inches or two feet in diameter. The roll consists of a number of skins of parchment, each from six to eight feet long, and two feet or so broad, stitched together at one end; at the extreme end of each skin is written the name of the county to which it refers; for the receipts on these rolls, like the general Pipe Rolls, are divided out into their special counties. For our present purposes we have only to turn to the skins labelled *Southampton*, or Hampshire, to see what special information they can give us.

The first year, as I have said, is 1590 A.D., after Elizabeth had been on the throne some two-and-thirty years. The Hampshire record for this year is contained on one skin of parchment, such as I have described, written on both sides. The usual method followed is first to account for the estates wholly or partially in the hands of the queen, "by reason of the recusancy" of their owners, and then to record the names of those who during the year in question had been fined for not going to service in their parish church. Thus we find recorded under the first heading that the tenants of various properties belonging to the gentry of the county had paid two-thirds of the value of their holdings to the royal officials because their owners were recusants, and their properties—or rather the rents—had been seized in payment of fines. In one or two cases the *property* itself had already been granted for a term of years to a tenant to farm for the queen's benefit. One gentleman,

Richard Warnford, is entered upon the roll as being behindhand in his fines to the amount of £1,540, and so his property was taken over under the Act of Parliament, about which Hallam has told us, which enabled the crown to take possession of two-thirds of the property of all who would not, or more probably could not, pay their fines for not going to the service in their parish churches. The present record shows that many of the gentry had already been reduced to this strait; amongst them we find the names of Gilbert Wells, of Brambridge, near Twyford, whose property had been granted out to a farmer by the crown in the thirteenth year of the queen's reign; of Thomas Poundes, of Beamond, or Beaumont, in the parish of Farlington—a very noted recusant, about whom I shall speak presently; of Anthony Udall, or Uvedale, of Woodcote, near Alresford, who had other property at Hambledon. To come nearer to this neighbourhood of Petersfield, we find the receipt of the sum of £72 4s. 4d. for two-thirds of the manor of Westbury, described as "situate on the road from Eastmeon," the property of "William Fawkenor, recusant." On the other side of the hills we have Humphrey Milles, or Clarke, paying over two-thirds of the value of the manors of Idsworth and Bannisters Court, the property of Edward Bannyster, "recusant;" and, to take one more example, the same fine of two-thirds is exacted on the property of one Stephen Vachell, "gentleman and recusant," who is described as of "Heath House, in Borryton, near Petersfield."

With these few examples I pass on to the second division of the record, which gives the names of those fined at the rate of £20 a month, and thirteen months in the year, "for not going to church, chapel, or other place of common prayer." First comes the name of George Cotton, of Warblington, near Havant, who pays £260 on this score. Then there is given a long list of all sorts and conditions of men and women called on to pay at the same rate for the same legal offence. Husbands are requested to pay for their wives—for the women clearly make what I may perhaps call a "manful" stand for the rights of conscience. To take a few examples in the Petersfield neighbourhood: amongst those who have been found absent from their churches for seven months, and who are consequently requested to pay down £140, are Elizabeth, wife of Giles Turner, gentleman, of Steep; Richard Strange of Barnes, of Buriton, gentleman; William Edmonds or Holloway, of Eastmeon, yeoman; Margery Vachell, of Catherington, spinster; Humphrey Milles or Clarke, of Idsworth, yeoman (you remember he was the tenant of Edward Bannister, the owner of Idsworth); and, not to mention others, Thomas Neave, of Petersfield, yeoman. Amongst those who had been convicted of having absented themselves from the common place of worship for four months, and were consequently asked only for £80, there is the following list of Buriton people:—Thomas Kent, yeoman; Thomas Crowcher, yeoman; Arthur Richman, yeoman; Mary Blackman, wife of Henry Blackman; Emma Okelie, widow; Elizabeth Geale, widow; Ralph Geale (her son, probably), yeoman.

I give this as merely a sample of the information which may be obtained by an examination of the *Recusant Rolls*. Year after year the same story is disclosed; not that the fines in money are levied constantly or regularly; at times there are long lists; at times the names are fewer, but the first part of the record—that which gives the rental of lands seized by the crown in payment of the recusant fines—practically changes only in two ways; fresh names are added from time to time, and here and there we have noticed the sales of timber, &c., upon the various estates, and the leases and other grants made by the crown from the lands of "obstinate recusants." Thus, for example, at Hinton, on two farms called Wetham's and Cook's, the property of Thomas and Benjamin Stockwith, "by reason of their recusancy," the goods and chattels were seized and sold to meet the deficiency of rent to pay their fines. At Newlands, in the parish of Southwick, the property of Anthony Uvedale, of Woodcote, near Alresford, the oak and beech woods were cut down, as well as his beech woods at Hambledon, to pay fines due to the crown. As time goes on, more property is discovered and noted as having to pay two-thirds of the rental to the royal receiver. Thus in the fortieth year of Elizabeth's reign a considerable addition appears to the rents received from the property of Stephen Vachell, of Heath House: thirteen acres of land, for example, at Charlton, lands in Catherington, Havant and Hayling, and Weston farm near Buriton, with house, garden, orchard, and some 200 acres of land, are made chargeable at two-thirds of their value. This same farm, on the 30th of September, 1600, was granted for twenty-one years to one Arthur West, by Sir Thomas West, and other royal commissioners. The tenants of two brothers, Robert and Anthony Joy, of Rothercombe, in the parish of Eastmeon, are ordered to pay their rents to the crown for various meadows named "long croft, cops close, square meadow, great combfield of 20 acres, green close, &c.," in the parish of Eastmeon. And to take but one more example, Henry Knight, the tenant of Anthony Norton of Blendworth, has to pay to the crown the rent of a house and 60 acres of land at Punsall (or Punsholt) in the parish of Eastmeon.

As to the money fines, the obvious question at once arises, how could they have been paid? We must bear in mind that money in the days of Elizabeth was at least ten or twelve times the value of money at the present time. Probably we shall be under the mark if we take a penny at the end of the sixteenth century to be equal to our shilling, and at that rate £20 a month would be the same as £240 of our coinage. It is obviously impossible that such a sum, or anything like it, could have been found by the class of people who were condemned to pay these fines for not going to church. For example, the *Recusant Roll* for the second year of James I. contains extraordinary lists of men and women of every kind and degree, each fined £120 for not appearing at church for six months. The Hampshire portion of the Roll alone gives the names of some five hundred people thus fined, and the list includes the names of millers, tailors, milliners, husbandmen, yeomen, shoemakers, labourers, blacksmiths, fishermen, &c., not to name numerous widows, spinsters, and other lone women who had no husbands to pay for them. For example, at Petersfield we have Stephen Neve, tailor, and his wife, together with Thomas Neve, each fined £140 for not going to church for the previous six months; also John Harris and his wife; Richard Dyling and his wife, and Richard Allen and his wife, all of Petersfield, for the same. At Hambledon there are given the names of some twenty, and at Warblington some six-and-twenty, men and women, all of the labouring classes, who were thus fined. At Buriton we have the names of Agnes Crowcher, and her husband Thomas Crowcher, labourer; of Arthur Rudesbye, haulier, and Elizabeth his wife; of Elizabeth Okelie, widow; of Mary Blackman, wife of Henry Blackman; of Joan Crowcher, widow, and of Ann

Crowcher, wife of Ralph Crowcher, labourer. Down by the coast recusancy is evidently rife. At Wymering the list is a long one, and at Westburant, near Havant, occurs the name of "Elizabeth Bulbeck, spinster"—a Catholic name still known in the same place. It is of course obvious that these people, and hundreds like them in the country, could never have found the money to pay. Still the mere fact of their being, as they were called, "convicted recusants," placed them within the power of the law, and the next step taken with them was to value, and, in the crown's behalf, lay claim to the goods and chattels of all indebted, for the amount of their fines. There are records of cows and cattle of all sorts, furniture—poor sticks of furniture enough, for the most part they seem to be—farming implements, hayricks, &c., &c., being declared of such and such a value, and the property of the crown. In some instances this embargo appears to have been bought off at the royal official valuation; but almost always these poor unfortunate creatures had to remain under the crushing sense that all their worldly goods were known to be the property of the crown, and held solely at the mercy of some official in the district. Instances are not wanting of the actual sales of every bit of furniture, and even of the home itself, over the heads of a family noted for its recusancy.

A series of Rolls little consulted for any purpose affords us some particulars about these debts owed by various recusants. They are called *Exannual Rolls*, and upon them are entered such debts to the crown as are never likely to be paid—debts for which it would be hopeless to prosecute. From the twenty-fifth year of Queen Elizabeth's reign these rolls contain long lists of *bad* debts owing by recusants who have nothing wherewith to pay. In some instances, at a later period, there is a record that payment, or part payment, of this or that debt has been obtained; as for example, when the lands of Stephen Vachell, of Heath House and Buriton, and Anthony Uvedale, of Hambledon, are taken possession of; but generally the debt is entered as hopeless.

There are some instances, however, on the *Recusant Rolls* in which, year after year, a recusant, somehow or other, managed to scrape together sufficient to pay the full penalty for refusing to attend his parish church. Thus, Mr. George Cotton, of Warblington, actually paid £260 each year for many years. I have followed the receipts for twenty years, from 1587 to 1607. Imagine what such payments mean; actually in hard cash this gentleman—a man of considerable property about Havant—in these twenty years paid in fines some £5,200 in money of those days, or something over £60,000 of our money. I did not myself for some time believe that this could have been the case, and supposed that although he was nominally fined that amount, the money was not actually paid. I have, however, satisfied myself that the cash was in fact handed into the royal treasury. There exist at the Record Office what are called the *Pells Receipt Books*, and day by day in these were entered the sums of money which were paid into the exchequer, and the source whence they came. I have followed out in these Pells receipts the sums of money obtained from Hampshire as noted on the Recusant Rolls. There, for example, duly noted as received will be found the rents of Stephen Vachell's property in Petersfield and Buriton, the rents of Heath House and Weston Farm; there are the payments of two-thirds of the rents of the Idsworth and of the Westbury property, and the rest; and there each six months is recorded the receipt of a moiety of the £260 which Mr. George Cotton is stated on the Recusant Roll to have paid for not attending the church service. He begins in 1586 by a small payment of £15 6s. 8d. In 1587, on May 29th, he pays £140, and the other moiety of the £260, namely £120, on November 24th; on this day he also pays £199 6s. 8d., said to be "in part payment of the sum of £1,199 6s. 8d.," arrears of fines for not going to his parish church. From 1587 till his name disappears from the treasury account books in 1607, Mr. George Cotton pays his £260 a year regularly. More than this; by degrees he is forced to pay off the arrears of which I have just spoken. Thus on November 28th, 1588, besides his usual six-monthly moiety of the £260, he pays into the queen's purse £433 6s. 8d.,[1] and a like sum at two subsequent dates.

I may add that the *Pells Receipt Book*, besides being a day book, gives what may be called a ledger account at the end of each volume. Here the various sums paid into the royal treasury are gathered together under their various headings. Thus there are the customs dues on wine, &c., the fines inflicted in the Star Chamber, the payment for renewal of crown leases, &c. One of the headings given is " *Fines de recusantibus accedere ad ecclesiam ubi communis oratio utitur* "—that is, " Fines from those refusing to come to church where the Common Prayer is used," and the totals show, when compared with other receipts, that the recusant fines were a very considerable source of revenue. There are, indeed, only one or two other sources that furnish more money to the exchequer of the country than what was obtained from Catholics refusing to be present at service in their several parishes. One example of the amount actually received under this head may be of interest. In the first half of the year 1601 the Treasury acknowledges the receipt of £4,856 15s. 9½d. from recusancy fines; in the second half £4,370 3s. 6½d., making a grand total of £9,226 19s. 4d. for the year, or, to put it into modern figures for comparison, some £110,719 8s. of our money.

[1] Pells Receipt Books, No. 51.

I will here give a balance-sheet showing the actual sums of money received by the exchequer each six months during the last twenty years of the reign of Queen Elizabeth, from Catholics who refused to come to their parish churches for service. It must be borne in mind, however, that the receipts of the exchequer were but a trifle compared to the losses sustained by the Catholics by the methods employed to collect the fines, and the consequent waste and wanton destruction of their goods, and, as has been pointed out, "of the vast sums which found their way into the hands of courtiers, parasites, and favourites to whom recusants were given to farm, and pursuivants and informers, who made Catholics pay for their forbearance." Even so, the total sum of money extracted from the recusants in the course of the last twenty years of the sixteenth century is sufficiently appalling, and as the details are taken from the Royal receipt books, there can be no question about the money not having been really paid. The average yearly payment, it will be seen, was, in round numbers, £6,000, whilst in each of the last three years it exceeded £8,000. In 1601, when the receipts from recusant fines amounted, as we have said, to £9,226 19s. 4d., the total revenue of the crown averaged £400,000[1], so that these fines were about a fiftieth part of the total exchequer receipts.

---

[1] J. C. Vincent, *Lancashire Lay Subsidies*, Introduction, p. xxix.

HAMPSHIRE RECUSANTS.

CASH RECEIVED BY THE EXCHEQUER FOR THE FINES OF CATHOLICS REFUSING TO BE PRESENT AT PROTESTANT SERVICE.

		£	s.	d.	£	s.	d.
1583	Easter term	285	0	0			
	Michaelmas	2077	2	8	2362	2	8
1584	Easter term	1005	19	11			
	Michaelmas	440	4	2	1446	4	1
1585	Easter term	1476	0	4			
	Michaelmas	1046	13	4	2522	13	8
1586	Easter term	535	19	4			
	Michaelmas	982	4	5	1518	3	9
1587	Easter term	2325	16	11			
	Michaelmas	3419	5	3	5745	2	2
1588	Easter term	2698	19	6			
	Michaelmas	5645	15	9½	8344	15	3½
1589	Easter term	1908	6	6½			
	Michaelmas	5433	15	4	7342	1	10½
1590	Easter term	3112	10	2			
	Michaelmas	3500	10	7½	6613	0	9½
1591	Easter term	2954	16	10½			
	Michaelmas	2955	0	4	5909	17	2½
1592	Easter term	3546	6	4½			
	Michaelmas	3000	0	0	6546	6	4½
1593	Easter term	3422	9	3½			
	Michaelmas	2587	10	8	6009	19	11½
1594	Easter term	3134	8	3			
	Michaelmas	3425	1	10	6559	10	1

		£	s.	d.	£	s.	d.
1595	Easter term	3326	4	1			
	Michaelmas	2987	12	2			
					6313	16	3
1596	Easter term	3185	15	4½			
	Michaelmas	3458	13	8			
					6644	9	0½
1597	Easter term	3189	9	8			
	Michaelmas	3449	17	2			
					6639	6	10
[1]1598	Easter term	3148	8	0½			
	Michaelmas	3539	5	8½			
					6687	13	9
1599	Easter term	3505	3	1½			
	Michaelmas	3998	14	6			
					7503	17	7½
1600	Easter term	3689	15	0½			
	Michaelmas	4788	4	1½			
					8477	19	2
1601	Easter term	4389	0	2½			
	Michaelmas	4443	18	10			
					8832	19	0½
1602	Easter term	4110	6	5½			
	Michaelmas	4176	13	6½			
					8287	0	0

Grand Total   £120,306   19   7½

I must not, however, delay longer over these accounts, for we have many other sources of information. My note-books of collections from the State papers of this period contain many notes and copies of documents relating to Hampshire and Hampshire recusants. For the purpose of this paper I have turned over the pages and marked several which were copied out years ago. There is, of course, not the least possibility of giving in a

[1] From Lansd. MS., f. 190.

mere paper any adequate notion of the story as it comes out from these records of the past. All I can do is to note some one or two points, which are, I fancy, most likely to be of interest. I begin with a list to be found in the Domestic State Papers of Elizabeth's reign.[1] It is headed: " The names of the recusants within the county of Southampton who refuse to come unto their several parish churches unto the divine service there said, whereof many of them were presented in the inquisition made through that shire in (April), 1583, and many of them hath been both then and in former inquisitions presented." The list contains the names of some 240 of the Hampshire gentry and their wives. It is impossible, of course, to give the details, and I only take as a sample the names entered as at Buriton: Henry Shelley, Marie his wife, Marie his daughter, Lawrence Young and two others, servants to Mr. Shelley; Stephen Vachell, gent, Marie his wife, Margery Vachell his sister, and a servant named William. To this list is appended another of names left out either by accident or design, and at the end are noted " those recusants who are committed and do remain in prison." In the gaol at Winchester there are some eight and twenty, including two priests and two nuns. In this company are Nicholas Tichborne, Gilbert Wells, of Twyford, William Beconshaw, Simon Cuffold of

[1] Vol. clx.; No. 26.

Basing, Edward Bannister of Idsworth, John Ludlowe of Fareham, and, to name but one more, our old friend of Heath House and Weston Farm, Stephen Vachell. At the same time four Hampshire gentlemen are in prison for recusancy in London, namely: John Beconshaw, Peter Tichborne, George Cotton of Warblington, about whom we have already heard so much, and Henry Shelley, of Buriton.[1] In the "house of correction" at Winchester there is Mrs. Edborow Bullacre, widow, of Warblington, Mr. Thomas Goter, of Timsbury, Mr. Bobert Joy of Eastmeon, and Nicholas Collyns of Meonstoke.

The circumstances which led to Mrs. Bullacre finding herself in the House of Correction are the following. In August, 1582, John Chapman, formerly rector of Langton Herring, in Dorsetshire, and now "a seminary and massing priest," as he is officially described, was discovered in the house of Mrs. Bullacre in Warblington, where he had been residing for some time. He was carried off to

---

[1] Mr. Henry Shelley, of Mapledurham House, was descended from the Shelleys of Michelgrove, Sussex. The last Abbess of St. Mary's, Winchester, was born at Mapledurham, and the family furnished many priests and religious in the sixteenth and seventeenth centuries. The house of Mapledurham was a large gabled building approached by an avenue of elms. Like Michelgrove, the family mansion of the Shelleys in Sussex, and one of the finest houses in the county, Mapledurham was destroyed only in this century, when the present farmhouse was built on the site. This Mapledurham is not to be confounded with another mansion of the same name situated on the Thames, about three miles from Reading.

Winchester together with the lady for harbouring him. After he had been examined before the Bishop of Winchester (Dr. John Watson), and two magistrates, the Bishop wrote to the Privy Council for further instructions, whether he should be sent up to London, or left to be dealt with by the judges at the forthcoming assizes. "He is in the meantime," writes the Bishop, "committed to a safe place in the correction house. The gaol hath so many backward people, that we thought not good to commit neither the priest nor the widow, Mrs. Bullacre, thither."

The four Hampshire gentlemen in the prison in London had probably been there for more than a couple of years, as their names appear in a list of recusant prisoners in the White Lion prison, Southwark, in December, 1581,[1] and two of them, John Beconshaw and Peter Tichborne in another "catalogue of papists imprisoned in 1579";[2] whilst in the same list are given the names of four widows in prison at Winchester, and against them is noted: "their husbands have died in prison."

I should be glad, had it been possible within the limits of this paper, to have followed the fortunes of a few more Hampshire recusants in the prison lists of which I have a great number. I must content myself with merely noting the name of "Benjamin

[1] State Papers Dom. Eliz., 1581, No. 240 A.
[2] Lansd. MS., 28, fol. 96.

Stockwith, gent." We have already referred to him as joint owner with his brother of some property at Hinton. In 1586 he is certified as being in the Clink prison, and the entry states that he was " sometime student in ye Inns of Court, imprisoned on March 24th : since arraigned at Newgate for hearing Mass, and then committed prisoner hither again." [1]

In turning over the parchment records of the Recusant Rolls the searcher is struck with the way in which the name of the husband of any female recusant is set down. It was done, of course, with the distinct policy of bringing the pressure of the husband's authority to put an end to the wife's recusancy, as the following paper, addressed by the Bishop of Winchester in 1580 to the Privy Council, shows :—" Touching the last letter we received from your honours containing an order how such women are to be dealt with as are relapsed in this diocese, whose husbands come to church and hear sermons and do according to her Majesty's laws in these points : we have called before us many of the husbands and mean to deal with the rest towards the latter end of this week, and hope we shall do some good therein. But at the beginning they thought it something strange that they shall be punished for their wives' faults. But . . . we have taken bonds . . . of them to keep their

---

[1] State Papers Dom. Eliz., vol. 190, No. 26 (June 12).

wives from conference, all manner of ways, with such as are backward in matters of religion, and also have imposed a mulct upon every of them weekly, till their wives shall come to church."[1]

In the year 1586 the Catholics were evidently given some hope that they might perhaps purchase toleration by the payment of a yearly sum to the Queen. Indeed, a commission was appointed on April 13th of that year to examine the recusants of Hampshire as to their ability to pay, and a list was sent for the use of the officials. The Lord la Warre and his fellow-commissioners certified after examination that they find only few who are able to pay anything. Many of the Catholic gentry are noted as being then in Wisbeach Castle for matters of religion, or otherwise confined to prison in Winchester. They forward certain letters, however, in which some of the Catholics state what they can pay, and were willing to pay if they were only left to follow their consciences. Thus Stephen Vachell, of Heath House, promises to pay £5 a year for the Queen's permission to follow his religion. Nicholas Tichborne declares that he has left out of his property only an annuity of £3, which the Queen may take. George Cotton, in his letter, says that he had received intimation from his brother, Sir Richard Cotton, " of her Majesty's most gracious favour, bent to the case and relief of her subjects, recu-

[1] State Papers, Dom. Eliz., vol. 144, No. 36.

sants." He will pay to the utmost of his power, which, however, is "but weak of itself, and hath been of late not a little diminished, as well by ordinary charges of children and servants necessarily depending on (him), as by manifold losses sustained, partly by long imprisonment, partly by the evicting of a great part of (his) living." He adds that he has lately married three daughters, and has seven children more depending on him. Still he concludes, " besides the great sums which I have paid for the statute of Recusancy," I offer £30 a year. This sum is changed into £40 by his son, Richard Cotton, with his authority.

One or two of the other answers are pathetically interesting. For example: Mrs. Katherine Henslow " protests before God" that she has only £20 to support herself and her servant, and offers the Queen 20s. " as a poor widow's mite," to be allowed to practise her religion. A friend, one Anthony Fortescue, subsequently promises to make this up to 40s. for her. Edward Bannister, of Idsworth, says he has already been called upon to pay in Surrey, where he is residing, for " I am," he writes, " still bound to remain with my cousin Bellingham of Putney, and I may not go any farther than I am licensed, or first have leave of the Council upon payment of my bond." Lastly, Mrs. Elizabeth Tichborne, of West Tisted, says upon being called upon to make a " personal appearance" before the Commissioners, " I hope you will by reason of my long infirmity hold me excused, the state of my body being such, I thank God for it, that this many year I have not been out of my chamber—nay, not in many months together out of my bed." She would willingly pay the Queen what she is able, but has twelve children "left in trust by my husband," and to them by his will " all my goods and stocks belong when it shall please God to call me." Still, with the aid of friends there is offered in her behalf £13 4s. 8d. a year.[1] But this slight hope of some better treatment, and of the possibility of the Catholics being allowed to purchase toleration was quickly disappointed, and the same, if not increased, rigour, was displayed towards them in the closing years of Elizabeth's reign.

It is evident from the nature of things that only a portion, and that probably by no means the greater portion, of the fines paid by Catholics under the recusant laws really passed into the State coffers. One of the worst results of penal laws was the creation of a body of informers, who traded upon the necessities of their fellow-countrymen, and either by rewards for discovering and detecting persons subject to the laws, but hitherto unknown, or by hush-money extracted from the unfortunate subjects, enriched themselves. Further than this, all during the later part of Elizabeth's reign and in the early years of her successor, it was the practice of the Crown to reward favourites and

[1] State Papers, Dom., Eliz. vol. 183, No. 16.

officials by what was called "the value of the recusancy" of this or that Catholic. In 1610, to take one example, Sir John Saville offered to pay to the King no less a sum than £8,000 a year for permission to farm the recusant fines in Yorkshire, and at the same time Sir George Manners and Sir Thomas Grantham asked for a grant of the fines for the county of Lincoln, promising to pay £2,000 a year more than the King had hitherto received from his Catholic subjects in that county who refused to go to their parish churches to service.[1] The extent to which this was done was much greater than may be supposed. "A memorial of things grievous and offensive to the Commonwealth which may be reformed by the King or by Parliament," drawn up in May, 1603, the first year of King James I., says: "The penaltie of Recusants (is) £20 a month by Act of Parliament for not comyng to church—a punishment no waie fittinge nor proportionable to that offence." There is a great "defrauding of the Prince of that penaltie due unto him . . . for whereas the penalties amount yearlie to the somme of £13,595, as appeareth by the accompt of the officer that is appointed for that purpose, there is paid into the Exchequer for the Prince's use but £3,900 or thereabouts. The rest goes to certain courtiers who have begged those penalties, and compounded with them, and by that means become

---

[1] State Papers, Dom., James I., vol. 54, No. 78.

Patrons and Protectors of Recusants, wherebie Poperie is maintayned and increased in the realm."[1]

With the coming of James I. the Catholics hoped for better treatment and liberty. They were, however, soon undeceived, and quite a volume might be made of the various suggestions proffered by hungry officials setting out how more might be made for the Royal Exchequer out of the recusants' lands. One paper sets forth particulars by which property leased at £2,210 4s. 3d. a year might be made to produce £5,779 8s. 9d. In Hampshire, for example, he desires to make Anthony Uvedale, of Woodcote, pay £40 instead of £13 6s. 8d., and our old friend Stephen Vachell, of Petersfield, £50 in place of £11.[2]

The amounts, as stated to have been forfeited in this latter reign, became so enormous that one almost hesitates to believe them. I give one entry exactly as it stands. It is endorsed "Recusants, 10 July, 1612," and is to the following effect: "The forfeiture of Recusants which have escheated into this court from the beginning of Michaelmas term in the 9th year of the King's Majesty's reign, to the end of Trinity term in the 10th year of his said Majesty's reign, do in the whole amount to, as by the estreats thereof, remaining in the custody of the clerk of the estreats of this court and by him cast up, particularly appeareth, £371,060." There would appear to be no reasonable doubt about this

---

[1] State Papers, Dom., 1 James I., vol. i., art., 68.
[2] Lansd. MS. 153, f. 178.

record; but the effect of it is to show that, in this one year, property of Catholic recusants was confiscated to the crown to the amount, in modern figures, of £4,452,720.

Hallam has told us how priests came over from abroad with their lives in their hands, and passed from one Catholic house to another, administering the rites of religion, and exhorting those whom they met with to suffer the extreme penalties of the law rather than abandon the Catholic religion. The coasts of Hampshire and Sussex were naturally the parts of England where these priests were landed, just as it was the part from which, in those days, many a Catholic youth departed, by stealth, to seek in the colleges established in France and Belgium the education denied to him here. Thus, in December, 1581, an informer, writing to Walsingham about one Mr. White, probably Mr. Thomas White, of Titchfield, near Fareham, says: "He imparted to me this day, although in Portsmouth he durst not enter into conference with me, that he was in France at Christmas last, from whence he conveyed over to England one Adams, a priest . . He conveyed over into this realm of late one Chapman, a priest, and landed him at Stokes Bay, by Portsmouth, and gave directions what course he should take."[1] The houses of the Catholic families in Hampshire were always open to shelter the priest on his landing. Mr. George Cotton's

[1] State Papers, Dom. Eliz., 1581, No. 231.

house, at Warblington, was conveniently situated near the coast, and in many State papers of the period it is noted as one of their chief places of abode, and in 1609 the Lord Treasurer was informed that " In the house of Mr. Cotton, of Hampshire, there is harboured a Jesuit who names himself Thomas Singleton. He teaches the grandchildren of the said Cotton."[1]

It is more than probable that priests landing at Portsmouth would pass along the London road through Petersfield. Be this as it may, it is certain that there was always a shelter for them at Buriton, and Mr. Shelley's large manor house at Mapledurham stood invitingly on the London road, a few hours' journey from the coast. There, and at the neighbouring farm of Weston, priests were always sure to find a welcome, a place to say their Mass, and, if necessary, a secure hiding place. A letter describing the state of the case in 1586 is of such local interest that I will give it entire :—" 15th of June, 1586. The declaration of Edward Jones, the Recusant. *In primis* Rt. Hon. . . . it happened that serving my master Tichebourne,[2] being his footboy, the young man being very desirous to travel, as fortune fell out, there came on a time unto his master's house a merchant named Hopton, being unto my knowledge but of small acquaintance, but they knew one another, his father being then

---

[1] Winwood's *Memorials*, iii., p. 43.
[2] This was Mr. Chidcock Tichborne, of Porchester.

in prison [1] unacquainted with this matter. The place is named Porchester. There they agreed between them that they would travel into France, so staying there, departed, going towards London wherein press of time met with was a week or thereabout, so briefly concluded that the next week they would take their journey towards Rye, where they were shipped privily and passed by sea to Dieppe, where they arrived safely, myself being then in London placed by my mother with one Mr. John Shelley, waiting on the Lord Montague and being in the house not passing a four days, but one of the Lord's sons named Mr. George Brown was very desirous to have me and in the end getting my mistress's good will and him I served a 3 weeks in his father's house. At length old Mr. Titchborne being then prisoner in the White Lion in Southwark, hearing of my being with him sent for me and placed me with this Shelley's brother [2] being prisoner too, where I waited on him and his wife and was reconciled there in my mistress's chamber by one Wrenche who died in London two years agone; but being alive went down to my mistress (Mrs. Henry Shelley) unto her house named Mapledurham, near unto Petersfield where he did say mass every day once; whither resorted certain priests more, named as followeth: Jasper Haywood, Jesuit, Shelborne, Chepnam, Adames, Warblington,

---

[1] Mr. Peter Tichborne, in the White Lion prison, 1583.
[2] Henry Shelley, of Buriton.

Farmer, Eskene, Stone. There I daily consociate withal and heard mass every day, thus passing the time a three quarters of the year in London at my Mrs. lodging and I came unto the prison and heard mass every morning there. My old master Mr. Tichborne's father, he being always timorous of the law, would never any these persons to have entertainment in the house by reason of the law."

On the back of this letter is noted:—"Mapledurham. Mr. Stephen Vachill and his wife, Marten Croucher and his wife, Mr. John Shelley and his wife. White Lion in Southwark, Mr. John Shelley, Mr. Chideock Tichebourne."

The endorsement is of some interest from the absence of the name of Henry Shelley, of Mapledurham. The fact is, however, that before October 23rd, 1585, he had already died in his prison at the White Lion, Southwark.[1] In the year 1587, in a small list of notable recusants, written in Lord Burghley's own hand, appear two Hampshire names I have already spoken a great deal about, George Cotton, of Warblington, and Gilbert Wells, of Twyford, about both of whom I shall have a word to say later.[2]

A glimpse—and perhaps the most interesting glimpse—of the life of the recusants in these parts at this period, is afforded by the information of an informer in 1594. He was a young Hampshire

[1] Harl. MS. 360, f. 22.
[2] State Papers, Dom., Eliz., vol. 183, No. 45 (6).

gentleman, signing himself "Ben. Beard," connected with the Tichborne family, and who, upon finding the Fleet prison in London too much for him, endeavoured to purchase his liberty by volunteering information about the doings of his Catholic relations and friends. He had seen such and such priests at his grandmother's house, and if the Privy Council would set him at liberty he would be able to find them. He had heard mass said at such and such a house, and the searchers could find the chapel hidden away by following his directions, and so on. Of course his chief information is about Hampshire, and a good deal is about the neighbourhood of Petersfield. For instance, he says: "If these parties (*i.e.*, two priests) be missed at Mr. Wells' house (at Brambridge) it is not unlikely but they will be found at Mapledurham, at Mr. Thomas Shelley's house in that county, where I think one Mr. Strange doth dwell.[1] Strange and Wells are great friends, and shift such persons between each other. At Mapledurham there is a hollow place in the parlour by the livery cupboard where two men may well lie together, which has many times deceived the searchers.

"Jerom Heath, who is not a recusant, he dwelling at Winchester, who, not being suspected for religion, was wont in time of any disturbance to harbour such persons, as when my grandmother

---

[1] Richard Strange *alias* Barnes of Buriton, gent., appears among the list of Hampshire recusants (Recusant Roll, I., A.D. 1590).

Mrs. Tichbourne lived, there were continually in her house one Fennell and Richards, priests, who upon any search did lightly fly thither for a three or four days together.

"If I were at liberty I could go but to the Castle at Winchester where presently my uncle, Gilbert Tichborne, and divers other my friends and kindred remain for their consciences, of whom I could understand anything, and no doubt do very good service."[1]

In a paper containing further information Ben. Beard says: Two Jesuits landed in Cornwall and were harboured there for three weeks "by a minister, and afterwards conducted by the same party to Hampshire to a place called Pitt Farm, where one Mr. Yate and his wife did abide. . . . have seen with my own eyes one John Shelley, who was with the old Lord Montague, carry Fennell and Richards (the two priests about whom he had spoken as having been sheltered by his grandmother, Mrs. Tichborne) about the country with him in my Lord Montague's livery, with chains about their necks. Whilst old Mr. Tichborne lived, this Simon Fennell abode with the other priest Richards at Mapledurham in Hampshire, where then one Strange did dwell."[2]

Upon this information Beard was apparently examined by the Lord Keeper Puckering, and we

---

[1] State Papers, Dom., Eliz., vol. 248 (March 15th, 1594), No. 30.
[2] Ibid., No. 105.

have the following notes by his lordship: "Hampshire. John Shelley lieth at Barnes Farm (or Bailes Farm), as it were in an old park, paled and locked that none can come in without a key.

"His consort is Strange (that was with my Lord Montague) and kept a college of priests (as it were) at Mapledurham.

"Robert Knight, of Lydshot, hard by Bramshot, where Mr. Marvyn dwelleth. This Mapledurham is Thomas Shelley's house. He was going over the sea to be a priest, and was taken, and now Strange farmeth it. . . .

"These houses are common receptacles for priests, and have great shift for the hiding of them: as in Mapledurham house, under a little table is a vault, with a grate of iron for a light into the garden, as if it were the window of a cellar, and against the grate groweth rosemary."[1]

In another examination, held in 1596, of one John Harrison, then prisoner in Bridewell, some slight information is afforded about Mapledurham, Petersfield. Harrison confessed that "he was married to his wife in Newgate by an old priest then in prison, himself nor his wife being no prisoner." He "served Robert Barnes by the space of eighteen years, and was with him at his house at Mapledurham, Hants, and was there when Mrs. Barnes died, which was about eight years past, and she was buried at the parish church at Buriton.

[1] State Papers, Dom., Eliz., vol. 248, No. 116.

He attended on his master, Barnes, at Bellamy's house, but his master was at Mapledurham when Babington resorted to Bellamy's house. He confesseth himself to be a Catholic of the Pope's religion, and so hath been before and since he came to Barnes' service," but he denied that he had ever seen any he knew to be priests in his master's house at Mapledurham.[1]

It was, of course, as Hallam has told us, highly dangerous to property, and even to life, to be known to shelter a priest; and curious devices were practised to be able to escape the penalty. Thus, in one case, a priest declares that to his knowledge the Catholic gentleman stood " behind the door to hear the masses, and not to be seen of his servants," as though he had not known the gentleman staying in his house to have been a priest at all. It is curious to find that, through the sympathy and contrivance of the gaolers, Catholics in prison for their recusancy were able to obtain many of the consolations of religion. We have already heard that people outside the walls of such a prison as the White Lion at Southwark, could often come and hear mass said by some priest confined there; and that marriage and other sacraments were administered within prison walls. This was the case even within the Tower, where, in 1588, it was discovered not only that at times, by means of keys, the prisoners had access to

[1] State Papers, Dom., Eliz. 1596 (March 3), No. 47.

each other's rooms; but even, for a certain period, had been able to have daily mass said "by all the priests that have been there these many years."[1] At Winchester gaol the compassion of the gaolers mitigated the strictness of the confinement of some of the recusant prisoners; but this was soon discovered, and a long enquiry led to the dismissal of the official, and the appointment of another who could be relied on "to correct" those under his care.

In 1583 "certain poor Catholics, who were unable to pay the heavy fine imposed upon them for neglecting to attend public service were publicly whipped through the streets of Winchester,"[2] and on Bishop Cooper succeeding to the See in 1584, he wrote to the Privy Council suggesting the following admirable mode of getting rid of the recusants from Hampshire, which he describes as over-run with them. His plan is "that a hundred or two of the obstinate recusants, lusty men, well able to labour, might by some convenient commission be taken up and sent to Flanders as pioneers and labourers, whereby the country would be disburdened of a company of dangerous people, and the rest that remained be put in some fear."[3]

It would appear that at this time, 1584, the number of recusants in Hampshire was very considerable; the Clerk of the Peace for the county

---

[1] State Papers, Dom., Eliz., 1588 (Oct. 26), No. 760.
[2] Milner, *Winchester*, p. 380.
[3] Cassan, *Lives of the Bishops of Winchester*, ii., p. 47.

states that, "at every sessions the indictments against them are in number seven score at the least." He adds, after suggesting some change in his duties: "The number of recusants which at every sessions are to be indicted is so great, that the Clerk of the Peace is driven to spend, not only by himself, or his deputy and a servant or two, a great deal of time before and after the sessions itself, in drawing and engrossing the indictments, judgments and processes, and the Justices most occupied about them, whereby the sessions are continued more days than heretofore, and almost all other causes and grievances of the shire omitted altogether."[1]

One other point only will I refer to here: the difficulty experienced by recusants in burying their dead; for, as a rule, the bodies were refused a resting place in the parish churchyards. I have mentioned already the name of the family of Wells, of Brambridge, near Twyford. One member of that family was Swithun Wells, whose house in Hampshire was the refuge of numerous priests, and in it were frequently celebrated two, and even three masses a day. In the last stage of his life he had taken a house at London, in Holborn, near Gray's Inn Fields. Here Topcliffe, the celebrated priest-catcher, broke in whilst Father Edmund Genings was saying mass, and carried off the priest and the

[1] State Papers, Dom., Eliz., vol. 183, No. 83.

whole congregation to Newgate. Mr. Wells was not present at the time, but was afterwards apprehended and condemned to death for harbouring a priest and having mass in his house. He, together with Mr. Genings, was actually hanged before his own door on December 10, 1598. The Twyford register of burials discloses the fact that in the century from 1663 (before which date such entries do not appear to have been set down) to 1767 some seventeen members of the Wells family were buried " as recusants, clandestinely, by night." During the same period some fifteen or sixteen other recusants were similarly buried.

The Cotton family were lords of the manors of Warblington and Bedhampton, and we have already seen what large sums Mr. George Cotton had paid to the crown in fines for not attending his parish church. He had likewise lost great estates in Cheshire, which, having been granted to his father, Sir Richard Cotton, and having come to him as part of his inheritance, passed again to their original owners.[1] A letter, written in 1614, records his end. " George Cotton," the writer says, " was despoiled of all his goods and consigned to a dungeon to the end of his days, which was hastened by hardships, filth, misery, and a chronic malady. The ministers, as if he were unworthy of Christian burial, would not allow his corpse to be buried in their church-

---

[1] Foley, *Collectanea*, part 2, p. 1040.

yards, hence his remains are deposited in an open field." [1]

Mr. Thomas Pounde, of Beamond or Belmont, near Farlington, spent nearly thirty years of his life in various prisons in England. His life presents a series of almost incredible sufferings for the rights of conscience, and most of his property passed to the crown in fines for obstinately refusing to attend the parish church. The register of Farlington records his burial thus: "1613 (1 March) Thomas Pounde, Esq., was buried *by night* the first of March."

In the year 1589 Nicholas Tichborne of Hartley Maudit, three miles from Alton, died. He had been in the gaol of Winchester for nine years a prisoner, as he says himself in his petition for relief "for not repairing unto my parish church," or as the sheriff puts it, "in execution for a great sum of money due unto Her Majesty by reason of his recusancy." We have a glimpse of his sad condition in a letter written by him in 1585. In October of that year orders were sent down to the officials in the various counties to demand from each recusant gentleman or woman one "light horse" for the Queen's service, or £25 in money. George Cotton, apparently, was the only one in this part of the country who was "contented" to furnish the horse. Poor Nicholas Tichborne pleaded "non-ability" to do what was required. "I and such other recusants," he writes,

[1] Harl. MS., 2083, fol. 127.

"have reported ourselves, notwithstanding our recusancy, to be as good subjects as any other Her Majesty's subjects, which before God I do acknowledge and profess. And hereupon, Her Majesty having present service for certain light horsemen to be sent into Flanders, Her Majesty's will and pleasure is to require of me to have a light horse in readiness, with all the furniture thereunto belonging, by the 26th day of the month of October, or else £25."

"I," he continues, "am a younger brother and son of a younger brother," and had only one little farm, "for the maintenance of myself, my poor wife, and eight young children." The "lease whereof with all such goods as I had upon the same was sold by Robert White, Esq., late sheriff of the said county, and the money for the same was paid into the receipt of Her Majesty's Exchequer, to Her Majesty's use in the Michaelmas term, in the 25th year of Her Majesty's reign." I may mention that in the Pells Receipt Book is entered on November 13th, 1584, the sum of £40 paid by Nicholas Tichborne in part payment. Whilst on the *Exannual Roll* of the following year this £40 is deducted from the £360 he is said to owe the Queen, but one sum of £260, and two of £120, are added to the debt at the same time.

To return to the letter of excuse. Tichborne declares that since he has been in prison and all his little property taken away, his family has lived upon the alms of the charitable. He is sorry he is unable to do anything in the way of finding the horse to show "his loyalty and true obedience to Her Majesty, who," he adds, "with all my heart I do acknowledge for my most dread sovereign lady and queen." He begs they will give him his liberty so that he may work for the support of his family, and promises, if possible, when free, to collect the money necessary to buy a horse from his friends.[1]

The sheriff himself testifies as to the miserable condition of poor Nicholas Tichborne, for on November 11th (1585) he writes that he "is utterly unable of himself to maintain his wife and children since the confiscation of his goods to Her Majesty for his contemptuous recusancy."[2]

He was left, consequently, in the Winchester gaol till he died, as I have said, in 1589. The Bishop of the diocese, Dr. Cooper, refused to allow his body to be buried in any church or cemetery, declaring that his conscience would not permit him to suffer a Papist to be buried in any of his churches or cemeteries. By the advice of an old Catholic the body was carried to the summit of a hill about a mile from the city and interred in the old disused cemetery of St. James, now known in Winchester as the Catholic Cemetery.

To these instances I must add that of the burial of Fr. Sigebert Buckley, the last of the old West-

[1] State Papers, Dom., Elizabeth, vol. 183, No. 45.
[2] Ibid., vol. 184, No. 17.

minster monks. For some time before his death he was living in the house belonging to Mr. Anthony Norton, called Punsholt, in the parish of Eastmeon, to which we have referred before. As they refused him burial in any churchyard, his friends carried his body and deposited it in the ruins of an old chapel, in the hopes, as the record says, that in happier times it might be removed to a more honourable sepulchre.

With this I must close my lengthy paper. I will ask you to believe that I have touched only the fringe of a large subject, and that the mass of material at hand to illustrate this page of English history is little short of appalling. One thing I hope I have made clear, and that is, that if we want to know the history of these times we cannot afford to ignore the penal laws or to underrate the amount of domestic misery of which they were the cause.

In these days people talk easily of liberty of conscience, but they are commonly ignorant of the means by which, and of the men by whom the liberty, now so highly prized, was really won. In a vague way it is imagined that the world was convinced of this by the philosophers; that Locke, for example, was the apostle of this liberty. The work, however, was not done by men who wrote at ease in their armchairs; but by the men, whatever their belief, who bore and suffered all things rather than be false to what appeared to them to be the leading light of conscience. In Elizabethan days, to do so was in some respects most difficult; for the immense majority of Catholics had no quarrel with the Queen's succession, and were quite ready to accept her as their legitimate sovereign. The politicians in this party, if potent, were few. On the other hand, Elizabeth was open in her declaration that all she required was external compliance with State regulations in matters of religion for the purposes of policy; yet, fortunately for true "liberty of conscience," she demanded conformity with externals, which, as anyone acquainted with the actual state of the Church of England in her reign knows, were quite incompatible with any continued belief in the Catholic religion.

There can be no question as to the fact that most of those who suffered under the penal laws, outside the ranks of those who actually sacrificed their lives for religion, were simple-minded Englishmen and Englishwomen, skilled neither in argument nor controversy; but from truthfulness and sincerity of conscience easily open to conviction from the logic of visible facts. They saw through the plea for mere external compliance, as the early Christian martyrs of old recognised the renunciation implied by the mere dropping of a few grains of incense before the statue of their Emperor.

The lives of the Recusants fell in days of that confusion and entanglement of ideas which must exist in an age of transition. Whilst, at whatever sacrifice, they refused to abandon what they felt to be good and holy coming to them from the past, they were unwitting instruments in preparing the only conditions possible for the public weal in days to come, when it should be seen that unity of religious faith in England had been broken, perhaps for ever.

One word more in conclusion. There is an idea abroad that it is in great measure to the Puritans that we owe liberty of conscience. It is true that in the issue they, or their descendants at all events, were one of the elements which contributed to this result. But liberty of conscience was in no degree the Puritan ideal. In fact, it directly ran counter to their ideal. According to their principles a church order and discipline existed by Divine right. To them only one form of religious belief was to be permitted in England; and not merely one form of belief, but one form only of church order, and that belief, and order theirs and theirs alone. Those who would not accept it must be made to do so, or suffer for their refusal.

NOTE on p. 161.

Mr. Kenyon, *Our Bible and the Ancient Manuscripts* (p. 206), has said that "it is only in rhetorical passages that the picture" of the Lollards persecuted for the making and use of the English Scriptures has been drawn. A friend has pointed out to me that the extract I have given from Taine in regard to this is, indeed, rhetorical, and may therefore suggest to those who do not possess special knowledge of the subject, that the observation is just. I add here, therefore, the remarks of two English writers, who speak in a sober and straightforward way. The first is taken from the *First Sketch of English Literature*, by Mr. Henry Morley, a work that has had the widest circulation, and which, by the year 1887, had passed through seven editions. The same statements, with a few verbal variations, are reproduced in Mr. Morley's *English Writers*, vol. vi. (London : Cassell, 1890), p. 139. I have made no attempt to find where the quotation of the law against the Lollards given by Mr. Morley in old English comes from. Possibly Foxe, the martyrologist, may be the authority. The original act was, of course, in Norman French.

Mr. Morley writes: "In the second year of Henry V., in 1414, a new law passed against the Lollards, which ordained that they should forfeit all the lands they had in fee simple, and all their goods and chattels to the king. The same act decreed that whatsoever they were *that should read the Scriptures in their mother tongue*, they should forfeit 'land, catel, lif, and godes from their heyres for ever, and so be condempned for heretykes to God, enemies to the crowne, and most errant traitors to the lande.'"[1]

---

[1] The act referred to is to be found in the Statutes (Record Commission ed.) ii., 181-184. In this there is not a syllable about the Holy Scriptures from beginning to end. The chief passage is as follows: "And also that all persons convict of heresy of what estate or degree that they be, by the said ordinaries or other commissaries left to the secular power, according to the laws of holy church, shall lose and forfeit all their lands and tenements, which they have in fee simple" (p. 182). The justices are given power to inquire concerning "the common writers of such books, as well as of the sermons, as of their schools, conventicles, congregations and confederacies."

The second writer whom I will quote is the present Bishop of Durham, to whose *General View of the History of the English Bible* most persons desiring to have a critical and reliable statement about the subject in question will naturally turn. This is what Dr. Westcott says about it: "As might be expected the revised text (by Purvey) displaced the original version (by Wyclif and Hereford), and in spite of its stern proscription in a convocation in 1408, under the influence of Archbishop Arundel, it was widely circulated through all classes, till it was at last superseded by the printed versions of the 16th century." Then in a note the Bishop adds: "It is scarcely necessary to add that Sir T. More's statement that the holy Bible was translated (into English) long before Wycliffe's days, is not supported by the least independent evidence. He may have seen a MS. of Wycliffe's version and (like Lambert) have miscalculated the date" (p. 15). Again, "In a convocation of the province of Canterbury, held at Oxford under Archbishop Arundel, several constitutions were enacted against the party of the Reformation. The one on the use of the vernacular Scriptures is important, both in form and substance." Then, after quoting the well known provision of the Synod, the writer continues: "Four years after came the insurrection and death of Sir John Oldcastle; a new and more stringent act was passed against heresy (2 Henry V.), and the Lollards, as a party, were destroyed. But the English Bible survived their destruction. The terms of the condemnation under Archbishop Arundel were explicit, but it was practically ineffectual. No such approbation as was required, so far as we know, was ever granted, but the work was still transcribed for private use, and the MSS. are themselves the best records of its history."

INDEX.

ABBEYS, the national archives, 58
ABINGDON ABBEY, books at, 19; professed scribes at, 52; materials for scriptorium work at, 46
ABUSES, Catholic clergy speak against, 97
ADAMES, 368
ADDITAMENTA, The, a collection of state papers, 61; the public records in, 62
ADMONT, Monastery of, 20, *note* 2
ALAN OF LYNN, his Summa predicantium, 213, 216
ALLEN, Richard, 349
ALNWICK, Bp. of Norwich, 232
ALNWICK, English testament at, 143
ALPHABETUM exemplorum, 218
ALPHABETUM predicantium, 214
ALRESFORD, 345, 347
AMIATINUS CODEX, history of, 55
ANECDOTES in sermons, use of, 209
ANGEL GUARDIANS, devotion to, 197, *note*
ANGLESEY PRIORY, Cambridge, books lent to, 32
ANGLO-SAXON GOSPELS, copies of, 151.
ANNE OF BOHEMIA, her love for vernacular Scriptures, 149
ANSELM, Abbot of Bury, 232; his tomb, 246
ANTIQUARII employed by Richard of Bury, 53
APOCALYPSE, The early translation of, not Wyclif's, 147

APOLLONIUS, Anglo-Saxon translation of, 24
AQUINAS, St. Thomas, his works brought to England, 37
ARAGON, King Peter III. of, his library, 18
ARCHCANTOR, John the Roman, 55
ARCHIVES of monasteries searched for state documents, 59
ARISTOTLE TO ALEXANDER, Book called, 296
ARMAGH, sermons preached by Fitz-Ralph at, 66
ARMARIUS, Directions for the office of, 20, *note* 2, 48
ARUNDEL, Archbishop, his gift of books to Canterbury, 9; orders instruction of people by clergy, 190; supposed hostility to English Bible, 163; on Wyclif's English Scriptures, 113; his Constitution on English Scriptures, 122 *seqq.*; Canon Dixon on his attitude to vernacular Bible, 125, *note*; his approval of some translation, 149, 178; proposal to Parliament, 150; examination of documents regarding, 166
ATHELSTAN, King, his presents to Bath, 29
AUGUSTINIANS, employment of professional scribes by, 52
AURORA MASS, The, 245
AUTHORISATION of vernacular Scrip-

tures, 148, 149, 155; admitted now, 159; evidence for, 134.

BABEES BOOK, The, 278
BACULARIUS, The, 266
BALDWIN, Abb. of Bury, 252
BALE, John, on the Carmelites, 223; on Leland, 23; his proposal for a library in every county, 39
BALL, John, the preacher, 87
BANNISTER, Edward, 345, 346, 358, 362
BARDNEY ABBEY, Henry IV. at, 7
BARNES, Robert, 372, 373
BARNWELL PRIORY, Book presses at, 15; employment of professional scribes at, 52; Lenten distribution of books at, 28
BARTHOLOMEUS, De proprietatibus rerum, 274
BASILICAS, Libraries attached to, 5.
BASING, 351
BATH, Books given to, 29
BEARD, Ben, an informer, 370
BECONSHAW, William, 357
    „   John, 358, 359
BEDFORD, The Regent duke of, 52
BEHAVIOUR, Tracts on, 278
BELLAMY, 372
BENEDICT, St., his rule, 1, 2
BENEDICTINE monks of England, their use of books, 36; Cardinal Pole's love for, 284, *note*
BENET BISCOP, St., his library, 54
BERE, Abbot of Glastonbury, his part in the revival of letters, 317 *seqq*.
BERNARD, St., describes monastic writing schools, 43; on chained books, 17
BESANÇON, Etienne de, his stories for sermons, 218
BIBLE, Hebrew MSS. in England, 54, *note*; Bohemian version of, 119, *note*
BIBLE, THE ENGLISH, 102; common in Middle ages, 146, *note* 2; in 16th century, 148; is given publicly in wills, 143

BIBLICAL literature attributed wrongly to Wyclif, 111
BIBLICAL studies of monks, 2, 16
BIBLIOTHECA, meaning of the word, 4
BISHOPS, The, their attitude towards evil, 73; character of Christian, 81
BLACK PRINCE, The, 67; character of, 99; the hope of the nation, 75; death of, 97; sermon on, 98
BLACKMAN, Mary, 349
BLESSED VIRGIN, Devotion to, 274.
BOHEMIAN Bible, versions of, 119, *note*
BOKENHAM, Dom Edmund, chaplain to Ed. III., 237
BOLOGNA, Greek studies at, 310
BONNER, Bp., owns a supposed Wyclif Bible, 143
BOOKCASES, 14, 15, 16
BOOKS, making of, a monastic work, 41; need of, in monasteries, 17; monastic care of, 20, *note* 2; price of, 29; bequeathed on death, 35, *note*; mediæval borrowing of, 8, 30; claiming of stray, 17; sold from St. Albans library, 53; presents of, 34; kept in the cloister at Durham, 11; chaining of, 17; destruction of, at Reformation, 23; care of, 268
BOROUGH, *see* Burgo
BOSTON OF BURY, his great index, 25, 216
BOTILLER, Ed., monk of Westminster, 280, *note*
BOTONER, family of, 289; William, *see* W. of Worcester; Adam, 289, *note*
BOULTON. Thomas de, gets books for Vale Royal, 37
BOYLION, Godfray de, The Viage of, 8
BOZON, Nicholas, his stories for sermons, 218
BRAMBRIDGE, 245, 370
BRAMSHOT, 372
BRETTON, The printer, 198, *note*
BREVES, The, 47

INDEX.

BRISTOL, St. Mary's, 296; Bible at, 144; the family of Botoner at, 288
BROMYARD, John, his aids to preachers, 212
BROWNE, George, 368
BRUNDISH, Abb. Edmund, 234, 237; his great antiphonal, 244
BRUNTON, Bp. Thomas, of Rochester, 66 seqq.; his sermons, 221; his social teachings, 87; his character as an orator, 101
BUCKLEY, Dom Sigebert, 379
BULBECK, Elizabeth, 350
BULLACRE, Mrs. Edborow, 358
BURGO, or Borough, John de, 197
BURIAL denied to Catholics, 379
BURITON, 346, 347, 349, 358
BURLEIGH, Lord, on the Mass, 322
BURTON-ON-TRENT, library at, 24, note 2; state papers in archives of, 59
BUBY, Richard of, Bp. of Durham, 11, note 6; 213, note; employs scribes, 52; buys books from St. Albans, 53; his *antiquarii*, 53
BURY ST. EDMUNDS, books given to, 38; books lent from, 38; ancient classic in library of, 54, note; Henry VI. at, 226; character of, 229; bronze gates of, 232; choir paintings at, 233; chalice given for ransom of Richard I. from, 237; ruin of, 239; the bells of, 240; boy school at, 251

CAMBRIDGE, William of Worcester visits the College libraries at, 302
CAMDEN on the destruction of Bury, 237; his assertion as to Catholic religion being connived at, 335
CANTERBURY, CHRIST CHURCH, law books given to, 39, note 2; size of the library at, 22; books lent from, 9, 32, 33, note; building of library at, 14; the prior's "gloriet" at, 14; librarian at, 20; burial of B. Prince at,

98, seqq.; school at, 270; letter from, 282; Card. Pole on return of Benedictines to, 284, note; Greek school at, 308, seqq.; visit of Greek Emperor to, 312; fire at, 315; classical MSS. at, 314
CANTERBURY, ST. AUGUSTINE'S, W. of Worcester at, 303; prayers for benefactors, at, 34
CANTERBURY TALES, The, 86; the character of the priest in, 181; on popular love of tales, 219
CANTOR, The, his charge of the monastic books, 18, 31
CARDIFF, Franciscan library burnt at, 33
CARTHUSIAN RULE on book making, 48
CATALOGUES in monastic libraries, 21, note, 26; at Durham, 27
CATHERINGTON, 346, 348
CATHOLIC DICTIONARY, The, on Wyclif, 106
CATHOLIC RITES prohibited by Elizabeth, 333, 337
CATHOLICS, possessed of supposed Wyclif Scriptures, 143, 152; forced to attend church under Elizabeth, 335; retired abroad for the exercise of their religion, 339, 366
CAXTON, his prints of the Liber Festivalis, 211
CEOLFRID, St., and the Codex Amiatinus, 55
CHAPMAN, John, priest, 358, 366
CHARLTON, 348
CHARTERHOUSE AT SHENE, 9
CHAUCER, his typical priest, 183
CHEPMAN, 268
CHRISTIAN DOCTRINE, Instructions on, 202
CHRONICLE OF ST. ALBANS, The suppressed, 69, 82
CHRONICLES, Writing of, 6
CHURCH, state of, in 11th century in England, 96; attitude to the verna-

cular Scriptures, 104, 133, *note*, 160; teaching of, in Middle Ages, 180

CICERO, *De Senectute*, W. of Worcester translates, 305; *De Republica*, a copy at Canterbury in 16th Century, 314, *seqq*.

CILIUM OCULI SACERDOTIS, The, 201, *note*

CLARKE, Humphrey, 345

CLASSES, The, in 14th century, 76; division between, 88

CLAYMOND, John, 318, *note*

CLERGY, The duties of, 79

CLOISTER, The monastic; books in, 10, 12; writing done in, 44, 47; the usual library, 12; glazed sometimes, 14; carrels for study in, 10, 14; schools in, 261; the workshop of the house, 263

CLUNY, Monastic library catalogue at, 27

COBHAM, Sermon of Bishop Brunton at, 93

CODEX AMIATINUS, its history, 55

COLET, DEAN, and the new learning, 314

COLLYNS, Nicholas, 358

COMMANDMENTS, Instructions on the, 199, 201, *note*

COMMONPLACE BOOKS of preachers, 212, *note*

CONCORDANCES of Scripture in 14th century, 216

CONFESSORS, Bishop Brunton on duties of, 73, 84, 85; their duty to instruct penitents, 201

CONFORMITY to State religion impossible to Catholics, 334

CONSCIENCE, Liberty of, won by Catholic suffering, 381 *seqq*.

COOK, Hugh, Abbot of Reading, his patronage of Greek studies, 317, *note*

COOPER, Bp. of Winchester, his advice as to Catholics, 374; refuses to permit Catholic burials, 379

CORBIE, writing school at, 51

CORNWALL, W. of Worcester on, 293

CORRECTOR, The, of manuscripts, 51

COTTON, George, 346, 351, 352, 358, 361, 366, 369, 376

COTTON, Richard, 361

COVENTRY, Founders of St. Michael's at, 289, *note*

Cox, Leonard, and instruction in Greek at Reading, 317

CRANMER, Archbishop, on vernacular Scriptures, 34; his copy of English Bible, 177; implies existence of an authorised translation, 135

CROWCHER, Agnes and Thomas, 349

,, Ralph, 350

,, Martin, 369

CROYLAND, Books lent from, 31

CUFFOLD, Simon, 357

CURTEYS, Abbot of Bury, 32

DAMASUS, Pope St., forms Roman library, 4

DANVERS, Thomas and Anne, 144, 145

DE ARTE PREDICANDI, by Walleys, 207, *note*

DE LIRA on the Bible, put for common use at Oxford, 18

DELISLE, M., on Mediæval book lending, 30; on Tours' school of writing, 57, *note*

DENHAM, Reginald de, gives bells to Bury, 240

DENMARK, W. of Worcester's notes upon, 224

DEPING, Library at, 24

DERNHALL, or Vale Royal, gift of books to, 37

DESTRUCTION of books, &c., at the Reformation, 23, 39, 54, *note*

DEXTRA PARS OCULI, Instructions named, 197

DIS, Walter de, 236

DURHAM, Rites of, 10; MSS. kept in various places at, 10; the library at

INDEX. 389

12; the school at, 264; catalogues of library at, 27; Robert Rypon, Sub-prior of, 27, *note*; St. Cuthbert's, Gospel at, 29; MS. Gospel of St. Luke at, 55

DUTCH versions of Scripture, 119 *note*

DYLING, Richard, 349

EASTMEON, 346, 358

EASTON, Cardinal Adam, 67; his gifts to Norwich, 34; his tomb in Rome, 35, *note*

EASTRY, Prior of Canterbury, his catalogue, 22, 33, *note*

EBRARD the Grecian, 279

ECCLESIASTICAL authorities, supposed hostility of, to vernacular Scriptures, 109, 119, 157, 161; on what assumption based, 159; real attitude of, 119, 122, *note*, 125, *note*

EDMUND, St., Hymn to, 233

EDUCATION in middle ages, 260

EDWARD the Confessor, his charters to Bury, 229

EDWARD III., state of England at the close of the reign of, 67; evil influence over, 71

ELEANOR, Queen of Henry II., gifts to Bury from, 237

ELIZABETH, Queen, religious difficulties on Accession of, 319; had no religious preferences, 322; penal laws of, 327; had no wish for severity, 335

ELMSWELL, The Bury manor at, 255

ENGLAND, state of, in 14th century, 70, 75, 85, 86; state of the Church in, 96; services in churches of, 145; sermons in, 222; *Abbeys of*, libraries not common in, 9; MSS. of classics in, 54, *note*; early writing schools in, 51; *Benedictines of*, chapter orders as to books, 27, 49; book-buying in 16th century, 36, *note*

ENGLISH BIBLE, Wyclifite tradition as to, 102-3; methods of translators, 118; supposed destruction by church authority, 104, 161, 383; Maitland as to, 104, *note*, 162, *note*; common use of, 146, *note* 2

ENGLISH LANGUAGE, first beginnings of, 109

ENGLISH TRACTS of 14th and 15th century, commonly attributed to Wyclif, 108

EPISCOPAL REGISTERS, evidence of instruction to people in, 193

EPISTLES AND GOSPELS, to be read in vernacular, 151

ERASMUS submits his translation to Abbot Bere, 317, *note*

ETIENNE de Besançon, his sermon aids, 219

EVANGELIUM ÆTERNUM, meaning of, 172

EVESHAM ABBEY, The cantor's office at, 19; Abbot Marleberge gives canon-law books to, 38; writing schools established at, 51

EXETER REGISTERS on religious instruction, 194

EXANNUAL ROLLS, The, 351

FAMILIAR INSTRUCTIONS as opposed to set sermons, 224

FASTOLF, Sir John, 287, 289, 301

FAWKENOR, William, 345

FELTON, John, his sermons, 207, 208, *note*

FENNEL, a priest, 371

FESTIVALE, The, MS. copies of, 192, *note*

FESTIVALS, collections of sermons for, 210

FINES for recusancy, 349, 352, *seqq*.

FIRES, danger of mediæval, 33, 34, 59

FISHER, Bishop, and the new learning, 314

FISH-STEWS at Bury, 254
FITZ-JAMES, Bp., destroys Hun's English Bible, 164
FITZ-RALPH, Archbp., 66, 219
FIVE AND TWENTY BOOKS, the prologues called, 141
FLOS FILIUS, the Bury *Benedicamus* called, 243
FLOS FLORUM, the book named, 201
FORSHALL AND MADDEN, their evidences as to Wyclif's Bible, 113, 154, 158; on hostility of church to Bible, 162, *note*
FOXE, John, on proposed authorised version, 150; his testimony as to authorised version, 136
FRANCISCAN library at Oxford, 25
,, ,, at Cardiff burnt, 33
FRATERNITY O.S.B. receptions at Bury, 256
FRENCH BIBLES, numbers of versions, 120 and *note*
FRENCH KING, audiences granted by the, 78
FRENCH LANGUAGE, late continuance in England of, 109
FROUDE, Mr., on Catholic ignorance of Scripture, 162

GATRYKE, his instruction book, 189
GAUNT, John of, evil influence of, 68, 82; supports the Lollards, 96; opposed English Bible in Parliament, 150
GENNINGS, Fr. Edmund, 375
GENTYLL, Umfrido—a bookseller, 306
GERMAN vernacular Scriptures, 119, *note*, 120
GESTA ROMANORUM, The, 218
GILDAS, copy of, at Oxford, 296
GLANVILLE, Bartholomew, 213
GLASTONBURY, Leland at, 292; size of library at, 22; Erasmus and Greek learning at, 317, *note*

GLORIET, a building at Canterbury called, 14
GLOUCESTER, Duke Humphrey of, 8; employs professional scribes, 52; presents books to Oxford, 25; his English Bible, 142; a *confrater* of St. Albans and Bury, 256
GOLDEN FOUNDATION, The, by Gorham, 214, *note*
GOLDEN LEGEND — a Bible history, 121
GOLDSTONE, Prior Reynold of Canterbury, 14, 271; revives Greek studies in Canterbury, 309
GOOD PARLIAMENT, Meeting of, 71, 75, 81
GORHAM, Nicholas, 214
GOSFORD, John, prior of Bury, 237; his bells, 240; his buildings, 254
GOSPEL, The, a common word for preaching, 172
GOSPELS, The, in English, in possession of Queen Anne of Bohemia, 150
GOTER, Thomas, 358
GÖTHE, W. von, 11
GOWER, the poet, tomb of, 303
GREEK MSS., secured for France at Reformation, 314; burnt at Canterbury, 315
GREEK STUDIES, revival of, 306; Professor Burrows on, 307; beginnings at Canterbury, 308-9; influence of visit of Greek Emperor to Canterbury, 312; put an end to by Reformation, 316; Cardinal Pole on need for, 316, *note*
GREEN, Mr. J. R., on Elizabeth's recusancy laws, 326 *seqq.*
GRINDAL advises torture for a priest, 331
GROCYN, 306-7; goes to Italy to study, 311; his books, 318, *note*
GROSSETESTE, Bp., 66; his works, 296; on popular instructions, 201; his unpublished sermons, 219

INDEX.

GUIGO, Prior of Carthusians, his legislation for the order, 48

HALLAM on the Elizabethan recusancy laws, 326 *seqq.*
HAMBLEDON, 345, 347, 349, 351
HAMPOLE, Richard Rolle of, his translation of the Psalms, 109, 115; his English Psalms used, 146; and interpolated by Lollards, 139
HARRIS, John, 349
HART, Walter le, Bp. of Norwich, 294
HARTWIG, 17, *note*
HAVANT, 346, 348, 350
HAYLES Abbey, Books brought from Avignon for, 37, *note*
HAYWOOD, Jasper, 368
HAYLING, 348
HEARNE on monastic libraries, 25
HEATH, Jerome, 370
HEATH, Nicholas, is connected with translation of Bible, 177
HEBREW Alphabet, W. of Worcester on, 302
HENRY III. begs books for Dernhall, 36; his gifts to Bury, 242; and Matthew Paris, 61
HENRY IV. at Bardney, 7; a borrower of books, 8
HENRY V., 8
HENRY VI. possessor of vernacular Scriptures, 140; his Christmas at Bury, 226; his coronation, 227; his reception as *confrater*, O.S.B., 257
HENRY VII. possessor of vernacular Bible, 151
HENSLOW, Mrs. Katherine, 362
HEREFORD, Adam de Orlton, Bp. of, brings books from Avignon, 37, *note*
HEREFORD, Nicholas, his work of translating Scripture, 115; his career, 116-137
HERIMANN, Abbot of Tournay, on studies in his monastery, 44
HERTLEY, John, prior of Rochester, 67

HINTON Charterhouse, Books lent from, 31
HINTON, Hampshire, 347
HISTORIETTES in Sermons, 209, 218
HISTORY and the people, 180
HOBBY, Friar, 290
HOBHOUSE, Bp., on mediæval instructions, 184
HOLCOT, Robert, 213, *note*
HOLY INNOCENTS Day at Bury, 251
HOLY-WATER-BELL, The, 240
HOLY WEEK, Instructions for, 210, *note*
HORWELL, John, a London Goldsmith, 238
HOSPITALITY in monasteries, 248
HUGH II., abbot of Bury, his vestments, 236
HUGH, the sacrist, at Bury, 237; his great rood, 244
HUMPHREY, D. of Gloucester, a *confrater*, O.S.B., 257
HUN, the London Lollard, Bible of, 128, 129, 164
HUS, John, or Wyclifite origin of the English Bible, 113; sole authority for the tradition, 174

IDLENESS, St. Benedict's legislation against, 3
IDSWORTH, 349, 352, 358, 362
ILLUMINATION OF MSS., St. Dunstan works at, 50, a monastic work, 49
INDEXES, the great work of making, 216
INGRAM, William, Monk of Canterbury, 270
INGULPH, Chronicle of, 31; evidence of late date of, 59
INQUISITION, The supposed, as to English Bible, 161
INSTRUCTION in religion, a duty of the Church, 182; ordered by Synod of Oxford, 187; how carried out, 188; character of, 192; manuals to aid clergy in, 195 *seqq.*, 214; need of popular and familiar, 224

INSURRECTION of 1381, 91 *seqq*.
INTELLECTUAL work, monastic, 1
ITALIAN VERNACULAR Scriptures, 120

JARROW, Writing school at, 56
JERUSALEM, The Chronicles of, 8
JOLY, William, a priest in the Tower, 333
JONES, Edward, an informer, 367
JONES, John, lesson book of, 275
JOY, Anthony, 348
JOY, Robert, 358
JUDGES in the 14th Century, 83

KENYON, Mr., on Wyclif's Bible tradition, 159, 161, 383
KINGSBERY, Dom Thomas, of St. Albans, and Leland, 22
KNIGHT, Henry, 348
KNIGHT, Robert, 372
KNYGHTON, Henry, on Wyclif and the English Bible, 113; his authority examined, 171

LABOUR OF HANDS only a partial pursuit of monks, 1
LACY, Henry, E. of Lincoln, his gifts to Bury, 234, 237
LAMBETH MS. of Council at Oxford, notes from, 170
LANCIANI on ancient Roman libraries, 5
LANFRANC, his Consuetudinary, 44
LANGHAM, Archbishop, 67; on instructions, 189
LANGTON HERRING, 358
LANTHONY Priory, Library at, 16, *note*
LATIMER'S sermons, value of, 64
LATIN, general knowledge of, in Middle Ages, 109, 272
LAVENHAM, Dom John, of Bury, 233, 235, 237, 240
LAW, administration of unjust, in regard to poor, 89

LAWRENCE, St., Library in Church of, at Rome, 5
LAYTON, Dr., at Canterbury, 315
LELAND, his visit to Bath, 29; to St. Albans, 22; on the destruction of books at Reformation, 23; on fire at Canterbury, 316
LENDING BOOKS, 19; services done by this in monasteries, 8, 30, 33, *note*
LENTEN READING in monasteries, 28
LEOFSTAN, Abb. of Bury, 235
LESSON BOOK, a mediæval example of 274
LIBER FESTIVALIS, 191, 209
LIBRARIAN, The mediæval office of, 18
LIBRARIES, need of, in monasteries, 2; freely used by monks, 28; large collections and modern growth, 26; connected with churches, 5, 6, 8; formation in distinct places, 9, 12; at Durham, 11; presents to, 39; catalogues of, 15, 16, *note*, 26
LILLY, Mr., on mediæval religious instruction, 189
LINACRE and the revival of Greek, 307; at the Canterbury school, 310; taken to Italy, 310; teacher of Sir Thomas More, 311
LINGARD, Dr., on the Wyclif translation of Scripture, 106
LIVY, the *Decades* of, 305
LOLLARDS, The, preaching of, 173, 190; search for writings of, 129, 139, 161; interpolation of Catholic books by, 139; not persecuted for the Bible, 104, 161, 163; their doctrines denounced by Bp. Brunton, 95; their preachers mostly laymen, 153; why called "Bible-men," 148; no evidence of persecution for English Bible, 126
LONDON, need of preaching in, 80
LOUIS, St., and the library of the Sainte Chapelle, 5
LUCA, a bookseller in London from, 306

INDEX.

LUDLOW, John, 358
LUTHER and the Bible, myth as to, 120 and *note*
LUTTERWORTH, Tradition as to Wyclif, 106, 112; Purvey at, 116
LYDGATE, Dom John, 255, 278
LYNDEWODE on the Council of Oxford, 124, 147, *note*

MACHLIN, William, the printer, 200
MAGNA CHARTA, Copies placed in Religious houses, 59
MAITLAND on the Wyclif tradition, 104
MALMESBURY ABBEY, St. Aldhelm's Psalter at, 29
MALMESBURY, William of, 43; on St. Dunstan's work, 50
MANNERS, Tracts on, 277
MANUALS for popular instruction, 195
MANUEL, The Greek Emperor, at Canterbury, 312
MANUSCRIPTS, The making of, 42, 51; each one unique, 21; cost of, 21; care taken of, 29; Mare, Abbot de la, of St. Albans, 13.
MAPLEDURHAM, 358, 368, 369, 372
MARVYN, Mr., 372
MASS, The, Questions as to, 276; instructions on, 199, *note*; Lord Burleigh on, 322; people in prison for hearing, 331; Scripture to be read in, 151; offered by stealth under Elizabeth, 337
MASSES AND CLASSES, Bp. Brunton on, 89
MATINS at Bury, description of, 243
MATTHEW, Mr. F. D., on Wyclif tradition, 103, 158; on hostility of English Church to the Bible, 121
MAUNDAY THURSDAY, Instructions on, 210, *note*
MEDIÆVAL SERMONS, character of, 65
MEDICAL WORKS given to Bury, 39
MENDICANT ORDERS, Libraries of, 11; popular teaching of, 203; Archbp.

Fitz-Ralph on, 219, *note*; powers of, 84; attacks on, 66
MENTMORE, Abbot Michael of St. Albans, 12
MEONSTOKE, 358
MERTON COLLEGE, Oxford, copy of Gildas at, 296
METHWOLD, Katherine, a nun, 143
METRICAL TRANSLATIONS of Scripture, 110
MICHELGROVE, 358
MILLES, Humphrey, 345
MOLASH, Dom William of, 9
MONASTIC LIBRARIES, the National Archives, 58; size of, 3, 22; for most part in the Cloister, 4, 6; Scribes to, 372; be set apart for work, 47
MONASTIC ORDERS, work of, 1; parish churches served by, 239; work common to all, 51; character of work, 57
MONK BRETTON, monastic library of, 39, *note* 3
MONKS, regulations for the reading of, 28
MONTAGUE, Lord, 368
MOORE, Prior of Worcester, his book buying, 35
MOOTE, John de la, Abbot of St. Albans, 13
MORE, Sir Thomas, his attachment to the new learning, 309; his teachers at Oxford, 311; his college at Oxford, 317; on authorised vernacular version of Scripture, 124, 136, 148, 164; on destruction of Hun's Bible, 128
MORLEY, Mr. H., on Wyclif, 383
MORRICE, Cranmer's Secretary, on preparation for the printed Bible, 177
MOUNT ST. MICHAEL, Cornwall, W. of Worcester at, 293, 295
MUSIC, The mediæval notion of "colours of," 303
MYRK, John, his sermons, 191, *note*, 209
MYRROURE of Our Lady, The, 145

INDEX.

NEAVE, Thomas, 346, 349
NEAVE, Stephens, 349
NEVILL, Archbp., orders religious instruction, 190
NEW LEARNING, 308 seqq.; destroyed at Reformation, 316
NEW TESTAMENT, Wyclif's connection with the translation, 112
NEWENHAM ABBEY, 295
NEWLANDS, 347
NEWPORT, Prior of Bury, his bell, 240
NORTHERN INSURRECTION for religion, 338
NORTON, Anthony, 348, 380
NORWICH, Cardinal Easton's gifts to, 34; fire at, 33, 59; archives destroyed, 39; Bp. Brunton at, 67
NOTE BOOKS, Information to be obtained from, 236
NOVICES at Westminster, Book set apart for, 12
NUNS in possession of supposed Wyclifite Scriptures, 142

OCULUS SACERDOTIS, The book named, 197
OKELIE, Widow, 349
OMONT, M. H., 17, note
O REX CLEMENS, The *Kyrie* named, 245
ORDINATION, Letter of a Canterbury monk on his, 282
ORLTON, Bp. of Hereford, 37, note
ORMULUM, The, a metrical translation of Scripture, 110
ORTHODOX possessors of English Bible, 140
OUEN, ST., Librarian's notes at, 30
OVID, Mediæval knowledge of, 301; French translation of, 302
OWEN GLENDOWER, Franciscan library at Cardiff destroyed by, 33
OXFORD, Council of, on Vernacular Bible, 122, 123, 148; meaning explained by Lyndewode, &c., 124; the provision examined, 169

OXFORD UNIVERSITY, catalogue of library at, 27; direction as to use of books at, 21; Duke Humphrey's present of books to, 25; chained books at, 17
   St. Mary's, de Lira's works in, 17
   Franciscan library at, 25
   Trinity College, foundation of, 316
   Canterbury College and Greek studies, 317

PADUA, *St. Justina's* library catalogue, 10, note; *St. Antonio* library catalogue, 11, note; books lent from, 32, note
PAGULA, William, 196
PARIS, Coronation of Henry VI. in, 227; *St. Victor's*, cantor to find material for books at, 47; *St. Denis* renowned for MSS. making, 53
PARIS, MATTHEW, 43; his character, 56; his career, 60; is State archivist, 61; at marriage of Henry III., 60
PARKER, Archbishop, on versions before Wyclif, 136
PARKER, Walter, 196
PARLIAMENT, The Good, 70, 75; praises of the institution of, 71
PARS OCULI SACERDOTIS, Instructions called, 196, 199, note
PASTON FAMILY, The, 288
PATER NOSTER, meaning of instructions on, 202
PEASANT RISING of 1381, 91
PECKHAM Archbp., loan of books to, 31; orders instructions, 187
PECOCK, Bp. Reginald, 147; on Bible reading, 148
PELL'S RECEIPT BOOK, 352
PENAL laws under Elizabeth, 332 seqq.
PEPWELL, The printer, 198, note
PERRERS, Alice, 67, 75, 78, 81
PERSECUTION of Lollards for English Bible, 104, note, 138

INDEX. 395

PETERBOROUGH, size of library at, 22; burnt by Danes, 33; Abbot Peter collects books for, 37
PETERHOUSE, Cambridge, 302
PETERSFIELD, 345, 346, 349, 352, 368.
PHILOBIBLON, The, 11, *note*
PIERS PLOUGHMAN, 86
PIUS V., Pope, Bull of, 338
POBLET, Cistercian abbey at, 18
POITIERS, The Victory of, 99
POLE, Cardinal, his education at Canterbury, 284, *note*
PONTISSARA, John de, Bp. of Winchester, 31, *note*
POOR, The, Bp. Brunton on, 88
"POOR PRIESTS," Wyclif's, 153
POPE, Sir Thomas, founds Trinity Coll., Oxford, 316
POPULAR INSTRUCTIONS, 204
PORCHESTER, 367
POUNDES, Thomas, 345, 377
PRAYERS, Beauty of old Catholic, 200
PREACHING, Mediæval, 63; instructions on the art of, 206; Bp. Brunton on, 73; Wyclifite, 153; helps for, 211, 212, *note*, 213
PRELATES, character of true Christian, 81
PRE-REFORMATION ENGLISH CHURCH HISTORY, still unknown, 179
PRIEST, Chaucer describes a pre-Reformation, 183; difficult position under Elizabeth, 337; laws against, 343
PRINTED VERNACULAR BIBLES, attitude of church to, 133
PROCESSIONS at Bury abbey, 246; at Bardney, 7; public, ordered in 14th century, 70, 100
PROLOGUES to English Scriptures, 117, 141, 175
PROTESTANT TRANSLATION OF BIBLE, errors in, 131, *note*
PSALMS, Early translation of, 109; in use, 146

PUNSHOLT, 348, 389
PUPILLA OCULI, Instruction book named, 197, 198, *note*
PURVEY, his connection with English Bible, 116, 137, 162
PYNSON prints the *Liber Festivalis*, 211

RACK, use of, on Catholics in Elizabeth's reign, 341
READING Abbey, State documents in Archives of, 59; Greek studies at, 317, *note*
RECUSANTS, laws as to, 324; chief points in, 325 *seqq.*; meaning of term, 326; goods sold to pay fines, 351; rolls of, 352; fines from, farmed 364; money levied upon, 365; hardships of, 374; numbers in diocese of Winchester, 374; burial in churchyards denied to, 379
RED BOOK OF EYE, 54, *note*
REFECTORY, reading books for, 11; Bible for, 38; the Bury, 248
REFORMATION designed to blot out the past, 40; put an end to learning, 316
REGIMEN ANIMARUM, The, 198, *note*
RELIGION, laws as to, 324; liberty as to, unknown in Tudor times, 321
RELIGIOUS INFLUENCES in Middle Ages, 273
RELIGIOUS Orders, supposed hostility to learning, 307
REPRESSOR, The, by Bp. Pecock, 147
RHEIMS, Writing school at, 57, *note*
RICH AND POOR, Bishop Brunton on, 89
RICHARD I., Bury chalice given for ransom, 237
RICHARD II., coronation of, 100; Queen of, and the Bible, 149
RICHARDS, a priest, 371

RIPON, Dom Robert of Durham, 27, 214
ROCHESTER, election of Bishop to, 67
ROKELAND, William de, Prior of Bury, 237
ROLLE, Richard of Hampole, his translation of Psalms, 109
ROLLESTON, Robert, 8
ROME, public libraries in, 4
ROSES, The wars of the, 304
ROSSI DE, Remarks on libraries, 5: on Codex Amiatinus, 56
ROYE, William, 130
RUBRICATOR, The, 52
RUDESBY, Arthur, 349
RUDHAM, Dom Thomas, 254
RULE OF ST. BENEDICT, 1; English copies in 16th century, 36; on Lenten reading, 28

SACRAMENTS, mediæval instruction on the, 198, *note*
ST. ALBANS, formation of library at, 5; historical school of, 6; building of library, 13; scriptorium of, 44; *Abbots*—Paul, 44; Simon, 5; Mentmore, 12; de la Mare, 13; de la Moote, 13; Whethamstede, 113; Lanfranc's Consuetudinary introduced, 44; books sold to Richard of Bury, 53; character of the writing peculiar, 56; foreign State, events known to, 62; suppressed chronicle of, 69; opposed to Lancastrians, 70, 82; great writing school at, 46, 51; Leland visits, 22; marked out for Tudor vengeance, 23; Humphrey, D. of Gloucester, a *confrater* of, 257; grammar school at, 267; frequent stay of Court at, 228
ST. ALDHELM, Psalter of, 29
ST. AMOUR, William de, 172
ST. AUGUSTINE, Works of, 16, 35
ST. BENET BISCOP, his writing school, 54

ST. BOTULPH, altar to, at Bury, 243
ST. BENET HULME, 62, 290, 296
ST. CLAUDE de Jura, library of, 17, *note*
ST. CUTHBERT, his Gospel book at Durham, 29
ST. DAVID writes out St. John's Gospel, 50
ST. DUNSTAN, a scribe and illuminator, 50
ST. EDMUND, Hymn to, 233; shrine of, 234, 243
ST. ETHELBERT, his epitaph at Canterbury, 303
ST. GALL, Scriptorium at, 44, *note* 2
ST. GREGORY, Works of, 9, 16
ST. MARY'S OTTERY, 294
ST. NECTAN, 295
ST. OYAN, chained dictionary at, 17
ST. PAUL'S CROSS, preaching at, 212 *note*, 220, 221
ST. PAUL'S SCHOOL, incident at, 266 *note*
ST. SABAS, altar to, in Bury, 242
ST. THOMAS, of Aquin, Works of, 303
ST. THOMAS OF VILLANOVA, on chained books, 17
SAMPSON, Abbot of Bury, his chasuble, 236; his cross, 237; his anniversary, 252; his vineyard, 254
SANDWICH, Nicholas, Prior of Canterbury, 82
ST. CECILIA, Rome, Cardinal Easton's tomb in, 35, *note*
SARUM Use, English Bible arranged for Mass according to, 151
SCHOOL, discipline of, 266; of writing in M. Ages, 53, 56
SCHORAM, William de, translates psalms, 107
SCRIBES, instruments for, 47; work in monasteries, 48; employment of professional, 52
SCRIPTORIA, true meaning of the word, 42; set places for, 44; silence kept

INDEX.

in, 45; Cistercian, 44, *note* 2; individual peculiarities in, 56
SCRIPTURES, Early English translations of, 109; study of, urged, 215
SEARCHES for Lollard literature, 129, 139
SELLYNG, Prior W. of Canterbury, 305; his influence on learning, 306, 309; his career, 308-10; his tract on Greek, 313; his MSS. burnt, 314
SERBOPOULOS, John, a Greek copyist at Reading, 318 *note*
SERMONS, Early printed, 191, 211; their form in M. Ages, 205; for Sundays, 208, *note*; different from instructions, 225; historical importance of, 65; how delivered, 68; little effect of, 94
SHELBORNE, the Jesuit, 368; John, 368, 369, 372; Thomas, 370
SHELLEY, Henry, 357, 358, 369; his family, 357, 368, 358, *note*
SHENE, Charterhouse, 9, 298
SHIRLEY, Professor, on Wyclif literature, 108
SINISTRA PARS OCULI, a book named, 198, *note*
SIXTUS V., Pope, 15, *note*
SOCIAL DISTURBANCE, 1381, 86
SOUTHWARK PRISON, 359
SPANISH VERNACULAR Bible, 120
SPECULUM CHRISTIANI, The, 198, 200
SPECULUM SPIRITUALIUM, The, 35
SPENDIMENT or treasury Durham, 10
STANS PUER AD MENSAM, The tract, 277
STAPELDON, Bp., his enquiries about religious instruction, 194
STAR CHAMBER fines, 353
STATE DOCUMENTS sent to monasteries, 58, 60
STEWS for fish at Bury, 254
STOCKWITH, Benjamin, 347, 360
STOKESLEY, Bp., and the new learning, 314
STONYHURST, The St. John's Gospel at, 56

STORY of the English Bible, The, 157
STORIES in mediæval sermons, 209, 217
STRANGE, R., 346, 370
SOUTHWICK, 347
SUDBURY, Archbp., his murder, 91
SUMMA CONFESSORUM, 199, *note*
SUMMA SUMMARUM RAYMUNDI, 198, *note*
SUPREMACY, The oath of, number of clergy refusing, 328, *note*; the purpose of, 334
SYON CONVENT, orthodoxy of, 145; English Bible at, 144

TABULÆ of devotion in English mediæval churches, 298
TAINE, M., on Wyclif's Bible, 105; on Lollard persecution, 138
TENEBRÆ, Instructions for, 210, *note*
TERENCE, mediæval knowledge of, 302; copies of, 53
TERRINGTON, 33
THEMA, The, of Gorham, 214
THETFORD, Dominican house at, 296
THOMAS, Abbot of Bury, 249
THOMPSON, Sir E. Maunde, on Wyclif, 115
THORESBY, Archbp., his directions as to instruction, 189
TIDMARSH, family of, 287
TIMSBURY, 358
TINTERN, W. of Worcester at, 295
TICHBORNE, Nicholas, 357, 361, 377, 378
,, Peter, 358, 359, 361
,, Elizabeth, 362, 371
,, Chidcock, 367, 369
,, Gilbert, 371
TITCHFIELD, library at, 15
TOURNAY, St. Martin's Abbey, 44
TOURS, writing school at, 51, 57, *note*
TRANSLATIONS of Scripture authorised by Church, 146, 164
TREASURY or Spendiment, The, at Durham, 10

INDEX.

TRINITY, The Holy, The Black Prince and devotion to, 100
TUDORS, The, and conscience, 323
TUNSTAL, Bp., his condemnation of Tyndale's Testament, 132; his connection with Cranmer's translation, 177
TURNER, Giles, 346
TWYFORD, 345, 369
TYNDALE, his N. Testament, 130; character of, 130, *note*; false translations in, 131, 133

UDALL, *alias* UVEDALE, Anthony, 345, 347, 351, 365
UNIFORMITY, the act of, 330; its object, 331
UTRECHT PSALTER, The, 55

VACHELL, Stephen, 345, 348, 351, 352, 357, 358, 361, 365, 369
VACHELL, Margaret, 346
VALE ROYAL, or Dernhall, 37
VATICAN LIBRARY, Book-cases in, 15; Virgil in, 53
VERITATES THEOLOGICÆ, The book called, 199
VERNACULAR SCRIPTURES, evidence as to early, 110; tendency to spread error by, 132; numbers of, 119, *note;* attitude of church to, 109, 119, 122 and *note*, 125, *note*, 145; unauthorised alone forbidden, 123
VESPERS at Bury, 241
VILLANOVA, St. Thomas of, on chained books, 17
VINCENT OF BEAUVAIS, 213
VIRGIL, mediæval knowledge of, 301; copies of, 53
VITÆ PATRUM, The, 218

WAGES, Bp. Brunton on, 90
WALDEN, on Wyclif, 114, 117
WALDEGRAVE, Sir Edward, in Tower, 331-2

WALEYS, Friar, on preaching, 207, *note*, 208
WALSINGHAM, Dom Thomas of, 13; forms the St. Albans scriptorium, 44; establishes the historical school, 46
WALTER de Dis, 236
WARBLINGTON, 346, 351, 358; priest's shelter at, 367
WARHAM, Archbp., visitation of, 20; assists revival of letters, 314
WARNFORD, Richard, 345
WARWICK, E. of, 232, 256
WATSON, Bp. of Winchester, 359; his dealing with Catholics, 360
WATTON, John, 198
WAYNFLEET, Bp., 305
WEARMOUTH, writing school at, 55
WELLS, Gilbert, 245, 357, 369, 370, 375
WELLS, Swithun, 375
WESTBURANT, 350
WESTBURY, 352
WEST TISTED, 362
WENLOCK priory, 280, *note*
WESTMINSTER, Archbp. Langham at, 67; book presses at, 12; directions as to writing at, 50; writing carrels at, 50; cloister school at, 262; the customs of, 265; Abbot Ware's customary, 265, *note*; Cardinal Pole on restoration of, 284
WESSINGTON, Prior of Durham, 11
WEST, Sir Thomas, 348.
WESTCOTT, Bp., on Wyclif, 384
WESTMORELAND, The Countess of, 8
WESTON FARM, Buriton, 348, 352, 367
WESTON, William, 143
WHARTON, Lady, in the Tower for religion, 383
WHETHAMSTEDE, Abb. of St. Alban's, 13; the friend of Duke Humphrey, 142; silent about Wyclif's Bible, 111
WHITE LION PRISON, Catholics in, 359, 368
WHITE, Thomas, 366

INDEX.

WHYTFORD, Richard, 145

WINCHESTER, MS. of Apollonius at, 24, *note* 2 ; Bible left to, 31; Matthew Paris at, 61

WINCHESTER, Catholics in gaol of, 357; hardships in, 374.

WINCHESTER, *St. James' Cemetery*, 379

WITNESSES, Bp. Brunton on, 83

WODECRAFT, Dom John, the Bury artist, 233

WOODFORD, silent as to Wyclif and the Bible, 114

WOODSTOCK, Thomas, 141

WOOKEY HOLE, Somerset, 297

WORCESTER library, books bought for, in 16th cent., 36

WORCESTER, William of, his note books, 285 *seqq.*; his birthplace, 288 ; his itinerary, 291 ; his tract on the religious orders, 303 ; his translation of Cicero, 305 ; visits Canterbury, 319.

WORSBOROUGH, Religious from Monk Bretton at, 39, *note*

WRITING, The art of, 280

WRITING PLACES, St. Bernard describes, 42

WYCLIF, Bp. Brunton on teaching of, 95 ; works wrongly ascribed to, 108,
111, 112 ; tradition as to English Scriptures, 102, 159 ; assertion as to translation, 105, 137 ; search for his writings, 129 ; his great personality, 108 ; his active mind, 114 ; propagates errors through vernacular translation of Scripture, 113 ; his position at Lutterworth misunderstood, 117, *note;* his retractation, 117, *note*

WYCLIFITE SCRIPTURES generally assumed as certain, 106, 157 ; evidence for, 112, 114 ; portions only Wyclif's, 112 ; questions as to, 109, 129, 156, 176 ; owned by Catholics, 140 *seqq.*, 163, 164 ; tradition as to origin based on false premises, 174

WYKEHAM, William of, Bp., 75, 162, 188, *note*

Wymering, 350

YATE, Mr., 371

YOUNG, Laurence, 357

YORK, Synod of, orders religious instruction, 190 ; marriage of a king of Scotland at, 61

YORK, *St. Mary's*, 189, 262

www.ingramcontent.com/pod-product-compliance
Lightning Source LLC
Chambersburg PA
CBHW051244300426
44114CB00011B/886